The  Oxford Guide to

# Effective Argument and Critical Thinking

Colin Swatridge

OXFORD

UNIVERSITY PRESS

UNIVERSITY PRESS

Great Clarendon Street, Oxford, OX2 6DP,
United Kingdom

Oxford University Press is a department of the University of Oxford.
It furthers the University's objective of excellence in research, scholarship,
and education by publishing worldwide. Oxford is a registered trade mark of
Oxford University Press in the UK and in certain other countries

First edition 2014

Impression: 1

Published in the United States of America by Oxford University Press
198 Madison Avenue, New York, NY 10016, United States of America

British Library Cataloguing in Publication Data

Data available

ISBN 978–0–19–967172–4

Printed in Great Britain by
Ashford Colour Press Ltd, Gosport, Hampshire

*'Life is the art of drawing sufficient conclusions from insufficient premises'*
(Samuel Butler, 1912)


This book is dedicated to my granddaughters:
Pauline, in fond memory, and Alice, in equally fond anticipation.

# Contents

# Figure Acknowledgements

# Introduction

You are someone who has to argue a case: you have a speech to make, or a letter, article, paper, essay, or dissertation to write. You are a student (most of us are at some stage), and you have been given a title, or you have to choose one, that requires you to advance an argument. You have to read relevant articles, books, websites; you have to decide where you stand on the subject, and make a case in such a way as to persuade your reader, or readers, to agree with the conclusion that you come to. You may have to write just a couple of pages; or you may have to write a paper, or essay, of 5,000 words; or, perhaps, a dissertation of 40,000 words or more.

This book is designed to help you to do this.

You have probably not been asked to write *about* a subject: what you already know about it or what you can find out about it; some *discussion* is probably expected—some *analysis*. The likely requirement is that you:

- address a question;
- decide where you stand on the question;
- review what claims others have made;
- offer a counter-claim;
- support this claim with reasons;
- come to a persuasive conclusion.

Let us imagine that you have been set this question:

> How realistic is the idea of a United States of Europe?

Your answer to this question (in however many words) will be one answer among many possible answers. Your job is to make a strong, persuasive case of *your* answer.

Central to your argument will be the claim that answers the question. It is the point that you want to make and that you want your reader to accept. It is the conclusion that you draw from the claims that others make, and from the evidence that is available to you. It is the conclusion that your reader will come to if the claims and the evidence give it strong enough support. It might be a conclusion like this:

> To be united, the peoples of Europe need to share a commitment to democratic ideals and consider themselves to be fairly represented by a single parliamentary government. We would seem to be a long way from this sort of unity.

The claims that you make and the evidence that you provide to support your conclusions we shall simply call reasons. This is what an argument is. It is a set of claims; one of them is the conclusion; and some (if not all) of the others are the reasons that you hope will support it.

The study of claims that make up an argument is the stuff of Critical Thinking. This is often taught as if it was a subject in its own right, to a small minority of students in their final years of school, or in their first year of a general humanities or philosophy course at college or university. This is a pity, since nearly all students have to advance and assess arguments at one time or another and it is highly desirable that they do this critically.

What does this mean: '*critically*'? The word often has a negative undertone: of carping; of fault-finding. In this context, though, it means using one's judgement: in Greek, a *kritikos* was a judge, examining evidence on two sides in a case, and judging which was the weightier.

This is what you do when you think 'critically': you judge what it is that makes an argument strong or weak; you learn how to put forward stronger arguments and how not to be seduced by weak ones. The *un*critical accept what they read or what they are told, at face value; critical thinkers weigh claims in the balance, and make—or reserve—judgement when the evidence has dispelled reasonable doubt.

This book is full of arguments put forward by thinkers and doers from across history and the (mostly western) world. These arguments illustrate aspects of conducting an argument, and they are numbered sequentially throughout the book, for easy reference. They are raw material for the critical thinker, too; but in this book, critical thinking is harnessed to the business of writing—as a means to a practical end.

Arguing is not about winning and losing. There are no 'model' arguments in this book, and there are no ticks for 'right answers'. The most that you can hope to do when you write is to persuade a reader that your conclusion is as safe and sound as you can make it for all the reasons that you give. Likewise, when you weigh up the arguments of other people it is wise neither to be too easily persuaded, nor too dismissive. You can be certain in an equation, but only rarely in an argument.

# 1 What do you do when you argue a case?

I shall aim in this chapter to explain:

- what an argument consists of;
- what we do when we reason;
- how an argument answers a question;
- what it means to draw a conclusion.

## Claims and conclusions

You have read the Introduction to this book, and you have turned the page to this chapter: so, you may well be someone with a case to make—an argument to advance—in writing or in a speech. Perhaps you have been given (or you have given yourself) a topic to write about or a question to answer; and your job is to persuade your readers or listeners to agree with your main claim.

Let us say that you are a student of geography and you have to write about:

Iceland and the European mainland

or you are studying American literature, and you have chosen this topic:

Political commitment in the novels of John Steinbeck

or you are writing in the field of business studies, on this subject:

The takeover of Cadbury by Kraft Foods

or you are a student of psychology and you are presented with this:

The importance of attachment in language acquisition

None of these 'titles' is a *question*, so none of them asks you to argue a case. They are just noun phrases which invite you to write, simply, 'what you know' about the topic. I shall have more to say about titles and questions—and titles-as-questions—later in this chapter.

Each phrase sets up an association between two objects, **P** and **Q**: for example, Iceland (in particular) and Europe (in general). This is how we advance knowledge—by investigating the association between two objects. In the physical sciences, the hope is that the association between **P** and **Q** might be so strong as to amount to a law; in the social sciences and humanities, the association is more open to question.

These objects might be *places* (Iceland); *people* (John Steinbeck); *institutions* (Cadbury); *ideas* (political commitment); *social behaviour* (language acquisition)—they can be anything at all.

> **1a.** Can you think of a title that you have been given, in any subject, that did **not** ask you about an association between two (or more) objects?

It is **implied** in each of the previous titles that the two objects referred to are associated in some significant way. We can easily make the phrases into sentences, and the sentences into **claims**.

> Iceland is a Nordic country nearly 1,000km distant from the European mainland.
> Steinbeck is a writer who made his political position quite clear.
> Cadbury was an iconic British brand when it was bought by US giant Kraft Foods.
> Attachment to a primary carer is important for a child's acquisition of language.

What was **implicit** in the phrases is now **explicit** in the claims. Claims on their own do not carry a lot of weight—though, perhaps, the more well known the claimants are, the more weight their claims carry. You have probably heard of these claimants:

> Communism fits Germany as a saddle fits a cow.
> JOSEPH STALIN, Soviet leader, 1944

> The one duty we owe to history is to rewrite it.
> OSCAR WILDE, Irish writer, 1891

There is only one really serious problem in philosophy, and that is suicide. To assess whether life is worth living or not is to answer the fundamental question of philosophy.

ALBERT CAMUS, French existentialist writer, 1942

The noblest prospect which a Scotchman ever sees is the high road that leads to England.

DR SAMUEL JOHNSON, English writer, 1763

No man is good enough to govern another man without that other's consent.

ABRAHAM LINCOLN, 16th US President, 1854

Whoever lights the torch of war in Europe can wish for nothing but chaos.

ADOLF HITLER, German Nazi Party leader, 1935

Lincoln's claim is weighty because of who he was and because we all believe in some sort of democracy now; Wilde's claim is weighty, as well as witty, because, though his observation would seem to be flippant, he has put his finger on precisely what it is that historians do; and Hitler's claim is weighty because, within ten years, he had lit the torch, and had indeed brought chaos down upon everybody's heads.

Each of these claims is, in effect, the **conclusion**—or *main claim*—of an implicit **argument**. Dr Johnson might have said: 'Scotland is a wet, wild, grim sort of place, whereas England is a thriving, balmy, lush arcadia'. His line about the high road to England would then have been his conclusion—the punchline with which he hoped we might agree. All but loyal Scots might have done so.

A claim might be a definition, such as this:

An expert is one who is familiar with some of the worst errors that can be made in his field, and who succeeds in avoiding them.

WERNER HEISENBERG, German physicist, 1969

It might be a recommendation:

In politics, if you want anything said, ask a man. If you want anything done, ask a woman.

MARGARET THATCHER, UK Conservative politician, 1975

It might be a prediction (or wishful thinking):

Palestine is a country without a people; the Jews are a people without a country. The regeneration of the soil would bring the regeneration of the people.

ISRAEL ZANGWILL, US author of *The Melting Pot*, 1901

Or it might—perhaps like most claims—be a simple expression of opinion:

> The man who is a pessimist before 48 knows too much; if he is an optimist after it, he knows too little.
>
> MARK TWAIN, US writer, 1902

A single claim is generally not persuasive on its own. Indeed, even a barrage of claims may not be persuasive:

> Franklin D. Roosevelt is no crusader. He is no tribune of the people. He is no enemy of entrenched privilege. He is a pleasant man who, without any important qualifications for the office, would very much like to be President.
>
> WALTER LIPPMANN, American journalist, 1932

> **1b.** How many claims does Lippmann make here? Which of them appears to be the **main** claim, the conclusion?

Lippmann wants us to believe two things: one is that it was Roosevelt's ambition to be president; and the other is that he was ill-qualified for the office. But he does not give us any **reasons** for believing either of these claims. I supplied two reasons for coming to Dr Johnson's conclusion and so constructed a simple argument:

[R1] Scotland is a wet, wild, grim sort of place.
[R2] England is a thriving, balmy, lush arcadia.

[C] The noblest prospect which a Scotchman ever sees is the high road that leads to England.

Reasons give *grounds* for accepting the conclusion—or not, as in this case (since neither reason is 'true'). Here are two rather better reasons for coming to Wilde's conclusion:

[R1] 'History' is what historians write, but they do not write it for all time.
[R2] We do not have to accept the judgements made by historians of an earlier generation.

[C] The one duty we owe to history is to rewrite it.

It is not enough merely to *assert* a claim if we wish to persuade an audience to accept it. We need to back that claim with reasons. Lippmann made a series of assertions about Roosevelt. If what he said is to be an argument, the grounds for claiming that Roosevelt was not qualified to be president would need to be made explicit.

# Reasons and inference

The difference between an argument and a non-argument is no sharper than the difference between fiction and non-fiction. This argument might have been written by a journalist:

1. The one great principle of the English law is to make business for itself. There is no other principle distinctly, certainly, and consistently maintained through all its narrow turnings. Viewed by this light it becomes a coherent scheme and not the monstrous maze the laity are apt to think it. Let them once clearly perceive that its grand principle is to make business for itself at their expense, and surely they will cease to grumble.

In fact, it comes from Chapter 39 of the novel *Bleak House*, by Charles Dickens. Many novels (and plays) are arguments in fictional disguise. One might, equally, come across an argument in verse:

2. The rain it raineth on the just | And also on the unjust fella | But chiefly on the just, because | The unjust steals the just's umbrella.
   CHARLES, LORD BOWEN, English judge (1835–94)

Bowen **explains** that the innocent may suffer as much as, if not more than, the guilty. It is sometimes difficult to tell **explanation** from argument, and, indeed, the difference is not hard and fast. It might be said that, when one explains, one is not trying to persuade; that persuasion is what marks out argument. Is the following an argument, or simply an explanation?

3. When a dog bites a man, that is not news, because it happens so often. But if a man bites a dog, that is news.

JOHN B. BOGART, US journalist, 1918

Bogart explains that only what is unusual is news. Bowen and Bogart are both explaining, but they are **reasoning**, too: they are both saying that one claim serves as a reason for another claim:

$$\textbf{P}, \text{ and so } \textbf{Q} \text{ (or } \textbf{P} \rightarrow \textbf{Q})$$

The unjust man steals the just man's umbrella (**P**), so the just man gets wetter than the unjust man (**Q**). A man biting a dog is unusual (**P**), so it's news (**Q**). **P** implies **Q**; from **P**, we can **infer Q**—that is, we understand **Q** to be a consequence of **P**. When the association between two claims, **P** and **Q**, is an **inference** of one from the other (**P**, and so **Q**) it is fair to say that we have an argument.

Explanation by itself may not equate to argument; but it may well be that explanation will play a *part* in argument. (I shall have a little more to say about this in Chapter 2.)

Was President Barack Obama arguing or explaining, in this extract from his January 2010 State of the Union Address?

4. From the first railroads to the interstate highway system, our nation has always been built to compete. There's no reason Europe or China should have the fastest trains, or the new factories that manufacture clean products.

China is not waiting to revamp its economy. Germany is not waiting. India is not waiting. These nations aren't playing for second place. They're putting more emphasis on math and science. They're building their infrastructure. They're making serious investments in clean energy because they want those jobs. Well, I do not accept second place for the United States of America.

He was certainly trying to persuade his listeners to think or to do something—and this is the conventional definition of an argument. He drew the conclusion—he inferred, and he wanted his listeners to infer—from his claims about the United States' past, and other countries' present policies, that the United States should invest in its infrastructure.

In the following passage, a journalist and BBC presenter explains why he is writing a history of the world:

5. Writing a history of the world is a ridiculous thing to do. The amount of information is too vast for any individual to absorb, the

reading limitless and the likelihood of error immense. The only case for doing it, and for reading it, is that not having a sense of world history is even more ridiculous. Looking back can make us better at looking about us. The better we understand how rulers lose touch with reality, or why revolutions produce dictators more often than they produce happiness, or why some parts of the world are richer than others, the easier it is to understand our own times.

ANDREW MARR, *A History of the World*,
London: Macmillan Publishers, 2012

> **1c.** To what extent would you say Marr's explanation is also an argument? Is there a **P** from which he infers a **Q**? Is there a claim or claims from which he draws a **conclusion**?

Perhaps when we make any claim, whether in speech or in writing, we want to persuade others to do or think something; but it may not be safe only to imply **Q**—readers or listeners may not infer the **Q** that you had in mind.

This warning—which is just about the shortest argument that can be imagined—could not leave it to drivers to infer what they should do or think:

---

SLOW

FOG

---

We have two one-word claims: one tries to persuade motorists to slow down—the conclusion; the other tells them why they should do so—the reason. And it is a good reason (as long as the fog has not lifted, and it is the sun that is the problem). The reason is not such a good one in this warning posted in an American washroom:

---

**MIRROR UNDER REPAIR**

**PLEASE DO NOT USE**

---

It is far from clear what danger one might pose to the mirror, or to oneself, just by looking at it. A claim-as-conclusion might come before a claim-as-reason, or it might follow it. It is not always obvious which is which. Dora Russell, second wife of the philosopher Bertrand Russell, made this claim in 1925:

> We want better reasons for having children than not knowing how to prevent them.

Is this claim the conclusion of an argument looking something like this?

[C]  We want better reasons for having children than not knowing to prevent them.

---

[R1]  One such reason is that having children is a life-affirming and fulfilling experience.

[R2]  Another is that the country's future depends upon couples wanting children and establishing families.

Or is it a reason in an argument looking something like this?

[R1]  Many couples who have children don't really want them.

[R2]  We want better reasons for having children than not knowing how to prevent them.

---

[C]  So, couples need help to prevent having children they don't really want.

This second argument is more likely to have been what Dora Russell meant; she was, after all, a doughty campaigner for better birth control.

Whether the main claim is made first or last, it is unlikely by itself to be as persuasive as one that has the backing of one or more claims-as-reasons.

> **1d.** Can you think of two claims (as reasons) that Hitler might have given for his claim (as a conclusion) in the previous section, p 3?

Consider this claim by the Scots-born journalist who founded the *New York Herald*:

> A newspaper can send more souls to Heaven, and save more from Hell, than all the churches or chapels in New York—besides making money at the same time.
>
> JAMES GORDON BENNETT Sr, 1831

By itself, this would seem a curious claim to make. Are we to infer from it that:

- There is more religion in newspapers than in churches and chapels?
- Journalists have more power to change lives than clergymen?
- The news teaches more moral lessons than sermons?
- One can do good and make money at the same time?

In fact, Bennett's claim was itself his (rather dubious) inference from a number of (rather dubious) claims-as-reasons:

6. What is to prevent a daily newspaper from being made the greatest organ of social life? Books have had their day—the theatres have had their day—the temple of religion has had its day. A newspaper can be made to take the lead of all these in the great movements of human thought and of human civilization. A newspaper can send more souls to Heaven, and save more from Hell, than all the churches or chapels in New York—besides making money at the same time.

Bennett's conclusion is a curious—perhaps even outrageous—inference from the other claims that he makes (each of them amply disproved); but it would have been even less persuasive on its own. (Or is the question at the beginning Bennett's main conclusion? Or is it the third sentence? Would Bennett have been able to tell us?)

We might say of a claim: 'Yes, I agree with that', or 'No, I don't agree with that' (or 'I would need to know more before I decide') and, indeed, this is often how a title for a piece of writing is presented. Here is an example from economics:

> 'Competition brings out the best in products and the worst in people' (David Sarnoff, US broadcasting pioneer).
>
> How far do you agree with this statement?

And here is another one from religious studies:

> 'The more the fruits of knowledge become accessible to men, the more widespread is the decline of religious belief' (Sigmund Freud, pioneer psychiatrist).
>
> To what extent, if at all, do you agree with this view?

Neither Sarnoff nor Freud backed up his claim. For all we know, the claims might have been made in a vacuum. It is likely, though, that both men gave some thought to the effects of competition and of the growth of knowledge, respectively, before making claims of such a resounding sort. In this case, their claims were inferences from experience. In answering these questions (or ones like them), you would have to provide reasons for agreeing or disagreeing with the claims—or for suspending judgement if you are simply not persuaded either way.

# Titles as questions

There is this, at least, to be said for the two previous questions: they are *questions*. All new knowledge is obtained by asking questions: it is how children learn, and it is where research begins. If we did not ask questions, we would have to make do with claims handed down to us, just as for centuries our forebears settled for the claims of Aristotle, and understanding of the world was held back until the Renaissance.

James Gordon Bennett asked himself a question quite explicitly, in Argument 6: 'What is to prevent a daily newspaper from being made the greatest organ of social life?'

> **1e.** What questions do Barack Obama and Andrew Marr ask themselves (implicitly) in Arguments 4 and 5?

Our original four titles could easily enough be reworded as questions:

To what extent can Iceland be called a European country?
In what sense did John Steinbeck write from a decided political position?
Why did the takeover of Cadbury by Kraft Foods prove to be controversial?
How important for language acquisition is attachment to a primary carer?

I have considered three sorts of title: the noun-phrase, the claim, and the question. When you ask a question (what is the precise relationship between **P** and **Q**?), you have a fixed target at which to aim; if you set yourself to write all you know, or all you can find out, *about* **P** and **Q**, your target is a pair of birds flying away from you in different directions.

Consider the political-science title: 'The idea of a united Europe': this noun-phrase seems to invite a simple display of knowledge, though it gives you little idea about where you might start. The title as a claim would, at least, invite an argument:

'The idea of a united Europe is unrealistic.' Discuss.

But it is still very open: the discussion could begin and end almost anywhere.

In the Introduction to this book, I gave this as an example of a title: 'How realistic is the idea of a United States of Europe?' Why is this a 'better' title? I will answer my own question in the form of a simple argument, marking my reasons, and the conclusion as I do so:

7. There are several reasons why it is a good idea to write in answer to a title in the form of a question. [R1] If you were to write to the title: 'The idea of a United Europe', it would be difficult to know where to start and where to finish—whole books have been written on the subject. Asking a specific question can give your writing a sharper focus than taking a statement as your title is likely to do. [R2] A question helps you to determine what material is relevant—what information actually answers the question—and what material you can discard because it doesn't. [R3] What is more, setting yourself a question makes what otherwise might seem to be an arid exercise in reproducing what others have written into a piece of (more or less) genuine research: it is your question and your answer; it is your argument and, therefore, you may be stimulated into making it as persuasive as possible. For these reasons, [C] *it is advisable to word, or to reword, a title as a question.*

> **1f.** Is my conclusion persuasive? Can you think of other reasons for coming to it? Can you think of reasons for coming to an alternative conclusion?

What I have tried to do in the previous argument is to reason: to engage with you in an act of reasoning. What I did was:

```
┌─────────────────────────────────┐
│        Address a question       │
│  (What sort of essay title is best?) │
└─────────────────────────────────┘
                  ↓
┌─────────────────────────────────┐
│   Make a statement as to the    │
│  conclusion that I would probably │
│            come to              │
└─────────────────────────────────┘
                  ↓
┌─────────────────────────────────┐
│  Identify my reasons for coming to │
│  this conclusion (three of them, in │
│            this case)           │
└─────────────────────────────────┘
                  ↓
┌─────────────────────────────────┐
│   State that conclusion so as to │
│  make it clear that it follows from │
│          the reasons.           │
└─────────────────────────────────┘
```

This is what an argument is; and it is the process you go through (not always systematically) when you argue (using the word in its reasoning, rather than quarrelling sense) in conversation.

When you are presented with a title that is not a question, you might convert it into one—if only at the planning stage—so that what you write will be an argument and not a mere catalogue of claims. Here is an example:

'Literature is news that STAYS news' (Ezra Pound). Discuss.

You might convert this to:

In what sense is literature 'news' that is always news?

Or you might convert it into two questions:

1. In what sense is literature 'news'? 2. How does it continue to be 'news'?

There has been a lot of 'literature'; so it would be wise to answer the question by reference to, say, one poem, one play, and one novel, as case studies (making reference to other works, perhaps, in less detail). Here is another example:

Analyse the part played by family breakdown in youth crime.

Here, too, there is a *what* question, and a *how* question:

1. What can we learn from the statistics about youth crime in the UK?
2. How big a proportion of crime is accounted for by youths from broken homes?

There has been a lot of family breakdown, and a lot of youth crime. If you were writing to a title like this, you would need either to refine it further ('What part was played by family breakdown in youth crime in the UK/United States/Illinois/1950–2000/what part does it play in the present?'); or you would need to make it clear in your opening **statement** that you will confine your attention to this or that place, at this or that time.

It is good practice to break a question down into *sub-questions*. Thus, the question:

> Why did the takeover of Cadbury by Kraft Foods prove to be controversial?

can be broken down into these (or other) sub-questions:

- What was Cadbury like before the takeover?
- How did Cadbury respond to Kraft's proposals?
- How far did this response affect the outcome?

A Word of Advice

By breaking down a question into sub-questions, you can begin to set the parts of your overall argument into a meaningful order, and give direction to your thinking.

## Support for a conclusion

Consider these claims:

> The French are a logical people, which is one reason the English dislike them so intensely. The other is that they own France, a country which we have always judged to be much too good for them.
>
> ROBERT MORLEY, English comic actor, 1974

Morley has asked himself why the English dislike the French and he gives two reasons to explain the dislike. He might have inferred from these two reasons that:

The English are justified in disliking the French.

Or that:

The English always will dislike the French.

Had he drawn either of these conclusions, he would have given us an argument; and he would probably have caused one, in the quarrelling sense, because his reasons do not **support** either conclusion. They might be said to give support to this one:

Logic being of less importance than cheese and wine, many English people have gone to live in France.

Morley was a comedian, so reasoning was not what he was about. The writer of the following was not reasoning, either:

I occasionally play works by contemporary composers and for two reasons. First, to discourage the composer from writing any more, and secondly to remind myself how much I appreciate Beethoven.
JASCHA HEIFETZ, Russian-Polish-born US violinist, 1961

Heifetz might have come to any one of these conclusions:

Music by contemporary composers isn't worth the paper it's written on.

Contemporary composers cannot write worthwhile music for the violin.

There's really only one composer of note, and that's Beethoven.

But his 'two reasons' would not have supported any of these conclusions; they go too far beyond what the reasons imply. All that is implied by what he wrote—all that he could reasonably want us to infer—is that his taste in music was rather late classical than modern.

Here is another set of 'reasons' that does not amount to an argument:

> Troops always ready to act, my well-filled treasury, and the liveliness of my disposition—these were my reasons for making war on Maria Theresa.
>
> FREDERICK II, King of Prussia, 1741

Frederick uses the word 'reasons', but he isn't *reasoning*; he might think he is explaining, but perhaps a despot does not need to do even this. Might is right, and there's an end to it.

Here is a set of reasons that *does* amount to an argument (whose conclusion is italicized):

8.  Our land is the dearer for our sacrifices. The blood of our martyrs sanctifies and enriches it. Their spirit passes into thousands of hearts. How costly is the progress of the race. *It is only by giving of life that we can have life.*

    E.J.YOUNG, US pastor, 1865

A great deal of young male blood was shed in the American Civil War, and it is understandable that a pastor should want to put a positive gloss on the waste; but his consecration of the slaughter cannot support the weight of his extravagant conclusion.

> **1g.** What alternative, less extravagant, conclusion might we draw from the claims that Young makes?

A comedian, a forthright violinist, a despot, a minister of religion might have been expected to overstate their case; a well-born lady, in the late 18th century, was more likely to understate it:

9.  Patriotism in the female sex is the most disinterested of all virtues. Excluded from honors and from offices, we cannot attach ourselves to the State or Government from having had a place of eminence. Even in the freest countries our property is subject to the control and disposal of our partners, to whom the laws have given a sovereign authority. Deprived of a voice in legislation, obliged to submit to those laws which are imposed upon us, is it not sufficient to make us indifferent to the public welfare? Yet all history and every age exhibit instances of patriotic virtue in the female sex; which considering our situation equals the most heroic of yours.

    ABIGAIL ADAMS, in a letter to her husband, John Adams, 1782

John Adams was one of the Founding Fathers (and the second president) of the United States; but he could not have acted upon her pioneering views if he had wanted to—for all that her 'reasons' give very adequate support to her modest conclusion.

We can set out her argument in much the same way that I set out my own argument, in the previous section.

**Question**

Why is it remarkable that females
are as patriotic as they are?

**Statement**

They have little enough cause to be patriotic.

**Reasons**

Females are excluded from exercising political
power; and their property on marriage comes under
the control of their husbands.

**Conclusion**

It is remarkable that they should be as patriotic as
they are, considering how little influence they have in
the affairs of state.

Here, now, is a longer argument, set out in a speech by the Irish president, on the 50th anniversary of the Easter Rising of 1916:

10. We cannot adequately honour the men of 1916 if we do not work and strive to bring about the Ireland of their desire. For this each one of us must do his part, and though the tasks immediately before us now are different from those of fifty years ago, we can have today, if we are sufficiently devoted and our will is firm, a national resurgence comparable to that which followed 1916.

    In the realization of this our national language has a vital role. Language is a chief characteristic of nationhood—the embodiment, as it were, of the personality and the closest bond between its people. No nation with a language of its own would willingly abandon it. The peoples of Denmark, Holland, Norway, for example, learn and know well one or more other languages, as we should, of course, for the sake of world communication, commerce and for cultural purposes; but they would never abandon their native language, the language of their ancestors, the language which enshrines all the memories of their past. They know that without it they would sink into an amorphous cosmopolitanism—without a past or a distinguishable future. To avoid such a fate, we of this generation must see to it that our language lives. That would be the resolve of the men and women of 1916.

EAMON DE VALERA, President of the
Republic of Ireland, 10 April 1966

> **1h.** What question would you think de Valera was addressing? And which of his claims would seem to be the 'conclusion' of his argument? (You might highlight this, and label the reasons that he puts forward to support it, as I did in Argument 7.)

So far, then, we have seen that when you argue a case, you:

> ➤ frame or reframe your title as a **question** that you may need to refine;
>
> ➤ make **claims** the most significant of which is your **conclusion**;
>
> ➤ present these claims as **reasons** from which you **infer** the conclusion;
>
> ➤ take care not to infer more than the reasons **imply**;
>
> ➤ and thus ensure that your reasons **support** the conclusion that you draw.

When you have framed the question that you will answer, you will have some idea what your response to this question will be—what your main claim, or conclusion, will be. Do you, though, make a claim and then look for evidence to support it:

Claim → Evidence

or do you look for evidence first and only then draw your conclusion?

Evidence → Claim

In a letter, dated 8 December 1874, Charles Darwin wrote:

I must begin with a good body of facts and not from a principle.

For Darwin, evidence came before claim—at least, this is what he implies here. In fact, he had a pretty good idea what he was looking for (a 'principle'; a theory; a claim that he would make) in order to know what facts would be of use to him. It is no good looking for evidence before knowing what it might be evidence *of*.

On the other hand, if you make a claim—or advance a theory—before you have the evidence to support it, you are all too likely to 'find' the evidence that suits your purpose. The safest way to proceed is to argue from claim (theory) to evidence, but to be prepared to revise your claim in the course of constructing your argument.

Claim ← → Evidence → Revised claim

Your first source of evidence will be what others have said in answer to the question—and I shall have more to say about this in Chapter 3. Meanwhile, though, how strong your own argument is going to be will depend, partly, on whether or not you make yourself clear. Chapter 2 is about how you might do this.

# 2 How will you make yourself clear?

I shall aim in this chapter to explain:

- why it is important to be precise;
- why you may need to be explicit about your claims;
- how the meanings of words might be misunderstood;
- how you might set claims in order.

## Vagueness and definition

Warning signs must make their point as clearly, and in as few words, as possible, but they must do this without sacrificing meaning. The meaning of the warning on cigarette packets

> SMOKING KILLS

is clear, but it risks overkill. 'Smoking *may* kill' would be more accurate, if less effective as a warning. Is the following safari park sign quite clear?

> ELEPHANTS
>
> PLEASE STAY
>
> IN YOUR CAR

Perhaps only highly literate elephants might wonder; but the word 'Danger', at the beginning might have cleared up any confusion.

**2a.** Can you recall seeing a public notice whose meaning was less than clear?

Clarity of meaning is vital in a title, too. A **vague** title is all too likely to result in a vague and unconvincing argument. The following three arguments are high-sounding, rhetorical—poetic even:

11. I am inclined to think that the far greater part, if not all, of those difficulties which have hitherto amused philosophers, and blocked up the way to knowledge, are entirely owing to ourselves—that we have first raised a dust and then complain we cannot see.

    GEORGE BERKELEY, Irish philosopher, 1710

12. If men could learn from history, what lessons it might teach us! But passion and party blind our eyes, and the light which experience gives is a lantern on the stern, which shines only on the waves behind us!

    S.T. COLERIDGE, English poet, 1831

13. Future historians will surely see us as having created in the media a Frankenstein monster whom no one knows how to control or direct and marvel that we should have so meekly subjected ourselves to its destructive and often malignant influence.

    MALCOLM MUGGERIDGE, English journalist, 1976

The targets at which these men were shooting were so large that they could scarcely have missed. A student of philosophy might ask:

In what respects can it justly be said that philosophers have raised a dust and blocked up the way to knowledge?

A student of history might ask:

In what sense do passion and party blind us to the lessons that we might learn from history?

And a student of the media might ask:

To what extent have the media been so destructive and malign as to amount to a 'Frankenstein monster'?

And they might (if they were Berkeleys, or Coleridges, or Muggeridges-to-be) make a good job of it; but if their arguments were not to be as vague as their titles, they would have to be very specific in what (in Chapter 1) I called the **Statement** (about which I shall say more later in this section). They would have to be **precise** about the dimensions of their targets (The speculations of English philosophers before 1710? The adverse effects of parliamentary debate on good government in England under the Georges? The 'power without responsibility' enjoyed by newspaper proprietors?) to save themselves having to write very large books.

One of the first things to be done, once you have settled on your title, is to determine the *scope* of your argument. Let us take this title, for example:

> Should we welcome the development of space tourism?

At the outset you would need to **define**:

- the *focus* of the enquiry: whether you will concern yourself with the brief history, the economics, the ethics, or the technological and environmental effects of space tourism, or all of these;
- the *time span* of the enquiry: whether you will start by looking at the very beginnings of space travel, or only of privately funded space travel; and how far into the future you will gaze;
- the *geography* of the enquiry: whether you will investigate developments only in the United States, or in Europe, or elsewhere, or everywhere.

You would expect terms used in a constitution to be very clearly defined; yet any discussion of US gun laws would have to take into account this famous argument:

14. **A well-regulated militia being necessary to the security of a free state, the right of the people to bear arms shall not be infringed.**
   SECOND AMENDMENT TO THE US CONSTITUTION

When this amendment was adopted, in 1791, it must have seemed clear enough; but one or two precise **definitions** might have saved many lives lost to the antics of too many gunmen who knew their rights.

> **2b.** How could those who framed the constitution have made their meaning clearer? What terms might they have defined in order to leave no room for doubt?

To save a title, and therefore perhaps an argument, from terminal vagueness you need to define your target: first, *identify* it; then, very likely, *reduce it in size*. (A small target is easier to hit than a big one if you stand up close to it.)

Ask not why banks failed in 2008; ask why Lehman Brothers failed, and then look at whether other banks failed for the same or similar reasons. Ask not what can be done to keep the world supplied with fresh water; ask what is being done to ensure supplies in the oil-rich, water-poor states of the Arabian peninsula, and perhaps whether this can be done elsewhere.

A Word of Advice

Someone said: 'To be sure of hitting the target, shoot first and call whatever you hit the target'.

There is something in this: whilst it is good to choose a precise title, it is wise to delay a too precise wording until you have seen what others have to say on the subject (see Chapter 3).

This short-story writer needed to do some defining if she wanted to persuade us that Forster the novelist was as ineffectual as she claims he was:

15. E.M. Forster never gets any further than warming the teapot. He's a rare fine hand at that. Feel this teapot. Is it not beautifully warm? Yes, but there ain't going to be no tea.

KATHARINE MANSFIELD, New Zealand-born short-story writer, in her journal, 1917

Mansfield does not appear to have been writing with her tongue in her cheek. This is serious stuff. If we were going to engage with her argument, though, we should want to know:

- how much of Forster's work she had read (some would say that the best was yet to come);
- specifically, whether she was referring only to his novels, or to his short stories also;
- what exactly she meant by 'tea'.

Were you to take as your title (in literary criticism, for example) the question:

> 'E.M. Forster never gets any further than warming the teapot. He's a rare fine hand at that. Feel this teapot. Is it not beautifully warm? Yes, but there ain't going to be no tea' (Katharine Mansfield).
>
> How far do you agree with this view?

you would need to be precise about which pieces of fiction she might have been writing about (anything before 1917), and what it was that she liked (the 'tea') in the fiction of others—that is, you would need to know something about her critical standards. You might make clear what these were in your initial **Statement**—a word that I am using in place of the more usual (and rather vague) 'introduction'.

A brave attempt is made to define terms in the following argument, by the great-grandniece of the author of Argument 12:

16. There are gifts that are no gifts, just as there are books that are no books. A donation is not a gift.

    A portrait painted—a teapot presented—by subscription is not a gift. The giving is divided among too many. The true gift is from one to one. Furthermore, tea, sugar, and flannel petticoats are not gifts. If I bestow these conveniences on one old woman, she may regard them in that aspect; but if I bestow them on eleven others at the same time, she looks upon them as her right. By giving more I have given less.

    MARY E. COLERIDGE, English writer, 1900

This argument comes from an essay entitled: 'Gifts'. Is it clearer at the end what a gift is, and what a 'no gift' is, any more than it is what a 'book' is and what a 'no book' is?

There are words that do have an *essential* meaning: earthworm, nostril, banana, wristwatch, trombone—there is seldom much confusion about the meanings of countable, concrete nouns such as these:

the names that we give to tangible things. Problems may (and do) arise, though, when we use words that mean different things at different times to different people.

17. The deterioration in meaning of the word 'propaganda' affords sad evidence of the stupidity of human beings. Originally, 'propaganda' meant a 'community of cardinals of the Roman Catholic Church having the care and oversight of foreign missions'.

SUSAN STEBBING, English philosopher, 1939

Why should the fact that we now use the word 'propaganda' in a different sense from the original (where we might well use a capital P) be considered 'stupid'? Even the meaning of the word 'stupid' (a synonym of 'ridiculous', or 'idiotic' now) has changed over time. 'Originally', it meant *senseless, stunned*—and the noun 'stupor' has retained something of this meaning.

'Decimate' is another word whose meaning has changed:

> Though it originally meant to kill one in every ten (as a punishment), *decimate* is legitimately used in the general sense of 'cause great loss or slaughter' in an army.

So wrote H.A. Treble and G.H. Vallins in *An ABC of English Usage*, in 1936. We may or may not find a change of sense disturbing:

18. A first difficulty of the Arab movement was to say who the Arabs were. Being a manufacturing people, their name had been changing in sense slowly year by year. Once it meant an Arabian. There was a country called Arabia; but this was nothing to the point. There was a language called Arabic; and in it lay the test. It was the current tongue of Syria and Palestine, of Mesopotamia, and of the great peninsula called Arabia on the map.

T.E. LAWRENCE ('Lawrence of Arabia'),<br>The Seven Pillars of Wisdom, 1935

The meaning of Lawrence's second sentence is not altogether clear (does he mean by 'manufacturing', literally, that Arabs made things by hand?); but, his main point is that, when he was writing (and possibly even now), there was no agreement about the definition of an 'Arab'—about the **extension** of the term (whether, that is, its use could be extended to people who lived in other countries or regions than those listed).

**2c.** Can you think of other words that have changed in meaning, so that we have to be careful in their use?

What is the difference between a 'politician' and a 'statesman'?

> A politician is a person with whose politics you don't agree; if you agree with him, he is a statesman.
>
> DAVID LLOYD GEORGE, UK Prime Minister, 1916–22

> A politician is a man who understands government, and it takes a politician to run a government. A statesman is a politician who has been dead 10 or 15 years.
>
> HARRY S. TRUMAN, US President, 1945–52

> At home you always have to be a politician. When you are abroad, you almost feel yourself to be a statesman.
>
> HAROLD MACMILLAN, UK Prime Minister, 1957–63

It seems the difference is that the word 'politician' has a negative, and a 'statesman' a positive, value. Mansfield was being negative in her assessment of Forster. His work was not her cup of tea, evidently— and perhaps we could not expect her to define terms in her journal.

# Assumptions

The meaning of the warning on this highway sign is reasonably clear:

DON'T DRINK AND DRIVE

At least, it is to native English-speakers, aware that if they have drunk alcohol and then drive erratically as they leave the pub car park, they may be stopped and breathalysed. An alien or foreign-language speaker might wonder whether it warns motorists against drinking of any kind— ever; or whether it permits a drink *before* driving but not *while* driving.

A road sign is no place for lengthy argument, but if the warning was set out in full, it might look like this:

IT IS A FACT THAT ALCOHOL SLOWS ONE'S REACTIONS
MANY ROAD ACCIDENTS ARE CAUSED BY DRUNK DRIVERS
SO DON'T DRINK ALCOHOL BEFORE DRIVING.

The first two lines are the premises, or reasons; they are missing from the warning sign. They are **assumed**, or taken for granted.

> That life is worth living is the most necessary of assumptions, and, were it not assumed, the most impossible of conclusions.

So wrote the Spanish-American philosopher George Santayana, in 1906. There is a great deal that we all take for granted; but in an argument it is wise to make our **assumptions** clear—to make them explicit.

Authors make assumptions because they suppose that they and their readers have a lot of experience in common: it would be tedious to give *all* the reasons for drawing the conclusions that they do, just as it would be tedious to define every word that you use. It is charitable to assume that your reader is not an utter fool. In a well-developed argument, though, it is best to make important assumptions explicit in your opening **Statement**. A statement is a standpoint: it is where you *stand*. Your reader needs to know where you stand.

In his famous *Essay on the Principle of Population*, Thomas Malthus called 'postulata' what I have been calling claims (and that might otherwise be called 'premises', which is what Samuel Butler called them in the quotation on the dedication page of this book):

19.  I think I may fairly make two postulata. First that food is necessary to the existence of man. Secondly, that the passion between the sexes is necessary and will remain nearly in its present state.

> These two laws ever since we have had any knowledge of mankind appear to have been fixed laws of our nature; and as we have not hitherto seen any alteration in them, we have no right to conclude that they will ever cease to be what they now are, without an immediate act of power in that Being who first arranged the system of the universe; and for the advantage of His creatures still executes, according to fixed laws, all its various operations.
>
> THOMAS MALTHUS, English clergyman and economist, 1798

His premises are the basis for the argument which follows, so he makes them explicit. Malthus can be reasonably sure that no one will counter these claims—we will all accept them—because they correspond with shared experience: we do all need food if we are to live; and, likewise, it is one of our biological drives to reproduce. Malthus is perfectly justified in making these assumptions.

He also assumes, though, that the premises were instituted by God. Religion was of some importance to most Britons in 1798, but what might have been a fair assumption then, might not be now.

Margaret Mead made the following observation in her book, *Coming of Age in Samoa*:

20. As the traveller who has once been from home is wiser than he who has never left his own doorstep, so a knowledge of one other culture should sharpen our ability to scrutinize more steadily, to appreciate more lovingly, our own.

    MARGARET MEAD, American anthropologist, 1928

Is the Dane who has been to the Alps necessarily 'wiser' than one who stayed at home on the plain? Is this a fair assumption to make— that travel broadens the mind? Whether it is or not, at least we know where Malthus and Mead are 'coming from', so we can understand why they draw the conclusions they do, even if we do not agree with them. It is only a matter for worry when an assumption is *implicit*, for then it is, in effect, a missing reason—and it may be that missing reason that contributes most to the conclusion. Until that reason is made *explicit*, the argument is incomplete and may fail to persuade.

Let us look again at what Harry Truman said about politicians:

> A politician is a man who understands government, and it takes a politician to run a government. A statesman is a politician who has been dead 10 or 15 years.

**2d.** What assumption, or assumptions, does Truman appear to be making here?

What he appears to have meant by his first sentence (substituting 'one' for 'a man') is:

> A politician is one who understands government, so only a politician can run a government.

We have here a reason and a conclusion, so it is an argument; what we do not have is a reason for the reason: how does one come to an understanding of government in the first place? There is something missing in Truman's definition of a politician. He is assuming something. His argument might have been:

> To be a politician, you have to have been born and raised in political circles; only then will you understand government. Only a

politician understands government, so only a politician can run a government.

He might not have meant this: he was not himself born and raised in political circles—far from it. So, he might have meant:

> To be a politician, you have to enjoy the support of the powerful, and you have to be in the right place at the right time; only then will you get to be a politician and so understand government.

The point is that, until we know why Truman thought that it is only a politician who understands government, we cannot make sense of his argument and be persuaded by it—or not.

Truman thought that only 'a man' could be a politician because he was a man of his time. He assumed it to be the case because this was the common assumption among men in 1958 (and a lot of women, too). So, there are (at least) two assumptions in his argument.

It had been the common assumption among men at the beginning of the 20th century in Britain that only a man could be entrusted with the vote. Sir Almroth Wright, a professor of experimental pathology, argued strongly against votes for women:

21. The primordial* argument against giving woman [*sic*] the vote is that that vote would not represent physical force. The woman voter would be pernicious to the State not only because she could not back her vote by physical force, but also by reason of her intellectual defects.

    * fundamental, elementary.

The Unexpurgated Case against Woman Suffrage, 1913

> **2e.** What assumption does Wright appear to be making in using the word 'primordial'?

The reference to 'intellectual defects' seems to be a secondary consideration (though, again, it would have been a common assumption among men); he is against giving votes to women because they cannot back their vote with 'physical force'. This enormous assumption—that a vote only has meaning when it can be upheld by manly muscle or the gun—is unlikely to have been any commoner in 1913 than his forename. But there are other assumptions that underlie this one that need to be made explicit if we are to judge whether Sir Almroth's (missing) reasons support his conclusion:

- the state is itself an expression of physical force;
- democracy can only work if it is guaranteed by physical force;
- the vote is a proxy, a stand-in, for physical force;
- only men (all men?) can wield this force and therefore be trusted with the vote.

Happily, a century of experiment has proved that all Sir Almroth's assumptions were mistaken.

Women have the vote; some are politicians; and some of them (along with some men) understand government. Zoe, a *Daily Mail* reader, argues that there is too little understanding of politics among young voters, male and female:

22.  As a 16-year-old soon to leave school, I feel that young people aren't being given an education in politics. Yet, at 18, we are expected to have enough understanding to vote. How can this vote mean anything if we don't have the necessary background knowledge? As long as it is taught on a non-partisan basis, I believe *politics should be a part of the core curriculum in schools*.

Adapted from a letter to the Daily Mail, 16 December 2009

I have italicized Zoe's conclusion. Her reasons for drawing this conclusion are that:

1. Young people are not being given an education in politics.
2. It cannot mean anything to vote unless the voter has the necessary background knowledge.

She takes as her premise that the teaching of politics should be non-partisan. This premise, though, rests on the assumption that: it is *possible* for politics to be taught in a non-partisan way; and, indeed, the whole argument rests on the assumption (the missing reason) that by learning about politics in school, young people will acquire the knowledge necessary for them to cast a meaningful vote.

Here are three arguments in which assumptions are made, but not explicitly. The first is by one who was well able to back his vote with physical force:

23. War alone can carry to the maximum tension all human energies and imprint with the seal of nobility those people who have the courage to confront it; every other test is a mere substitute.

BENITO MUSSOLINI, Italian fascist leader, 1930

24. All the old parties are in the pockets of the banks and big business. They all pretend to be worried about job losses but have allowed globalisation to destroy jobs and drag down wages. Fortunately there's now a real choice—the British National Party. We will protect British jobs from cut-throat foreign competition and put British workers first—every time!

BNP, European parliamentary election campaign leaflet, 2009

25. I think we ought to read only the kind of books that wound and stab us. We need the books that affect us like a disaster, that grieve us deeply, like the death of someone we loved more than ourselves, like being banished into forests far from everyone, like a suicide. A book must be the axe for the frozen sea inside us.

FRANZ KAFKA, Austrian novelist, in a letter, 1904

> **2f.** Can you identify any assumptions, any missing reasons, in these arguments?

# Ambiguity and conflation

For the meaning of an argument to be clear it must be as free as possible from **ambiguity**—from a confusion of meanings. There are simple sorts of ambiguity that arise from careless punctuation or turns of phrase. Consider this sentence:

Behind the scenes last minute details were added.

Is this 'last-minute (eleventh hour) details'; or is it 'last, minute (terribly small) details'? The meaning of the sentence would be clear in speech, but it is **ambiguous** in writing without the hyphen, or the comma.

A hyphen would have been useful in the following *Guardian* headline, in May 1990:

# BOGUS CHILD VISITS FOX POLICE

Who was this 'bogus child'? Who were these 'fox police'? A hyphen between 'child' and 'visits' would have made it clearer that the visits were bogus (paedophiles posing as social workers) and the police were foxed (that is, they were confused as to who these people were, and how they gained entry to family homes).

On Good Friday, in 2006, a clergyman, on the BBC Radio 4 *Today* programme, said this:

> The debate [about AIDS in Africa] gives the impression that it's all about money and condoms. No one would argue that these are necessary.

The verb 'argue' (one that I am using a lot in this book) is ambiguous unless it is followed either by 'for' or 'against'. The speaker here plainly meant: no one would argue *against* their being necessary; but he risked being understood to mean the opposite. So did the speaker who said:

> Fitness regimes may do more harm than good. We can't work our bodies too hard.

It is only the first of these two claims that makes it clear that the speaker meant: we *can* work our bodies too hard—and often do.

Ambiguities of this sort are minor matters. The sign in the window of a Spanish café probably raised a smile among English-speakers:

> Try our SANGRIA
>
> You will never get better

but the risk of misinterpretation was small. It gets more serious when we use abstract terms—uncountable nouns—whose meaning is open, or that might have one meaning in one subject (or discourse, or 'language game') and a different one in another. The word 'art' is such a word:

26. I believe that the scientist is trying to expand absolute truth and the artist absolute beauty, so that I find in **art** and science, and in an attempt to live the good life, all the religion I want.

J.B.S. HALDANE, Anglo-Indian biologist, 1931

27. One is alive, properly speaking, only in the act of creation; one is then a self-consciously artistic being. When it is performed consciously, even the act of peeling potatoes can be a work of **art**.

JOSEPH BEUYS, German sculptor, 1969

Art is what we say it is; it might be a French realist portrait of a peasant peeling potatoes; it might be the act of peeling them.

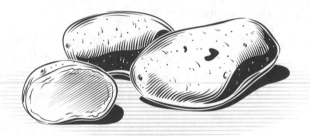

It matters little whether we prefer to use a word as it was used 'originally'; what matters in a piece of writing, as elsewhere, is that we make it clear what sense it is we are giving to a word, especially if it is a word we shall be using often, or that is a key word in a subject. Agnes Arber might almost have been thinking of Malthus, and his use of the word 'law' (in Argument 19):

28. When a theory is well established, and can claim a high degree of generality, it is often called a 'law'; but, at least, in the biological field, it is doubtful whether bestowal of this title can be justified. Originally the expression 'laws of **nature**', when used in science, referred to those direct edicts of the Almighty which were held to control material things; in this sense there was a clear analogy with human law, so that the term was fully applicable. In modern writing, however, in which a 'law' of nature stands for a 'theoretical principle deduced from particular facts', the word 'law', which suggests compulsion, is obviously out of place.

AGNES ARBER and P.R. BELL, *The Mind and the Eye*, Cambridge: Cambridge University Press, 1953

The word 'nature' (and its derivatives 'natural' and 'supernatural') will have different meanings for the philosopher, the physical scientist, and the man of letters:

29. If the universe had a beginning, its beginning, by the very condition of the cases, was **supernatural**; the laws of **Nature** cannot account for their own origin.

JOHN STUART MILL, English philosopher, 1865

30. **Natural** science does not merely describe and explain **nature**; it is one aspect of the interaction between nature and ourselves; it describes nature as revealed to us by the scientific method.

WERNER HEISENBERG, German physicist, 1959

31. It is so far from being **natural** for a man and woman to live in a state of marriage, that we find all the motives which they have for remaining in that connection, and the restraints which civilized society imposes to prevent separation, are hardly sufficient to keep them together.

DR SAMUEL JOHNSON, 1772

> **2g.** In what ways might Johnson's ambiguous use of the word 'natural' weaken his argument?

Was this writer to *The Guardian*, in July 2010, justified in calling the editor to account?

> 'Choosing a German president is boring by design, largely because the last head of state to make the job exciting was Adolf Hitler' (Editorial, 1 July). Let me just read that again. And again. Then I'll ask my mother's cousin how excited he was to be **murdered** at Auschwitz.

Was the meaning of the sentence quoted not clear? Was the meaning of 'exciting' ambiguous (in its playful opposition to the word 'boring')? Or was the letter-writer guilty of **conflation**—of conflating, or fusing together two meanings of the word 'exciting' (inflaming and enrapturing)? It is all too easy to do this when strong feelings are involved. An American Catholic theologian (whom, again, I shall not name) wrote as follows, in 1975:

32. The precise time at which the fetus becomes 'animated' has no bearing on the morality of abortion. However we define 'animation', abortion is plainly wrong. And it is wrong because every deliberate act of abortion is **murder**: it is killing with intent. It is

fair to say that every developing fetus is a human being. To kill a human being deliberately is murder.

The letter-writer was justified in using the word 'murder'. Was this theologian justified in using it? Was the equally anonymous writer of *Le Chronique de Paris*, who witnessed the first use of the guillotine in 1792 (he or his translator), justified in using it?

33. Yesterday, at half past three, there was used for the first time the machine destined to cut off the heads of criminals condemned to death. This machine was rightfully preferred to other forms of execution; it in no way soils the hands of the man who **murders** his fellow man, and the promptness with which it strikes the condemned is more in the spirit of the law, which may often be stern, but must never be cruel.

'Murder', after all, is the name we give in law to an act of 'unlawful killing'. Abortion and execution—at certain times and in certain places, and whatever one's views about them may be—are lawful.

'Mrs Grundy' was an offstage character in a play by Thomas Morton, in 1798: she was a gossip whose name has become a byword for anyone who minds other people's business. The philosopher Herbert Spencer wrote, in 1861:

The tyranny of Mrs Grundy is worse than any other tyranny we suffer under.

The same word ('tyranny') is used in the following argument:

34 You may talk of the tyranny of Nero and Tiberius; but the real tyranny is the tyranny of your next-door neighbour, and it exacts obedience to itself; it requires us to think other men's thoughts, to speak other men's words, to follow other men's habits.

WALTER BAGEHOT, English economist, 1907

> **2h.** Does it weaken Bagehot's argument, in your view, or strengthen it, that he calls both Nero and his next-door neighbour a 'tyrant'?

Generally a slippery use of words is merely self-defeating. The Slovenian philosopher Slavoj Žižek said this to the Australian founder of WikiLeaks, Julian Assange, in a London theatre, in July 2011:

35. You are a terrorist in the way that Gandhi was. In what sense was Gandhi a terrorist? He tried to stop the normal functioning of the British state in India. You are trying to stop the normal functioning of information circulation.

It might be said that if peeling potatoes is art, then everything is art; and if everything is art, then nothing is 'art'. If Gandhi—of all people—was a terrorist, then we are all terrorists, and no one is. When we over-extend the meaning of a word we risk emptying it of meaning altogether.

# Ordering and indicating

I said in Chapter 1 that the most basic argument is an inference from a claim ($P \rightarrow Q$); here, the inference comes first ($Q \rightarrow P$):

36. I think of NATO as an enemy only with some difficulty, for Russia is a part of European culture.
VLADIMIR PUTIN, President of Russia, 5 March 2000

I have emboldened the word 'for', since this word is a common **reason indicator**. I have emboldened the word 'since' in my simple argument which follows, because this is another.

**Since** a claim by itself will seldom be very persuasive, its *significance* may have to be explained; so, a more developed argument will look like this:

Claim (**P**) → Explanation (**E**) → Inference (**Q**)

I have separated the claim and the explanation in the following argument, but, in practice, reasons and explanations may well overlap:

37. [P] Private property is acceptable only as a concession to human weakness, not as something desirable in itself. [E] People work more and dispute less when goods are privately owned than when they are held in common. [Q] Private property is, therefore, a necessary evil.
Adapted from R.H. Tawney, British economic historian, 1926

In a still more developed argument, of course, there will be several claims leading to the conclusion. How clear your argument is will depend, to some extent, upon the order in which you place these claims in what has often, rather unhelpfully, been called the 'main body' of your argument.

Political parties have to give electors reasons for voting for them. Sometimes these reasons are placed in what seems to be a random order. The UK Independence Party (UKIP) would have Britain withdraw from the European Union. Here are the reasons it gave for voting for the party before the European elections of 2004:

38. Your UKIP MEPs will:

SAY NO to EU membership, we want to run our own country
SAY NO to the EU constitution
SAY NO to unlimited EU immigration
SAY NO to the euro. Keep the pound and keep control
SAY NO to paying £25m into the EU every day—money which could build 100 new hospitals every year.
Vote UKIP: the party saying no to the EU.

> **2i.** Are the five imperatives to say no placed in a sensible order? Are all five necessary? Is their significance explained?

There is reasoning in the order, in this address by the then leader of the UK Conservative Party, before the same European elections (**because** is another very common reason indicator):

39. This election won't change the current government of Britain, but it will help to decide how Britain is governed in the future. And a vote for the Conservatives will send the Labour Government at home a very clear message.

Why will this election influence how Britain is governed? Because, just one week after polling day, Tony Blair plans to agree to sign a European Constitution that will give more and more powers to Brussels at the expense of the British Parliament. A vote for the Conservatives makes it clear that we want to be governed by Britain not Brussels.

Why will a vote for the Conservatives send the Labour Government a message? **Because** after all the promises, all the extra taxes and all the additional spending, the British people are sick and tired of being let down by Labour. A strong vote for the Conservative opposition tells them that time is running out.

MICHAEL HOWARD, Conservative Party leader, 2004

Howard gave two reasons for voting Conservative: the first was *specific*, and the second was *general*.

This writer to *The Times* newspaper made three (or four) claims, or suggestions, in what seems like a reasonable order. His first sentence serves as his **Statement** and is an argument in itself (and, again, I have emboldened the reason indicators):

40. **Inasmuch as** plastic is a rich source of energy we ought not to be dumping it in landfill sites.

    **In the first place,** a lot of the waste of plastic is accounted for by the bottled water industry. We Britons consume enough bottled water to go through 13 billion plastic bottles in a year, only three billion of which we recycle. Why on earth do we do this when water is on tap, and costs 500 times less than bottled water?

    Restaurants should serve filtered, chilled tap-water in reusable glass bottles; **moreover,** businesses in general could install water-coolers at much less cost than the 'spring' water that they buy to serve in their canteens.

    **Finally,** the Government could levy a tax on bottled water as Chicago has done with some success. Measures such as these would encourage us to treat plastic as the precious resource that it is.

    Adapted from a letter to *The Times*, August 2008

The writer focuses first on the consumer; then on particular businesses; then businesses in general; and then the government. The order is from *individual* to *society*, or, to put it simply, from *small* to *big*.

In the following philosophical argument (large parts of which I have omitted) the order is reasoned, as you would expect:

41. All our knowledge, both knowledge of things and knowledge of truths, rests upon acquaintance as its foundation...

    Sense-data are among the things with which we are acquainted; in fact, they supply the most obvious and striking example of knowledge by acquaintance...

The first extension beyond sense-data to be considered is acquaintance by *memory*. It is obvious that we often remember what we have seen or heard or had otherwise present to our senses, and that in such cases we are still immediately aware of what we remember, in spite of the fact that it appears as past and not as present...

The next extension to be considered is acquaintance by *introspection*. We are not only aware of things, but we are often aware of being aware of them...

We may, **therefore**, sum up as follows what has been said concerning acquaintance with things that exist. We have acquaintance in sensation with the data of the outer senses, and in introspection with the data of what may be called the inner sense; and we have acquaintance in memory with things which have been data either of the outer senses or of the inner sense.

BERTRAND RUSSELL, *The Problems of Philosophy*,
1912. By permission of Oxford University Press

The reason indicators are easily identified here; and 'therefore' is a common **conclusion indicator** (along with '**so**', '**hence**', '**thus**'), particularly in short arguments.

Russell's order might be said to be one from *simple* (things that we know by sensing them directly), to *complex* (things that we know by thinking); or—another way of putting it—the order is from *concrete* to *abstract*.

The politician who spoke the following fateful words also placed his claims in a rational order. He did not come to an explicit conclusion—but we can come to it for him:

42. We shall never sheathe the sword, which we have not lightly drawn, until Belgium recovers in full measure all, and more than all, that she has sacrificed; until France is adequately secured against the menace of aggression; until the rights of the smaller nationalities of Europe are placed upon an unassailable foundation; and until the military domination of Prussia is wholly and finally destroyed.

HERBERT ASQUITH, UK Prime Minister, 9 November 1914

Therefore, so, hence, thus, in sum, in consequence, we can infer that, taking all this into consideration, I conclude that, in light of this:

> it will be some time, and there will be much hardship, before we
> sheathe our swords again.

Asquith might not have wanted to be too explicit, since there were those who thought they might have put the 'Prussians' to the sword by Christmas.

> **2j.** Asquith lists four aims to be achieved before the war could be said to be over. What seems to be the basis for the order in which he has placed these aims?

So, having chosen and refined the **Question** that you will answer, you will need to do the following in your:

---

**Statement**

➤ avoid **vagueness** by **defining** the key terms that you will use;

➤ be **precise** about the scope of your argument;

➤ be aware of any **assumptions** that you may be making;

➤ take care not to use **ambiguous** language;

➤ be wary of **conflating** terms that ordinarily have different uses.

---

You have some idea what your main claim (your conclusion) will be before you begin to gather evidence. As we saw in Chapter 1, there will be interaction between claim and evidence, as you select and study your sources:

Claim ← → Evidence

You might even start jotting down the reasons that you think you will give for coming to your conclusion, and putting them in order:

- from *specific* to *general*;*
- from *small* to *big*;
- from *simple* to *complex*;
- from *less significant* to *more significant*;
- from *early* to *late* (i.e. chronological order).

(*There seems to be an east–west difference here: Western Europeans seem to think *specific-to-general*, and Eastern Europeans to think *general-to-specific*. See Chapter 6.)

The question of the order in which you place the claims, or points, that you want to make is of some importance in a long argument, so I shall have more to say about it in Chapter 10.

Having outlined your own argument, though (and before developing it any further), you will need to find out what answers other people have come up with to the question that you have chosen to answer.

# 3   What case have others made?

I shall aim in this chapter to explain:

- what it is to oppose others' claims;
- the value of considering an opposing argument first;
- where you might get your information from, or not;
- why it matters who the author is.

## Counter-claims

What is the point of advancing an argument? It must be to say something fresh—or at least to say something said already, in a *refreshing* way. There is no point in rewriting what has been written before. It would neither be stimulating to write, nor interesting to read; and, perhaps more to the point, there would be no addition to understanding.

Every new piece of writing—however short—should be seen as a chance to add to understanding, by however little. It is the perception that an essay, or seminar paper, or dissertation is an exercise in rewriting, in re-presenting what has been said many times before, that leads to the cynicism of downloading, and of accessing ready-made essays on the Internet.

What you say will be different—not new, perhaps, but different—because it will be *you* who is saying it; and you who is selecting and ordering the reasons to support the claims you make. It may differ from the *received opinion* on the subject; from a common assumption; or from the position taken by an institution or individual, for example:

| Common claim | Your claim |
|---|---|
| Schooling is vital if children are to be socialized and receive a rounded education. | Education is vital, but not schooling; home education has its advantages for some. |

Many letters to the editors of newspapers are responses to claims made in a recent edition. Here is just one:

> Peter Watson claims that there have only been three significant scientific breakthroughs since 1950: the contraceptive pill, the internet, and—potentially—the cloning of a human embryo. Surely he must recognize the relevance of such developments as the mapping of the human genome, the microchip, laser technology, and artificial satellite communication.
>
> Adapted from a letter to *The Observer*, May 2005

Peter Watson (in a book in which he compared 1905 with 2005) had made a claim; this letter-writer made a **counter-claim**. It is difficult to see how either of the claims might have been supported: what counts as 'significant' in science is as open as what counts as 'significant' in art. Anyone can play the game of claim and counter-claim—and most of us do.

In the three passages that follow, the counter-claims oppose (anonymous) claims:

> Whereas it has long been known and declared that the poor have no right to the property of the rich, I wish it to be known and declared that the rich have no right to the property of the poor.
>
> JOHN RUSKIN, English art critic, 1862

> The alternative to economic growth is not, as some occasionally seem to suppose, an England of quiet market towns linked only by trains puffing slowly and peacefully through green meadows. The alternative is slums, dangerous roads, old factories, cramped schools, stunted lives.
>
> EDWARD HEATH, UK Prime Minister, 1973

> There are two ideas of government. There are those who believe that, if you will only legislate to make the well-to-do prosperous, their prosperity will leak through on those below. The Democratic idea, however, has been that if you legislate to make the masses prosperous, their prosperity will find its way up through every class which rests upon them.
>
> WILLIAM JENNINGS BRYAN, US politician, 1896

These are not arguments, strictly speaking (all three lack a reason, or reasons, to support their main claim): the authors simply present a claim (made by others), and a counter-claim—or *counter-assertion*—of their own (William Jennings Bryan was a Democrat). They are not arguments because the authors give us no grounds for agreeing with them that Claim B is superior to Claim A; they simply present, first, the claim that they disagree with, then they juxtapose their own claim:

| Claim A | Claim B |
|---|---|
| The poor have no right to the property of the rich. | The rich have no right to the property of the poor. |
| The alternative to economic growth is a green and pleasant England. | The alternative is slums, desolation, stunted lives. |
| Increase general prosperity by favouring the well-to-do. | Increase it by legislating to benefit the masses. |

Two claims are offered and you make your choice. In an argument, though, you are not offering your readers a choice; you are trying to persuade them to agree with Claim B.

> **3a.** Can you think of reasons that John Ruskin might have given to support his counter-claim?

In the following counter-claim, there is a hint of a reason ('our present experience') for preferring Claim B to Claim A; but the author would need to be more precise about what that experience was if he was to convince us:

> It had been boldly predicted by some of the early Christians that the conversion of the world would lead to the establishment of perpetual peace. In looking back, with our present experience, we are driven to the melancholy conclusion that, instead of diminishing the number of wars, ecclesiastical influence has actually and very seriously increased it.
> WILLIAM EDWARD HARTPOLE LECKY, Irish historian, 1869

Hindsight, as they say, is a wonderful thing; but it does not speak for itself. A second historian might object that the world had not been converted, and that the world would have been a much better place if it had. A third might claim that things might have been a lot worse if there had not been monasteries, for example (see Argument 121 in Chapter 5).

In these offerings, Alistair Cooke and Queen Elizabeth II *do* give us reasons for preferring Claim B to Claim A—for inferring Claim B from Claim A—so they *are* arguments:

43. No American institution is worse understood abroad than American football. British sportsmen who know their way around a rugby field, a billiard table, and even a chess-board succumb without a second thought to the facetious view of American football as a mindless bout of mayhem between brutes got up in spacemen outfits. But it would not take more than a couple of weeks of careful instruction from a coach or a fan to realize that American football is an open-air chess game disguised as warfare. It is without question the most scientific of all outdoor games.

   ALISTAIR COOKE, US-based British broadcaster, 1971

44. It is rightly acknowledged that people of faith have no monopoly of virtue and that the wellbeing and prosperity of the nation depend on the contribution of individuals and groups of all faiths and none. Yet, as the recent visit of his holiness the Pope reminded us, churches and the other great faith traditions retain the potential to inspire great enthusiasm, loyalty, and a concern for the common good.

   QUEEN ELIZABETH II, November 2010

> **3b.** What is Claim **A**, in Argument 43, and what is Cooke's counter-claim (**B**)? What is his conclusion, and what reasons does he give to support it?

Cooke is scornful of what British sportsmen think of American football; but he does go further than merely to place his own opinion alongside someone else's. The Queen goes further still:

| Claim A | Claim B |
|---|---|
| Non-religious people are as likely to be virtuous, and to make as valuable a contribution to the nation as religious people. | Religious people do have a special gift for enthusiasm, loyalty, and a concern for the common good. |

The Queen (or her speech-writer) has to be careful with her words: she cannot appear to favour her religious over her non-religious subjects, and—though she is the Supreme Governor of the Church of England—she cannot appear to favour Anglican Christians above other believers. What she does do is give us some grounds for assenting to her very measured counter-claim (Claim B): the fact that the visit of the Pope was an acknowledged success. It is a low-key argument; but it is an argument.

Why present Claim A (or a fully developed **Argument A**) at all? Why not just go straight into the case that you want to make? There are good reasons for considering what others have said first:

- it gives your reader(s) a point of reference, a sort of 'story so far'; a *context* in which to weigh your **Argument B**;
- it shows that you acknowledge that there are other points of view than your own;
- in a comparison with **Argument A** (which you show to be defective in some way), your own (well-supported) **Argument B** is given extra weight;
- and your **Argument B** leads straight into your intermediate (see Chapter 10) or main conclusion.

# Counter-argument

When you make a case, you place claims in a balance: the claims (reasons and conclusions) of others [A] go in one pan, and your **Argument B** goes in the other. Your job is to ensure that your Argument B is the weightier one.

Of course, there may be more than two 'sides' to the question; and you might want to include a number of perhaps quite diverse claims in a composite **A** argument. When you write a dissertation, or thesis, for example, you will very likely present **Argument A** in the form of a *review of literature*, where you give an account of the views of several authors who have made contributions to the position that you seek to counter.

Each time you find a reference in a book, journal, or website that is relevant to your question make a note of the title, the author's and publisher's names, the date and place of publication, and the page number, or URL, so that you can be sure to find it again, and make full reference to it in your own work.

Minutes spent making a note of these details when you first find the reference will save you hours of chasing later.

Here, a reader in Los Angeles replies to a claim concerning the performance of Irish children in maths tests:

45. Many have proposed that the solution to the decline in the standard of maths in Irish schools is to improve teaching methods. Findings of research done by a private firm in the US and England would suggest that a major factor is the lack of parental involvement. In these countries, and probably in Ireland, too, the level of support given by parents—assistance with homework, providing extra tutoring, keeping up with developments in the maths curriculum— is much lower than in Asian countries.

    In Singapore, for instance, parents are much more likely to be kept informed about maths assignments and forthcoming exams; and, whereas parents in the US and England may be able to help their children with basic arithmetic, but flounder when it comes to algebra and geometry, parents in Singapore—knowing their limitations—lay on extra tuition.

    Improvements to maths teaching in Irish schools might be part of the answer; but more might be achieved if parents themselves went back to school.

    Adapted from a letter to *The Irish Times*, December 2010

Claim A appears to be that what is needed is better maths teaching. No reason is given to support this claim—it is rather a commonsense intuition, perhaps, than an argument. The letter-writer does give a reason for his Claim B, though, so he does offer a **counter-argument**.

**3c.** What seems to be the letter-writer's conclusion, and what reason does he give to support it?

It may not be a strong argument, and it may not persuade us that what is done in Singapore could be done in England, the United States, and Ireland. But his Argument B is definitely weightier than Claim A. He points to research to support his conclusion, which the 'many' who advocate improved teaching methods fail to do.

This letter-writer does a little more to tip the balance:

46 The so-called 'Arab Spring' has seen the removal of some rather unsavoury heads of state; but we should not expect that democracy will come to the Middle East any time soon. England has not been a democracy for long. What held democracy back was the monopoly of power enjoyed by the state religion. Pluralism was at a discount until well into the 19th Century—and even more recently where women and gays were concerned. As long as those in power in Libya, Egypt, Iraq, Syria and the states and statelets of the Arabian peninsula suppose that their power is God-given, and as long as they persecute and discriminate against those who do not share their particular religious beliefs, there is no hope of western-style democracy in the Middle East.

Adapted from a letter to *The Independent*, 15 July 2013

There are the makings of a developed argument here:

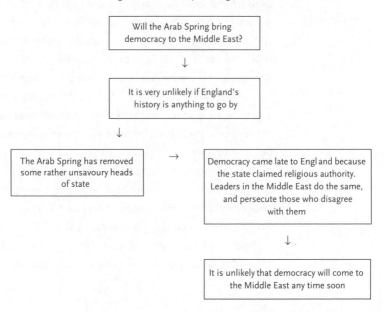

The letter-writer raises a question; states her position; presents a reason for optimism; counters this with a reason for pessimism; and reaches a conclusion in line with the earlier statement. We are not given a lot of information, and would certainly need more before we could know whether to agree or to disagree with the conclusion.

> **3d.** What would you infer from what little information we have here? What more information might we need?

Here is a further, more developed argument, adapted from the original. It is a review of the impact of psychology 50 years after the pioneering work of William James:

47. What have been the effects of the new psychology?

Much is to its credit—the Victorians distrusted pleasure, and were skilful at rationalising their impulses; but much has been lost, too.

It is impossible not to approve of many of the signs of the new spirit. Partly as a result of the new psychology, men and women today are more honest, more open—there is less hypocrisy. They know more about themselves and what it is to be psychologically healthy. But the new psychology poses a real danger. It has given rise to a distrust of reason which has led people to favour *un*reason; to think that instinct provides a short cut to truth and that impulse is a guide to good behaviour. Secondly, it may be doubted whether the distinctions that psychoanalysis makes between reason, will, and instinct—and, indeed, between consciousness and the unconscious—can be justified. It makes more sense to regard active life as single and continuous. This activity moves us to acquire food when we are hungry and to resolve mathematical equations when we are inquisitive. It is the same activity in mankind as in animals, but it is directed to different ends.

Reason is not something tacked on to instinct; it is simply instinct at a higher level. It is possible to maintain a view of life as freely-willed, dynamic, and creative, without thinking of reason as the evolutionary outcome of irrational instinct.

Psychology has led us to concede a far greater importance to the understanding of instinct and impulse than the Victorians did;

but we should not let it scoff at the higher expressions of will and reason as psychoanalysis has been inclined to do.

Adapted from C.E.M. JOAD, *Guide to Modern Thought*, 1933

Joad was a philosopher, not a psychologist, so it is understandable that he should have privileged reason over instinct.

> **3e.** How would you summarize **Argument A**, countered by Joad? What reasons does he give, in his own **Argument B**, for coming to the conclusion that he does?

# Selection and evaluation of sources

When you write—on any subject—you are going where many have gone before. You owe it to your own argument to look at the argument of at least one of your predecessors in the field.

Where will you look? You will look in books, in journals, and on websites—and in each case you will expect to find the name of the author, or authors, concerned; the name of the publisher; and the date of publication. Without these, you must judge the source to be **unreliable**, and therefore one that you might prefer not to use.

An advertisement used to appear regularly in the British press, from which this is an extract:

> **Shamed By Your English?**
> A world-famous educational publisher reports that there is a simple technique for acquiring a swift mastery of good English.
>
> It can double your powers of self-expression. It can pay you real dividends in business and social advancement, and give you added poise, self-confidence and personal effectiveness.
>
> The details of this method are described in his fascinating book *Good English—the Language of Success*, sent free on request.

According to this publisher, many people do not realize how much they could influence others simply by speaking and writing with greater power, authority, and precision.

Who was this 'world-famous educational publisher', author of this 'fascinating book'? All the advertisement told us about him was that he lived at a post office box in Stockport, Cheshire. How **credible**, how trustworthy, can a claim be when its author remains anonymous? And if it was such a good book, why was it not available 'in all good bookshops'? Why was it 'free'? Where's the catch?

Ordinarily, when we consider whether a source is reliable or not, we judge:

1. The book, journal, or website, itself; and
2. The author or authors of the text.

In this case, both fall under suspicion before we have even set eyes on the book.

We might be sceptical about any advertisement—as we might be of letters to the press. The following extract is from a letter sent to the *Irish Independent*, in 2010, by a correspondent (who did give his name and his PhD) from County Wexford:

> The most recent Intergovernmental Panel on Climate Change report has been shown to be full of errors exaggerating the effects of global warming [for example] on Himalayan glaciers.
>
> Now, even London's *Guardian* newspaper, long a 'warmist' bastion, is starting to question the 'settled science'.
>
> But don't expect our Government to notice. Despite repeated requests to the Government's Committee on Climate Change and Energy Security to make a presentation properly discussing the underlying science, I have been refused because of lack of time.

*The Guardian* gave space to the chairman of the Panel, one month later, to reply to such critics (again, this is an extract, from a 750-word article):

> To dismiss the implications of climate change based on an error about the rate at which Himalayan glaciers are melting is an act of astonishing intellectual legerdemain.* Yet this is what some doubters of climate change are claiming...
>
> The Intergovernmental Panel on Climate Change (IPCC) has published four comprehensive assessments of climate change and several important special reports since its founding in 1988. The last such document, the fourth assessment report from 2007, mobilised 450 scientists from all over the world to write the report. An

additional 800 contributing authors gave specialised inputs and about 2,500 expert reviewers provided 90,000 comments.

In this mammoth task, which yielded a finished product of nearly 3,000 pages, there was a regrettable error indicating the Himalayan glaciers were likely to melt by the year 2035. This mistake has been acknowledged by the IPCC. Learning from this error, the IPCC has requested, in tandem with the United Nations' secretary general, an independent review of its procedures and practices by the Inter-Academy Council (IAC).

© DR RAJENDRA PACHAURI, Guardian News & Media, 2010

\* Sleight of hand.

Whom do we trust? It may not be a question of whether an author has, or does not have, a PhD; or whether one writes a letter or an article. It may have something to do with the newspaper that publishes the letter or the article (in this case, both newspapers referred to are as trustworthy as any); it may have a lot to do with who the writer is, and what the writer represents—what group of people, or institution.

An article published in July 2012 commemorated the 400th anniversary of the trials of the 12 'Pendle witches', in Lancashire: it led to a flurry of blog-posts, as follows:

> **Coffee6:** Stories of witches unite us with our Celtic past. They were wise, prophetic healers whom the Church demonized. They were not the ill-willed evil-doers of myth.
>
> **SamsonJS:** You're wrong about witches being healers and benign seers. They weren't benevolent at all: they cursed those who crossed them, and used magic to cause harm. The sort of innocent herbalists you talk about weren't called witches.
>
> **Coffee6:** You can't be serious. Herbalists were among the very first to be burnt.
>
> **JamezJohnz:** Do you have any evidence for that? The victims of the Salem Witch trials, for instance, weren't exactly innocent herbalists. In England, women who were guilty of the evils of witchcraft weren't burnt, they were hanged.
>
> **Susanlily:** Not burnt? Some witches were hanged, it's true; but being burnt at the stake was the standard punishment for witches convicted of so-called petty treason, as it was for heretics. The last woman burnt at the stake was in 1789, the year of the French Revolution.
>
> Adapted from *The Guardian Review*, July 2012
> (all names are changed)

Who is to say who is right? One writer alleges one thing, and the next counter-claims. The boon of blogging—that there is no fussy editor between the blogger and the reader—is what makes a blog such a defective source of information. It is the editing that counts: an article (in a newspaper, but more especially in an academic journal) is edited; a book is edited; a government website is edited. This means it is read by other writers in the field, and checked, and approved before publication. A blog-post (to all intents and purposes anonymous) is not.

There are journals, of course, that are not 'academic', in the scholarly sense of that term. The following writer refers to a self-styled nutritionist whom I shall not name:

> She produces lengthy documents that have an air of 'referenciness', with nice little superscript numbers, which talk about trials and studies, and research, and papers...but when you follow the numbers, and check the references, it's shocking how often they aren't what she claimed them to be in the main body of the text, or they refer to funny little magazines and books, such as *Delicious*, *Creative Living*, *Healthy Eating*, and my favourite, *Spiritual Nutrition and the Rainbow Diet*, rather than proper academic journals.
>
> BEN GOLDACRE, *Bad Science*, London: Fourth Estate, 2008

And not all books will inspire trust, just because they are books: the United Russia party commissioned academics to write a history of Russia of which the party could approve. Andrei Loginov was Vladimir Putin's envoy to the Russian parliament, in 2010, when he said:

48. There exists a uniform text for science, physics and maths—why not for literature and history? We're talking about the history of Russia—the basic textbook must be unified across the country. Otherwise, you get too varied a version and people can't sit down and have a conversation together.

Conversations in united Russia are not expected to extend to more than two words: 'How true!'

> **3f.** Why might a 'western' historian treat such a 'uniform text' with caution?

When it comes to judging whether or not a source of information is *trustworthy*, it is wise to check that:

- the author's name is given in full (or the authors' names), and there is some information given about the author's qualifications for writing the book—whether he or she has written other, acclaimed, books, for example; and whether other authors have testified to his or her *expertise* (see the following section);
- the publisher is named. This may not be a commercial publisher; it may be an institution, a university, a pressure group, a government department; how well known, and how well established it is, and what else it publishes will all be clues;
- the date of publication is given, and the date of any new edition, so that you know the text is reasonably up to date (if this matters—some findings date faster than others);
- the place and circumstances of the publication are made clear. (Was the publication sponsored by a commercial, voluntary, or party-political organization? What might have been its motives for wanting the document to be published?).

In general, if 'two heads are better than one' many heads may be better still. The more hands a text has passed through, the more reliable (though not always the more readable) it is likely to be.

# Reputation and expertise

You will want to be sure that the argument that you are countering is one that is *worth* countering. To argue against a weak argument is to punch a cushion. An argument is more likely to be worthwhile if its author has a **reputation**, or 'good name'.

49. The plough is one of the most ancient and most valuable of man's inventions; but long before he existed the land was in fact regularly ploughed, and still continues to be thus ploughed by earthworms. It may be doubted whether there are many other animals which have played so important a part in the history of the world, as have these lowly organized creatures.

    CHARLES DARWIN, evolutionary biologist, 1881

50. In gravitational fields there are no such things as rigid bodies with Euclidean properties; thus the fictitious rigid body of reference is of no avail in the general theory of relativity. The motion of clocks

is also influenced by gravitational fields, and in such a way that a physical definition of time which is made directly with the aid of clocks has by no means the same degree of plausibility as in the special theory of relativity.

ALBERT EINSTEIN, German-born physicist, 1916

51. As a military man who has given half a century of active service, I say in all sincerity that the nuclear arms race has no military purpose. Wars cannot be fought with nuclear weapons; their existence only adds to our perils because of the illusions that they have generated. The world now stands on the brink of the final abyss. Let us resolve to take all possible practicable steps to ensure that we do not, through our own folly, go over the edge.

LORD LOUIS MOUNTBATTEN, English naval
commander and statesman, 1979

Each of these writers achieved a certain reputation in their lifetimes, and they have held on to it. We are inclined to trust Darwin on evolutionary biology, Einstein on physics (even if we seldom understand him), and Mountbatten on military matters (even if, or because, few politicians took any notice). The claims of these writers have high **credibility** because they were acknowledged **experts** in their fields.

They may not be experts, though, in someone else's field, as Flaubert tartly observed:

52. A novelist, in my view, does not have the right to give advice on the issues of his time. His vocation is to imitate God in His: that is to say, to create and to maintain a lofty silence.

GUSTAVE FLAUBERT, French novelist, 1866

In February 1963, a group of fair-minded intellectuals signed a public statement calling for the abolition of military rule over Israel's Arab population. The prime minister of the time said in the Israeli parliament:

53. If I shall need an expert opinion in matters of Talmudic commentary I shall gladly refer to Professor Urbach, in Godly matters to Professor Buber, and in matters of wheeling and dealing and economics to Professor Patinkin. But I do not recognize the supreme expertise of these distinguished professors in matters of security or in matters of political ethics.

DAVID BEN GURION, Israeli Prime Minister and
Defence Minister, 1963

**3g.** What counter-argument might the 'distinguished professors' have offered to the prime minister?

Experts take risks, even in their own fields, when they plough close to the edge:

54. Historians, I believe, should study the process of history and not merely the detail of the narrow sector in which, perforce, they specialise; and if this means that they must occasionally trespass into less familiar sectors, they must be prepared for the consequences.

    HUGH TREVOR-ROPER, *The Rise of Christian Europe*, London: Thames & Hudson, 1966. Reprinted by permission of Thames & Hudson Ltd, London

As an expert on the Third Reich, Trevor-Roper declared as authentic 'Hitler Diaries' that later proved to have been forged. The 'consequences' were that Trevor-Roper's reputation was seriously damaged. Expertise only stretches so far. For another prime minister, the credibility of experts was very close to zero:

55. No lesson seems to be so deeply inculcated by the experience of life as that you never should trust experts. If you believe the doctors, nothing is wholesome; if you believe the theologians, nothing is innocent; if you believe the soldiers, nothing is safe. They all require to have their strong wine diluted by a very large admixture of insipid common sense.

    LORD SALISBURY, British Prime Minister, 1877

Even experts might be *biased* (I shall have more to say about bias in Chapter 7); and they might stand to gain from the acceptance of their claims—when, that is, they have a **vested interest** in the outcome of a debate. George F. Baer was a mine owner, so he certainly had a vested (financial) interest in preventing his miners from joining a union. His argument is more than a century old:

56. The rights and interest of the labouring man will be protected and cared for—not by the labour agitators, but by the Christian men to whom God in his infinite wisdom has given the control of the property interests of the country, and upon the successful management of which so much depends.

    GEORGE F. BAER, Pennsylvania mine owner, 1902

But Baer's torch was taken up in recent years by the chairman of a mining company that blew the tops off mountains in Central Appalachia to extract coal. He defended what his company did, in a debate with Robert F. Kennedy Jr, in these terms:

57. This industry is what made this country great. If we forget that, we are going to have to learn to speak Chinese. Coal is what made the industrial revolution possible. If windmills were the thing to do, if solar panels were, it would happen naturally.

    Anyone who says they know what the temperature of Earth is going to be in 2020, or 2030, needs to be put in an asylum, because they don't. This whole thing is designed to transfer wealth from the US to other countries.

    DON BLANKENSHIP, Chairman of Massey Energy, 2010

By 'this whole thing', Blankenship meant attempts by environmentalists to curb his company's activities. (It is less clear what he might have meant by 'happen naturally'—see Chapter 2). We would not go to a mine owner, perhaps, for an objective assessment of the impact of burning fossil fuels; but we might expect that papers published by bodies called the Institute for Humane Studies and the Foundation for Research on Economics and the Environment would be 'scientific'. According to the environmental campaign group Greenpeace USA, however, these and other think-tanks are handsomely funded by a Kansas-based oil company:

The company's network of lobbyists, former executives and organisations has created a forceful stream of misinformation that company-funded entities produce and disseminate. The propaganda is then replicated, repackaged and echoed many times across a web of political front-groups and think-tanks. On repeated occasions, organisations funded by this corporation have led the assault on climate science and scientists, 'green jobs', renewable energy and climate policy progress.

Adapted from the website of greenpeace.org/usa, March 2010

Papers written by 'scientists' paid to toe a company line have a clear vested interest: their claims are no more credible than those of historians paid to toe a party line.

> **3h.** To whom *would* you go for 'an objective assessment of the impact of burning fossil fuels'?

Reviewers of books may have a vested interest in a book that they review: the billionaire, former Conservative Party Chairman Lord Ashcroft reviewed a book about the Conservative UK Chancellor of the Exchequer, *George Osborne: The Austerity Chancellor*, by Janan Ganesh. The book was published by Biteback. This was the final paragraph of what the author will have been relieved to acknowledge was a friendly review:

> [T]his is by no means a one-sided account, and ends with a description of the 'curious mix of vulnerability and over-confidence' that produced the omnishambolic* budget of 2012. Ganesh has produced an important biography of a man who is the deputy prime minister in all but name.
> © MICHAEL ASHCROFT, Guardian News & Media, 27 October 2012

> * This derives from the neologism 'omnishambles' to mean an utter mess.

This line was then appended to the review: 'Lord Ashcroft has an interest in Biteback Publishing'. The statement does not justify us in distrusting Lord Ashcroft's judgement; but we would probably not have expected a man with (presumably) a financial interest in the publisher to write an *un*friendly review.

We need not (and perhaps should not) go as far as Lord Salisbury in his scepticism, though: if you do not trust acknowledged experts, you will not be able to call on them to support your own argument when you come to it.

So far, then, the steps on the path to an argument are these:

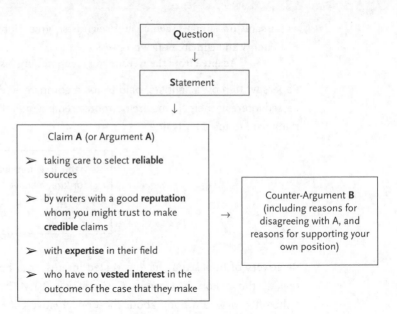

In laying out the argument, or arguments, that you will counter (or modify, or differ from, or add to in some way), it is important that you are fair to it—that you take it seriously. Having taken it seriously, though, you will want to point out the weaknesses in it.

I said at the beginning of this chapter that you should aim to say something a bit different. It may be that the difference will lie less in your answer to the question than in your critique of the weaknesses in other people's answers. There will be some weaknesses, because if there were not you would have no case of your own to make. You would be like the conversationalists in Loginov's Russia with nothing more to say than: 'How true!'

# 4

# What do you make of these arguments?

I shall aim in this chapter to explain:

- the risk of misrepresenting others' claims;
- and of confusing causes and effects;
- of drawing conclusions from history;
- and of appealing to ours and others' emotions.

## Overstatement and straw man

When we counter an argument, we may be tempted to *misrepresent* it: we exaggerate its defects, in order to make it look weaker than it is. Karl Marx countered the claims of the bourgeoisie to their private property. Understandably, the bourgeoisie was horrified:

58. You are horrified at our intending to do away with private property. But in your existing society, private property is already done away with for nine tenths of the population; its existence for the few is solely due to its non-existence in the hands of those nine tenths.

KARL MARX (with FRIEDRICH ENGELS),
*The Communist Manifesto*, 1848

Marx rather **overstated** his case: he was going too far in wanting to do away with private property altogether. He was very poor himself; but he would have been still poorer if his friend Friedrich Engels had not been a property owner, and sent him cash in the post.

One of the 'horrified' property owners was the very bourgeois barrister and Clerk of the House of Commons, Erskine May. He was rather given to **overstatement** himself:

59. According to [Marx]: 'From everyone according to his abilities; to everyone according to his needs.' In other words, no man is to

profit by his own strength, abilities, or industry; but is to minister
to the wants of the weak, the stupid and the idle.

SIR THOMAS ERSKINE MAY, English constitutional theorist, 1877

Sir Thomas went rather further than overstatement. Are his 'other
words'—the interpretation that he puts on Marx's slogan—ones
that Marx would have recognized or used? Probably not: Marx's plea
for classlessness has been misrepresented. The 'everyone', who has
both abilities and needs, has become two kinds of people: those who
have abilities and those who have needs. Sir Thomas might not have
come across many people, like Marx, who had both.

Sir Thomas set up a **straw man**. Literally, a straw man is a manne-
quin made of straw set up as a target. Sir Thomas set up a caricature
of Marx's vision so that he might more easily ridicule it. Fear and
loathing of 'the masses' did not die with Sir Thomas Erskine May:

60. Democracy: A government of the masses. Authority derived
through mass meeting or any other form of 'direct' expression.
Results in mobocracy. Attitude toward property is communistic—
negating property rights. Attitude toward law is that the will of the
majority shall regulate, whether it be based upon deliberation or
governed by passion, prejudice and impulse, without restraint or
regard for consequences. Results in demagogism, license, agitation,
discontent and anarchy.

US Army Training Manual, 1932

The propertied and the powerful—whether in uniform or not—always
have been suspicious of democracy. But is this a version of democracy that the Founding Fathers of America would have recognized?
Probably not. Has democracy in America meant the negation of property rights? Has it meant mob rule? When we do not like something,
we exaggerate its worst features. We make a straw man of it.

In 2008, Sir David King, the UK government's one-time chief scientific adviser, was critical of 'green' activists. He believed that there
could only be technological solutions to climate change—and that
one of these solutions was nuclear energy. Did John Sauven, then
executive director of Greenpeace UK, take a radically different view?

61. There is a suspicion, and I have that suspicion myself, that a large
number of people who label themselves 'green' are actually keen to
take us back to the 18th or even the 17th century. . . . They say: 'Let's
get away from all the technological gizmos and developments of

the 20th century'.... And then there's the real world, where everyone is aspiring to the sort of standard of living that we have, which is based on a large energy consumption.

SIR DAVID KING, January 2008

62. We need science to get us out of the climate change hole we're in. . . We're talking about technical solutions that can also be safely spread to every country in the world, no matter how unstable. Nuclear power isn't that technology, but Sir David wants to take us back to the 1950s, the last time we were told it would solve all our problems.

JOHN SAUVEN, © Guardian News & Media Ltd, January 2008

Did Sir David really think that 'greens' wanted to take us back to the 1600s? Did he really imagine they wanted to abandon all that was accomplished in the 20th century? Did Mr Sauven really think that Sir David wanted to take us back to the 1950s? And did he know anyone who said nuclear energy would 'solve all our problems'? Probably not: they might have disagreed about the need for nuclear energy; but they both looked to science to combat climate change.

> **4a.** Which of the two arguments, 61 or 62, is the stronger, in your view, and why?

A straw man may scare the crows, but it need not deceive the rest of us.

If the author, or any of the authors, of **Argument A** (the argument, or arguments, that you will counter) sets up a straw man, it is not difficult to spot that this is what they are doing. It is a weakness in an argument that you might legitimately point out; and, of course, it is a weakness that you might hope to avoid in **Argument B**.

An author who sets up a straw man makes the argument he would counter so weak that it is highly unlikely that anyone would put it forward. Defoe's stuffed-headed scholar is a genuine straw man:

63. We must distinguish between a man of polite learning and a mere scholar: the first is a gentleman and what a gentleman should be; the last is a mere book-case, a bundle of letters, a head stuffed with the jargon of languages, a man that understands everybody but is understood by nobody.

DANIEL DEFOE, English novelist and journalist, 1729

When an author is sure of his ground (or he thinks he is; see Chapter 6), or he argues emotionally (see later in this chapter), he is tempted into overstatement. There may be something in the distinction between the man who wears his learning lightly, and the 'ivory-tower' academic (though any division of the world into two is risky; see Chapter 8); but was it necessary for Defoe to go as far as he does in his final claim?

It is all too easy to get carried away—as Burke was when he reflected on the French Revolution, and Parisian 'mobocracy':

The age of chivalry is gone. That of sophisters,* economists, and calculators has succeeded; and the glory of Europe is extinguished for ever.

EDMUND BURKE, Irish politician and political thinker, 1790

\* Subtle speech-makers? 'Mere scholars'?

The Paris mob was a pretty fearsome spectacle; but history seems to have demonstrated that Burke's final claim was an overstatement. Politicians, advertisers, headline-writers are rather given to overstatement. Norman Tebbit, a politician through and through, targeted the 'permissive society' of the 1960s in this extract from his 1985 Disraeli lecture:

64. The permissives scorned traditional standards. Bad art was as good as good art. Grammar and spelling were no longer important. To be clean was no better than to be filthy. Good manners

were no better than bad. Family life was derided as an outdated bourgeois concept. Criminals deserved as much sympathy as their victims. Many homes and classrooms became disorderly—if there was neither right nor wrong there could be no bases for punishment or reward. Violence and soft pornography became accepted in the media. Thus was sown the wind; and we are now reaping the whirlwind.

NORMAN TEBBIT, Chairman of the UK Conservative Party, 1985

Tebbit was overstating his case; but he also made a straw man of the 'permissives': was there anybody in the 1960s who claimed that to be filthy, to produce bad art, and to be ill-mannered was acceptable, and that there was nothing that was wrong? Probably not.

Jeremy Collier, an English clergyman, was a vehement critic of the theatre of his day (the Restoration theatre of Wycherley, Vanbrugh, Congreve); HM was a *Guardian* reader passionate about drama (his name has been withheld here, and his letter has been adapted):

65. Nothing can be more disserviceable to probity and religion than the management of the stage. It cherishes those passions, and rewards those vices, which 'tis the business of reason to discountenance. It strikes at the root of principle, draws off the inclinations from virtue, and spoils good education: 'tis the most effective means to baffle the force of discipline, to emasculate people's spirits, and debauch their manners.

JEREMY COLLIER, 1698

66. We should be up in arms about the depths to which drama has sunk in this country. Condemned to die for lack of funding by idiots in government whose sole memory of our literature is from their dull school days, we are denied a share in our great inheritance. Drama should be everywhere: on the streets, in the public park, in every pub and club across the land, 24/7, both free of charge, and paid for.

HM, Somerset, December 2004

Collier might have had a point when he railed against the theatre of his day: Shakespeare it was not—but did he (like Burke, lamenting the end of the age of chivalry) have to accuse it of bringing civilization as we know it to an end? HM's enthusiasm for drama is admirable—but did he have to insist that it be in our face everywhere, all the time? Overstatement is overstatement whether it is in the service of praise or blame.

Your own argument is more likely to be accepted if you 'tell it like it is'. Keep your claims modest, measured, even *under*stated, and your argument will be the stronger for it, not the weaker.

Overstatement appears to lend weight to argument, and therefore it is common. But force is not weight. Here is one more argument that may be thought to be overstated:

67. 'They have no work', you say. Say rather that they either refuse work or quickly turn themselves out of it. They are simply good-for-nothings, who in one way or another live on the good-for-somethings—vagrants and sots, criminals and those on the way to crime, youth who are burdens on hard-worked parents, men who appropriate the wages of their wives, fellows who share the gains of prostitutes, and then, less visible and less numerous, there is a corresponding class of women.

HERBERT SPENCER, English apostle of laissez-faire, 1884

> **4b.** In what respects would you say Spencer has overstated his case, and so, perhaps, weakened it? And is there a straw man here?

# Causes and conditions

In Chapter 1, I suggested that when we make a claim (when we hope to advance knowledge) we make an association between two objects: **P** and **Q**. One of the simplest sorts of association is **cause and effect**: **P** causes **Q**; **Q** is the effect of **P**. This American warning notice made the association clear:

---

### WARNING

Falling Will Cause Injury or Death

Stay Back From Cliff Edges

---

If only life (and death) were that simple. The relationship between **P** and **Q** is rarely as clear as this: cause and effect are sometimes mistaken for each other.

68.  Aristotle said that men are not equal by nature: some are born to slavery, and others to rule. Aristotle was right; but he mistook the effect for the cause. It is certain that a man who is born a slave will live as a slave. But he is only a slave 'by nature' because his forefathers were slaves *against* nature. The first slaves were enslaved by force, and inertia has kept them in that state.

JEAN-JACQUES ROUSSEAU, French philosopher, 1762

Aristotle appears to have thought that 'nature' (**P**) was the cause, and slavery (**Q**) was the effect. Not so, said Rousseau (speaking from within a very different culture from that of Aristotle): enslavement of certain men by force was the cause, and what Greeks thought was 'natural' (the enslavement of the children of the enslaved) was the effect. Here is another Frenchman:

69.  Architecture is an art which is basically geometrical. The cube is the basis of architecture because the right angle is necessary—the steps of a staircase consist of vertical and horizontal planes and the corners of rooms are nearly always right angles. We need right angles.

ROBERT MALLET-STEVENS, French architect, 1924

Mallet-Stevens assumes that the right angle is necessary (**P**), and as a result, the cube is the basis of architecture (**Q**). It is true enough that when a building is rectangular (**P**), the staircase and the rooms are generally rectangular (**Q**); but the circle is no less geometrical than the cube. The horizontal planes of a spiral staircase are not rectangular. It may be that it is out of force of habit (**P**) that most of our buildings are rectangular (**Q**), and not out of necessity.

Telling causes from effects can be tricky: we need, first of all, to be sure that **P** did come before **Q**, and then we need to be sure that **Q** only happened because of **P**. Only then can we claim **causation**.

Even the relationship between smoking and dying as we saw in Chapter 2 ('Smoking Kills') is not clear-cut. Smoking is a contributory factor in many cancers, but the relationship is not strictly causative; rather the two 'objects' are observed to occur together very frequently—that is, there is a relation of correspondence or **correlation** between them. There is a strong correlation between smoking and death from, particularly, lung cancer. Causation and correlation are easily confused:

70. As education has increased amidst the people, infidelity, vice and crime have increased. At this moment, the people are far more vicious and criminal, in proportion to their numbers, than they were when they were comparatively uneducated. The majority of criminals consist of those who have been 'educated'.

ANONYMOUS, *Blackwood's (Edinburgh) Magazine*, 1827

The writer claims that education has *caused* a rise in crime; it may well be that there is a correlation between education and crime—but the typically low level of education among today's prisoners would suggest that it is a negative, not a positive correlation—that is, the *less* educated one is, the more likely one is to commit crime.

Some would suggest that it is a certain kind of education that causes bad behaviour:

71. [It may be] correct to blame the foul-mouthed antics of footballers for encouraging spiralling misbehaviour in schools. And teachers are right to complain about a lack of support from parents in controlling children.

But wouldn't it be really heartening to hear for once that much of the responsibility for loutishness in our schools lies at the feet of an educational establishment that for years adopted a politically correct dogma of hostility to classroom discipline because it was seen as 'restricting' young minds.

EDITORIAL, the *Daily Mail*, March 2005

Three factors are given that are said to be involved in misbehaviour in schools:

- the offensive behaviour of some footballers;
- the failure of parents to support schools in the control of their children;
- the 'hostility' on the part of the teaching profession towards enforcing classroom discipline.

> **4c.** Are these three factors *causes* of the misbehaviour, in your view, or are they simply *correlated* with it? Can you think of other factors that may be correlated with the alleged misbehaviour in schools?

Just because **Q** happens after **P** (is post hoc, or 'after this'), we may be inclined to think that **P** has *caused* **Q**—for example, because there is a clap of thunder and then your dog dies, you may infer that the thunder caused your dog's death. There is a name for this: *post hoc, ergo propter hoc*, or 'after this, therefore because of this'. Campaigners often make this mistake when they claim credit for some reform that they have urged on government—campaigning newspapers, for instance:

72. We're getting there. This week the Sunday Express Crusade to put more officers on the beat* scored a major victory. The Police and Criminal Evidence Act, which governs police powers, published its long-awaited reform proposals…and they have backed our demands. For the police to be effective they say there should be less red tape and 'more operational activity on the street'. We couldn't agree more.

   EDITORIAL, the *Sunday Express*, March 2007

   \* 'The beat' is the network of streets that a UK police officer patrols.

It may be that the *Sunday Express* was a factor in bringing the change about; and it may be that the wishes of the newspaper happened to coincide with those of the Home Secretary of the time. It is often safer to talk about *conditions* (or enabling circumstances) for a change, than causes. Some conditions are **necessary** for something else to happen, and some of *these* may be **sufficient** to make it happen.

The philosopher Susan Stebbing (already quoted in Argument 17 in Chapter 2) made this claim:

   A necessary and sufficient condition of asking a question is being puzzled about something.

   *Thinking To Some Purpose*, 1939

A condition may well be either necessary *or* sufficient. It is only when a condition is both necessary *and* sufficient that we can talk about a cause. It is, perhaps, necessary to be puzzled to want to ask a question (though I might want to ask it out of casual curiosity or devilment); but is it sufficient? I may need self-confidence, too, if I am not to look foolish in front of my classmates.

The UK online campaign group '38 Degrees' made a claim very similar to that made by the *Sunday Express*:

73. We were outraged to see bankers awarding themselves massive bonuses just after the government had to bail them out with our money. When plans to put a 50% tax on bankers' bonuses leaked out, bankers went into overdrive trying to force government to back down. We stepped up to outweigh the banks' pressure—in just 48 hours, thousands of us pressed the Chancellor to stand up to the banks' lobbyists. People power worked: the Chancellor stood up to the bankers and imposed the tax.

<http://www.38degrees.org.uk>, December 2009

The conditions in this case (five of them in a sequence of six events) were these:

there was the **bail-out** → the **bonuses** were awarded →
the **tax plan** was **leaked** → there was **lobbying** by the banks →
there was the **petition** → [the tax was **imposed**]

The bail-out seems to have been a **necessary condition** of the bonuses—if there had been no bail-out, there would have been no bonuses; and the tax plan was a necessary condition of the lobbying; but was the presentation of the petition a necessary condition of the tax? The Chancellor might have imposed the tax anyway. Leaking of the tax plan was a **sufficient condition** of the lobbying by the banks (the one was all that was needed for the other); and the lobbying by the banks was a sufficient condition for 38 Degrees to swing into action. But if there is any cause-and-effect relationship there, it is not between the petition and the imposition of the tax.

Rousseau, in Argument 74, seems to mean by 'a political group' a system of government. For a government to be good, all it has to do (the *sufficient* condition) is to urge people to breed:

74. What is the point of forming a political group? It is to ensure the continuity and welfare of the members of the group. And what is the surest sign that they are prospering as a group? It is the extent to which they grow in number. We need not look for a sign any-where else. All things being equal, that government under which, without foreign help or colonial annexations, the citizens increase in number is incontestably the best. That under which there is pop-ulation decline is the worst.

JEAN-JACQUES ROUSSEAU, *The Social Contract*, 1762

If Rousseau is right, it was a sufficient condition of a good government that it order its people to 'Go forth and multiply' and ensure that the order was obeyed: 250 years on, it may be necessary to our future prosperity that we urge people *not* to breed. But even in Rousseau's day, there must have been other conditions necessary for a government to be considered good.

The writer of 'The First Letter of John' attached a necessary condition to loving God:

75. Anyone who says 'I love God' yet hates his brother is a liar; for whoever does not love his brother whom he has seen cannot love God whom he has not seen.

THE BIBLE, 1 John 4:20

The writer claims that it is *necessary* to love your brother (sister, uncle, colleague) if it is to mean anything to say that you love God; but loving your brother cannot be a *sufficient* condition of loving God—you might need to 'see' him first.

Orson Welles had this to say about brotherly love:

76. In Italy for thirty years under the Borgias they had warfare, terror, murder, bloodshed—they produced Michelangelo, Leonardo da Vinci, and the Renaissance. In Switzerland they had brotherly love, five hundred years of democracy and peace and what did that produce? The cuckoo-clock.

ORSON WELLES, US actor and film director, 1949

> **4d.** Did Welles say anything that we can take seriously about the conditions necessary for creativity?

In assessing the claims made by others, then—and in testing how strong your own claims are—judge whether:

- causes and effects are as claimed, and are the right way round;
- a relationship said to be causative is, in fact, a simple correlation;
- conditions that are said to be necessary or sufficient really are.

**4e.** Take a look at **Argument A** in Exemplar Argument 1, on p 208: the reasons given for restricting access to higher education in pre-1960s Britain—are they *causes* of the restriction, would you say, or *conditions* for it?

And the reasons given for opening up higher education in **Argument B**: are they *causes* of the expansion after 1961 (and right through until c.2010), or *conditions* for it?

# Appeals to the past

A writer might appeal to someone or something from the past to support a claim—and this is perfectly legitimate; you might do this yourself. An appeal to the past can take a number of forms: it might, for example, call on **history** in general to bolster a claim. Jefferson appealed to history certain that history would support his case for democratic government:

77. Sometimes it is said that man cannot be trusted with the government of himself. Can he, then, be trusted with the government of others? Or have we found angels in the forms of kings to govern him? Let history answer this question.

THOMAS JEFFERSON, 3rd US President, 1801

Jefferson asked two **rhetorical questions** (ones to which he did not expect answers) to the second of which there was no other possible answer, than the answer 'No'. Angelic kings have been no commoner than unicorns. It was entirely possible, though, that history would prove this diplomat wrong:

78. I say that Fascism is not suited to England. In Italy there was a long history of secret societies. In Germany there was a long tradition of militarism. Neither had a sense of humour. In England anything on those lines is doomed to failure and ridicule.

SIR HAROLD NICHOLSON, English diplomat and politician, 1931

It is risky to call upon history to forecast the future: history is like the Bible; it can be called upon to support almost any position one might occupy. Nicholson joined Sir Oswald Mosley's New Party, in 1931, but left when it became the British Union of Fascists in 1932. Nazism, if not fascism, came close to proving him wrong; but history has a sense of humour, and proved him right.

The state of Israel appeals to history and to the Bible for its very existence:

79. We were granted our right to exist by the God of our fathers at the glimmer of the dawn of human civilisation nearly four thousand years ago. For that right, which has been sanctified in Jewish blood from generation to generation, we have paid a price unexampled in the annals of the nations.

MENACHEM BEGIN, Israeli Prime Minister, 1977

Begin appealed to **tradition**, perhaps, as much as to history: that is, he appealed to a well-established folk-narrative, handed down 'from generation to generation'. The Jews have suffered, to be sure; so, too, have the Romani, the Copts, Armenians, Muslims in Bosnia, and Native Americans:

80. These lands are ours. No-one has a right to remove us, because we were the first owners. The Great Spirit above has appointed this place for us, on which to light our fires, and here we will remain. As to boundaries, the Great Spirit knows no boundaries, nor will his red children acknowledge any.

TECUMSEH, Chief of the Shawnees, 1810

Whether or not one believes in the Great Spirit, Tecumseh's argument is a strong one: Native Americans had more right to occupy the land than newcomers did—the right conferred by being there first. The European conquest of South America was seldom gentle, yet here is a Colombian appealing to the 'Latin' past against an increasingly American present—and, like Nicholson, he appeals from the past to the future.

81. Europe is the matrix of our culture and the well-spring from which we have drunk Graeco-Roman civilisation, of which we are so justly proud. [Latin] America—which is the continent of the future—cannot lose permanent contact with mother Europe without bastardising its most noble traditions or disowning a glorious past.

JESÚS MARÍA YEPES, Colombian politician, 1929

The United States has a tradition of its own, of course; every country does—or it invents one. By 'those attacks' in Argument 82, Bush means those on '9/11':

82. With those attacks, the terrorists and their supporters declared war on the United States. And war is what they got...Our commitment to liberty is in America's tradition, declared at our founding, affirmed in Franklin, Roosevelt's Four Freedoms, asserted in the Truman Doctrine and in Ronald Reagan's challenge to an evil empire. We are committed to freedom in Afghanistan, in Iraq and in a peaceful Palestine. The advance of freedom is the surest strategy to undermine the appeal of terror in the world.

GEORGE W. BUSH, US President, May 2003

> **4f.** Why might an appeal to tradition not always be very persuasive?

Begin appealed not only to tradition, but to God; Tecumseh appealed to the Great Spirit; and Bush appealed to four famous Americans. In doing this, they were all appealing to **authority**—to something, or someone whose word is considered to transcend history and remain for ever 'true'. By appealing to authority, one hopes to borrow some of that transcendent 'truth'.

For Jews and Christians of all stripes, God has always been considered the ultimate authority; and the Bible his 'word'. Notice, though, how in the following argument, the anonymous writer appeals, in addition, to a famous scientist:

83. There are those who tremble to think of 'the last days' (2 Timothy 3:1). They imagine a time of harsh judgment. Why then do so

many people look forward to this time? They do so because the last days will also usher in greater happiness. For example, Sir Isaac Newton lived in the conviction that at the last, there would be an ingathering of all mankind in the Kingdom of God: a new order of peace and well-being. He declared that the prophecies of Micah 4:3, and of Isaiah 2:4, would be fulfilled in those last days.

Adapted from an article in an evangelical tract, April 2008

Scripture was authority enough for these evangelicals; but Newton's name added (what appeared to be) scientific authority to religious belief. Scripture was the ultimate authority for Erasmus, the Renaissance scholar; but like Yepes he paid homage to the Graeco-Roman world as well:

84. Holy Scripture is of course the authority in all things; but I do sometimes come across pagan writings and passages from antiquity—even among poets—expressed so wisely and reverently, so seemingly inspired, that I cannot but wonder whether their authors were not moved by some divine power.

DESIDERIUS ERASMUS, Dutch scholar, 1518

Plato and Aristotle were considered by western scholars to be particularly authoritative. Montaigne was another Renaissance man; unlike Rousseau (in Argument 68), he acknowledges the authority of Aristotle (or seems to):

85. We produce three varieties of wind: the one which comes from our nether regions is too obnoxious; the one coming from the mouth accuses the owner of over-eating; the third, sneezing, which comes from the head is involuntary and we do honour to the sneezer when we say: 'Bless you!'. You mustn't laugh at these subtle distinctions; they were made by Aristotle himself.

MICHEL DE MONTAIGNE, French essayist, 1580

Aristotle had been appealed to as an 'authority in all things' for centuries, but Montaigne was ready enough to laugh at his 'subtlety'. Marx and Lenin have been invoked in similar fashion by Communist Party cadres, unlaughingly; and equally great names are invoked by democrats:

86. The Soviet Union, faithful to the policy of peace and support for the struggle of oppressed peoples for their national independence, the policy proclaimed by Vladimir Ilyich Lenin, founder of the Soviet State, calls upon the United Nations to raise its voice in

defence of the just liberation of the colonies and to take immediate steps toward the complete abolition of the colonial system of government.

NIKITA KHRUSHCHEV, General Secretary of the<br>USSR Communist Party, 1960

87. There are still principles, ideas and ideals, hard as flint and clear as crystal. They are the principles of Adam Smith and Karl Popper, of Tocqueville, Burke and Mill, the principles that uphold political freedom and economic liberty, the principles that helped create and sustain open, plural societies, prospering mightily, trading freely, treating their citizens decently. Those are principles that we must hold on to and fight for, East and West, even when the barbarians appear to have melted away from the city's walls, because we know from all history that the barbarians always, always return.

CHRIS PATTEN, *East and West*, Basingstoke:<br>Macmillan Publishers, 1998

Had Khrushchev read Lenin's telegrams to party apparatchiks ordering them to terrorize 'kulaks' into giving up their grain to feed the populations of the cities, in 1918? Lenin was not an obvious candidate for the Nobel Peace Prize. Patten makes an appeal to 'all history' and to five men of firm principle. (Is the principle the same for each of the five men?)

> **4g.** Of course, it is quite legitimate and often effective to appeal to authority. Who are the authorities in your own subject to whom you might appeal in order to strengthen an argument?

It is a problem where appeals to history, tradition, and authority are concerned that the past, the writings of the past, and the people of the past, are like a ventriloquist's dummy: you can make it say what you want it to say. When you are assessing the claims of authors collected under **Argument A**, therefore, be alert to where a claim may be weakened by an appeal to a tradition better buried than honoured, or to an authority all too human.

Don't make a fetish of scepticism, though: just as we saw with 'experts' in Chapter 3, you will need to appeal to 'authorities' yourself. If they've written in your field, think of them as having done your dirty work; it is for you to reap what they have sown.

# Appeals to feelings

Just as it is perfectly acceptable to appeal to the past—where that past is genuinely instructive—so it is acceptable to appeal to feelings. Philosophers (like C.E.M. Joad, in Argument 47 in Chapter 3) have, perhaps, made too much of the distinction between *reason* and *feelings*, **logic** and **rhetoric**. They have elevated the former over the latter and claimed that, when they philosophize, they reason, detachedly. Indeed, rhetoric is thought of as improper—as an attempt to persuade by underhand means.

It is not improper to appeal to our emotions, as long as we know when we are doing it, and we can recognize when others are doing it. There are pluses and minuses—pluses first:

| + | − |
|---|---|
| We are more immediately susceptible to an appeal to feelings than we are to reasons. | We can be 'carried away' by feelings and so neglect commonsense considerations. |
| There are issues whose significance for us is more visceral than logical. | Emotion sidesteps reasoning and may make dispassionate argument difficult. |

Politicians commonly use **emotive language**. The British politician Neville Chamberlain used it in this implied criticism of Roosevelt's New Deal:

88. Without underrating the hardships of our situation, the **long tragedy** of the unemployed, the **grievous burden** of taxation, the **arduous and painful struggle** of those engaged in trade and industry, at any rate we are free from that fear which besets so many less fortunately placed, the fear that things are going to get worse. We owe our freedom from that fear to the fact that we have balanced our budget.

NEVILLE CHAMBERLAIN, Chancellor of the Exchequer, 1933

Particular terms carry emotive overtones that may make it hazardous to use them: the words 'nature', 'murder', and 'terrorist' are among them, as we saw in Chapter 2. 'Vivisection' is another:

89. The word 'vivisection' is itself an unfortunate one. It intimates the cutting up alive of a sensitive, terrified, and helpless animal, and that never occurs. The 'anti-vivisectionists', however, wrung by the horrible suggestions of the word, do seem to believe, in spite of all evidence to the contrary, that this is the normal method of experimental biology and the anti-vivisection campaign displays all the unscrupulous exaggerations natural to tender and imaginative minds tormented beyond any possibility of patient and sober judgment.

H.G. WELLS, JULIAN HUXLEY, and G.P. WELLS,<br/>The Science of Life, 1931

Anti-vivisectionists have typically appealed to **pity**. Wilfred Owen famously appealed to it in his First World War poetry ('…this book is not concerned with Poetry. The subject of it is War, and the pity of War. The Poetry is in the pity'). Pity is a powerful emotion; the problem is that it can be exploited by both sides in a dispute. Rousseau had appealed to reason in the slavery debate; Boswell and Charles Darwin's grandfather Erasmus appeal to pity—but they ask us to pity two very different sets of people:

90. To abolish a *status*, which in all ages God has sanctioned, and man has continued, would not only be *robbery* to an innumerable class of our fellow-subjects, but it would be extreme cruelty to the African savages, a portion of whom it saves from massacre, or intolerable bondage in their own country, and introduces into a much happier state of life, especially now when their passage to the West Indies and their treatment there is humanely regulated. To abolish that trade would be to 'shut the gates of mercy on mankind'.

JAMES BOSWELL, 1777

91. Hear, oh Britannia! Potent Queen of ideas
    On whom fair Art, and meek Religion smiles,
    How Afric's coasts thy craftier sons invade
    With murder, rapine, theft—and call it Trade!
    The Slave, in chains on supplicating knee,
    Spreads his wide arms & lifts his eyes to Thee;
    With hunger pale, with wounds & toil oppressed,
    'Are we not brethren?' sorrow chokes the rest;
    Air! Bear to heaven upon thy azure flood
    Their innocent cries! Earth! Cover not their blood.

ERASMUS DARWIN, 1791

Which is the more effective argument? Boswell appeals to authority (God), and contrasts 'bondage' in Africa with the 'humaneness' of slavery. Darwin seems to have been better informed about the viciousness of the trade—but it was his appeal to pity that outdid the cold rationalism of the slave traders in the long run. (The trade—though not slavery itself—was abolished in Britain and America in 1807.)

Homelessness is an evil unlikely to be abolished; there are still too many rough sleepers in London, though perhaps not as many as in 1901:

92. Something ought to be done by the authorities to wipe out the scandal of the homeless people who are forced to sleep out on these wintry nights. I walked home with Byron Curtis, editor of the *Standard*. Every bench from Blackfriars to Westminster Bridge was filled with shivering people, all huddled up—men, women, and children. The Salvation Army people were out giving away hot broth, but even this was merely a temporary palliative against the bitter night.

R.D. BLUMENFELD, US-born journalist,
editor of UK papers, diary entry, 24 December 1901

Homelessness charities still appeal to pity to bring the 'scandal' to our attention, and who would say they are wrong to do so? Marx, who must often have wondered where home was, appeals to other feelings than pity here; and so do many advertisers:

93. Within a communist framework, where no-one is confined to one single field of activity but everyone can develop a talent in any field he wishes, society controls overall production and so enables me to do one thing today and another tomorrow, to go hunting in the morning, fishing in the afternoon, rearing cattle in the evening or engaging in criticism after dinner, just as I please, without becoming hunter, fisherman, shepherd or critic.

KARL MARX, *The German Ideology*, 1845

94. Embark on a magnificent no-fly voyage to the Baltic visiting some fascinating ports of call on a ship that, though small and intimate, has a wealth of facilities. Relax with friends in the Morning Light pub, or enjoy wonderful views over the bow from the Observatory Lounge. Enjoy a choice of restaurants, a selection of entertainment options and activity programmes. We guarantee that you will be totally spoilt, thoroughly entertained and utterly pampered. Please do not delay as cabins at these fantastic prices will sell fast.

Adapted from an advertisement for Fred. Olsen Cruise Lines

**4h.** What feelings would you say these two arguments (93 and 94) are trying to appeal to in their readers?

Edmund Burke (whose reflection on the French Revolution has already been quoted in this chapter) knew well that:

> No passion so effectually robs the mind of all its powers of acting and reasoning as fear.

Winston Churchill was not above appealing to **fear**, in very much the same way as Burke:

95. The loss of India would mark and consummate the downfall of the British Empire. That great organism would pass at a stroke out of life into history. From such a catastrophe there could be no recovery.
    WINSTON S. CHURCHILL, as a Conservative back-bench MP, 1930

Burke forecast the extinction of 'the glory of Europe'; Churchill forecast the downfall of the British Empire if India was given its independence; the Director of the FBI forecast the end of the American way of life; and another British politician, infamously, borrowed lines from Virgil's *Aeneid* to prophesy against passage of race relations legislation:

96. The Communist propaganda technique is designed to promote emotional response with the hope that the victim will be attracted by what he is told the Communist way of life holds in store for him. The objective, of course, is to develop discontent and hasten the day when the Communists can gather sufficient support and following to overthrow the American way of life.
    J. EDGAR HOOVER, in testimony to the House Un-American Activities Committee, 1947

97. We must be mad, literally mad, as a nation, to be permitting the annual inflow of 50,000 dependants who are for the most part the material of the future growth of the immigrant-descended popula-tion. It is like watching a nation busily heaping up its own funeral pyre. So insane are we that we actually permit unmarried persons to immigrate for the purpose of founding a family with spouses and fiancées whom they have never seen... As I look ahead I am filled with foreboding. Like the Roman, I seem to see 'the River Tiber foaming with much blood'!
    ENOCH POWELL, Conservative politician, in a speech in Birmingham, April 1968

Powell's appeal to fear cost him his shadow-cabinet post, and his reputation for classical cool-headedness. More seriously, it cost him the argument: most people could see for themselves that this was the rhetoric of fascism (see Argument 24 in Chapter 2 and Argument 78 earlier in this chapter).

Just as the bright future anticipated in Arguments 93 and 94 might be compared with that predicted by the evangelical tract (Argument 83); so this 16th-century claim might be compared with that of George W. Bush (Argument 82):

98. It is true that there does exist a common right to all to navigate the seas and in Europe we recognize the rights which others hold against us; but the right does not exist beyond Europe and therefore the Portuguese as Lords of the sea are justified in confiscating the goods of all those who navigate the seas without their permission.

JOÃO DE BARROS, Portuguese chronicler, c.1560

99. You cannot fight against the future. Time is on our side. The great social forces which move onward in their might and majesty and which the tumult of your debates does not for a moment impede or disturb are against you. They are marshalled on our side. And the banner which we now carry in this fight, though perhaps at some moment it may droop over our sinking heads, yet it soon again will float in the eye of Heaven, and it will be borne by the firm hands of the united people of the three kingdoms, perhaps not to an easy, but to a certain and to a not far distant victory.

W.E. GLADSTONE, UK Prime Minister, in a speech on the 1867 Reform Act, 1866

> **4i.** What feelings do de Barros and Gladstone appear to be trying to arouse in their audiences?

Aside from appeals to pity, fear, and animal pleasures, you might be alert to appeals to novelty, greed, envy, the herd instinct—to any number of unworthy emotions; but there are nobler feelings (generosity, patriotism, tenderness, duty) that may be appealed to effectively and allowably. Here is one last example, where an appeal is made to fellow feeling. Jenny Tonge was a British MP, and Liberal Democrat opposition spokeswoman for children; she felt strongly about the Israel–Palestine impasse, and the violence that it was breeding—and she said this about Palestinian suicide-bombing:

100. This particular brand of terrorism, the suicide bomber, is truly born out of desperation. Many many people criticise, many many people say it is just another form of terrorism, but I can understand, and I am a fairly emotional person and I am a mother and a grandmother. I think if I had to live in that situation, and I say this advisedly, I might just consider becoming one myself. And that is a terrible thing to say.

JENNY TONGE, British MP, January 2004

She meant that it was a terrible thing to *have* to say; but she was taken at her word, and, like Enoch Powell, removed from her front-bench post. Some commentators called her brave; others—perhaps, who could not or would not 'understand'—called her foolish, and worse. Was it an 'effective' argument? If effectiveness can be measured in media time given to an issue, then it undoubtedly was.

When you have settled upon your **Question**

and you have made your **Statement**

and laid out the claims and arguments assembled under

**Argument A**

you are entitled to point out what you take to be the weaknesses in that composite case:

> It may be that:
>
> ➢ a **straw man** was set up;
> ➢ there was exaggeration or **overstatement**;
> ➢ a **cause-effect** relationship may be suggested mistakenly;
> ➢ a **correlation** may be mistaken for **causation**;
> ➢ there may be misunderstanding or confusion of **necessary** and **sufficient conditions**;
> ➢ an **appeal to history, tradition, authority** may be open to question;
> ➢ likewise, an **(emotive)** appeal to any one of many **feelings** may misfire.

We have identified a number of weaknesses in the arguments collected in this chapter—but there were some perfectly respectable arguments there as well. By pointing up the weaknesses in the composite **Argument A** (without overstating them), you will lend strength to your counter-argument—if you can avoid repeating them.

The chief weakness in the arguments of others may simply be that the claims made are not reasons: they are assertions unsupported by **evidence**; or the evidence presented is questionable. Either way, reasons and conclusion are unpersuasive.

We shall consider the nature of evidence next.

# 5 How will you support your case?

I shall aim in this chapter to explain:

- how examples may work as evidence, or not;
- how there might be different sorts of fact;
- why you should be careful how you use numbers;
- what it is that makes evidence believable.

## Examples and anecdotes

Making claims is all very well; giving reasons is all very well; but a judge in a court of law gives a verdict on the basis of **evidence**. We make a judgement (as the word *e-vidence* implies) 'from what we can see'—and, by extension, hear, touch, smell, taste, feel. Claims made in argument will not persuade unless there is some visible, tangible, *concrete* support for them—something not talked about, but shown.

One form of evidence is **examples**. Consider this claim:

> Much of the world's work, it has been said, is done by men who do not feel quite well.

The claim sounds reasonable enough—or, at least, not unreasonable. We cannot test how strong the claim is, though, until we have one or more examples of men (and women?) who were hard-working, but unwell—and, indeed, Galbraith gives us one example:

> Much of the world's work, it has been said, is done by men who do not feel quite well. Marx is a case in point.
>
> J.K. GALBRAITH, US economist, 1977

Once we have that example, we can make better sense of the claim. We can make better sense of an argument, too, when we have one or two concrete examples to bring it to life. Adam Smith's argument is quite dry until he mentions water:

101. The word VALUE, it is to be observed, has two different meanings, and sometimes the utility of some particular object, and sometimes the power of purchasing other goods, which the possession of that object conveys. This one may be called 'value in use'; the other, 'value in exchange'. The things which have the greatest value in use have frequently little or no value in exchange; and on the contrary, those which have the greatest value in exchange have frequently little or no value in use. Nothing is more useful than **water**: but it will purchase scarce anything; scarce anything can be had in exchange for it. A **diamond**, on the contrary, has scarce any value in use; but a very great quantity of other goods may frequently be had in exchange.

ADAM SMITH, Scottish economist, 1776

The references to the water and the diamond are the point at which a non-economist might say: 'Ah, right. I see what you mean.'

Galbraith gives us one example of a man who did great things and felt unwell. (Marx appears to have suffered from boils, headaches, and piles, to say nothing of the effects of London sanitation). But is one example enough to support the point that Galbraith wants to make?

Emerson gives us seven examples, and, what is more, he rules out in advance any evidence that might contradict his case:

102. Is it so bad to be misunderstood? Pythagoras was misunderstood, and Socrates, and Jesus, and Luther, and Copernicus, and Galileo, and Newton, and every pure and wise spirit that ever took flesh. To be great is to be misunderstood.

RALPH WALDO EMERSON, US philosopher and poet, 1841

It may be a necessary condition of being great to be misunderstood; but it is not a sufficient condition. We have all been misunderstood at some time in our lives. Hazlitt misunderstood, and was misunderstood; but this did not make him 'great'—it made him peevish:

103. No man is truly great who is great only in his lifetime. The test of greatness is the page of history. Nothing can be said to be great that has a distinct limit, or that borders on something evidently greater than itself. Besides, what is short-lived and pampered into mere notoriety is of a gross and vulgar quality in itself. A lord mayor is hardly a great man. A city orator or patriot of the day

only show, by reaching the height of their wishes, the distance they are at from any true ambition...Lord Nelson was a great naval commander; but for myself, I have not much opinion of a seafaring life. Sir Humphrey Davy is a great chemist, but I am not sure that he is a great man. I am not a bit the wiser for any of his discoveries, and I never met anyone that was.

WILLIAM HAZLITT, English essayist and journalist, 1821

A well-chosen example is like a picture in a dense text: it may be worth a thousand generalizations. The mayor, the orator, the patriot—these are *general* examples. Whether or not Nelson and Davy were 'great' men, these two *specific* examples enable us to judge the strength of Hazlitt's claim (in his first line). That claim is intuitively persuasive— but should he not have chosen examples of dead men who had been 'great' only while they lived? Nelson's greatness was already beyond dispute (he had been given a state funeral in St Paul's Cathedral, London, in 1806); and Davy was still very much alive—so it was too early, in 1821, to say whether he would be considered 'great' by posterity, or not.

Just as examples might support a case, so they might help to defeat one: Galbraith gave us one example of a man who did 'great work' but who was unwell; if we could think of one **counter-example** of a man (or woman) who did great things, but felt quite well (Shakespeare? Florence Nightingale?), would that defeat Galbraith's claim?

Tom Driberg questions the value attached to sincerity. It ought to be easy to give examples of people who were sincere and 'right' (the Chartists? the Suffragettes? campaigners for an end to slavery?). Instead, Driberg gives us four counter-examples:

104. 'Sincerity is what counts' is a widespread modern heresy. Think again. Bolsheviks are sincere. Fascists are sincere. Lunatics are sincere. People who believe that the Earth is flat are sincere. They can't all be right.

TOM DRIBERG, British journalist, 1937

His counter-examples do appear to defeat the view that 'sincerity is what counts'; but surely the groups he cites were deluded as well as sincere—and it was their deludedness that made them 'wrong'. Besides, 'rightness' is a matter of degree. Here is an argument that contends for degrees of 'evil'. It would undoubtedly benefit from one or two examples (though not of people, this time) by way of illustration:

105. There has been a strong focus on the dangers of smoking in pubs, in recent correspondence. This sidesteps the main problem, which

is alcohol. Regular, excessive drinking is a factor in many health and social problems. The effects of 'secondary smoking' have been a cause for concern; but what about the much more serious effects of what might be called 'secondary drinking'?

Why is it that campaigners concentrate their efforts on banning smoking—the lesser evil from many points of view—and neglect the effects of heavy drinking, which is the greater evil?

Adapted from a letter to *The Times*, January 2005

The letter-writer suggests that smoking is not the 'main problem': his counter-example, excessive drinking, is 'the greater evil'.

> **5a.** What do you think the writer means by 'secondary drinking'? Is 'regular, excessive drinking' a fair counter-example to 'smoking in pubs', in terms of its effects on others?

Hazlitt chose examples from close to home. Though he was ill-advised to choose Davy whom he confessed he did not understand, it is often a good idea to reach for examples drawn from one's own experience:

106. If you want to know the taste of a pear, you must taste the pear by eating it yourself. If you want to know the theory and methods of revolution, you must take part in revolution. All genuine knowledge originates in direct experience.

MAO ZEDONG, leader of the Chinese Communist Party, 1937

There is a lot in this, though, of course, experience only stretches so far. We would not have much knowledge—genuine or otherwise—if we had to depend on direct experience to vouch for it. I have not (yet) read Tolstoy's *War and Peace*, but I am prepared to believe it is a 'great' novel; I have never looked down a microscope, but I am inclined to believe in bacteria.

Telling a story, or **anecdote**, of an incident from personal experience can be an effective way of making a point—howbeit a point has position but no size. The lesson that can be learnt from **anecdotal evidence** may be limited: it is one example, only, like the Marx example in Galbraith's claim. There may be many counter-examples that would defeat it.

Here are two arguments that rely on anecdotal evidence:

107. It is quite absurd that there are no trains leaving from Manchester Victoria Station after 10.30pm, when concerts don't normally finish until 11.00pm. I took my mother to a concert on Sunday 12 December, having checked train times, so I was confident of getting home with my mother, who is 89. Imagine my surprise, therefore, to discover that the last train on a Sunday leaves at 10.30pm. Having had a very enjoyable evening, our pleasure was marred by the fact that I had to spend £45 on a taxi home. When will the train companies learn to put passengers' needs before their own convenience?

Adapted from a letter to the Manchester Evening News,<br>December 2010

108. I flew home from a skiing trip via Geneva recently. I passed through airport security in the normal way, screened for sharp objects or anything that might be used as a weapon; and then I entered the duty-free shop in the departure lounge. I was aghast to find wine and spirits being sold in glass bottles. Anyone who frequents pubs in run-down areas knows that a broken bottle can be a very effective weapon. What price all those ludicrous security checks, when one can buy a deadly weapon immediately before boarding the plane?

Adapted from a letter to The Mail on Sunday, March 2005

Apart from any weaknesses there may be in the claims made (why had the concert-goer not checked the times of trains on *Sundays* as well as on weekdays? Is the departure lounge at Geneva Airport very much like a pub in a slum?), it is unclear whether these indignant anecdotes have much to say beyond themselves.

Nevertheless, when you draw on first-hand experience, you are the authority. No one can ask: 'How do you know?' You yourself are the example, and no one can contradict your experience. Are you an example, though, that others would want to follow?

109. A scout has to sleep very much in the open, and a boy who is accustomed to sleep with his window shut will probably suffer, like many a tenderfoot* has done, by catching cold and rheumatism when he first tries sleeping out. The thing is always to sleep with your windows open, summer and winter, and you will never catch cold. Personally, I cannot sleep with my window shut or

with blind down, and when living in the country I always sleep outside the house, summer and winter alike. A soft bed and too many blankets make a boy dream bad dreams, which weaken him.

SIR ROBERT BADEN-POWELL,
founder of the Scout movement, 1908

\* An unhardened beginner.

> **5b.** Why might Baden-Powell's own experience not set the example that he intended it to?

# Facts and factual claims

Policeman, prosecutor, lawyer, judge—all want hard evidence; and the hardest sort of evidence is a **fact**. What is a fact? It is something 'made' or 'done'; something complete; something that has passed beyond disagreement and the possibility of disagreement. Darwin was quoted in Chapter 1 as writing, in 1874: 'I must begin with a good body of facts'. Among the facts he established were these:

- Coral polyps can live only in clear salt water less than 20 fathoms deep, at temperatures not less than 68°F.
- No plant that is pollinated by wind has coloured flowers.
- The birds and tortoises of each Galápagos island are different, although the physical conditions of the islands seem identical.

SIR GAVIN DE BEER, *Encyclopædia Britannica*, vol. 5, Washington DC:
Benton Foundation, 1976

These facts, it might be said, were facts by **discovery**. It just happened that this is how things were. They are **contingent** facts: they might have been otherwise. It would not have been shocking if the beaks of all the finches that Darwin observed had been much the same—it was that there were differences that needed explaining. Indeed, these facts are only facts because Darwin 'discovered' them, after very close and careful observation. (He discovered them, as we might otherwise say, *empirically*.)

In the same way, we have discovered that:

- A thin film of linseed oil when exposed to the air dries to a hard, elastic substance.
- The north-east and south-east trade winds meet near the equator, creating the doldrums.
- Between the two world wars, Romania produced more oil than any other European country.

Facts by discovery might have turned out differently; but, once 'made' (established by repeated observation, and by the absence of counter-examples), they are facts for good. Many facts are ones that we have made, and that we can unmake; these we might call facts by **definition**. One such is that when New Year's Eve falls on a Saturday, New Year's Day falls on a Sunday. This is a **necessary** fact: as long as we call the days of the week by their present names (in English), Sunday must come after Saturday. Facts by definition may cease to be 'necessary', however:

- The capital city of Nigeria is Abuja.
- An American president can serve for a maximum of two four-year terms.
- There are eight planets in the solar system.

Until 1991, the capital city of Nigeria was Lagos; F.D. Roosevelt served as US president for 12 years (1933–45); and Pluto was reckoned to be the ninth planet of the solar system, until 24 August 2006, when it was demoted. (It is now a mere dwarf planet.) A fact by discovery may be displaced by a new discovery; and we may revise a fact by definition by changing the definition. I do not want to draw a firm, vertical line between facts by discovery and facts by definition; some facts are the product of both discovery and definition.

**5c.** 'Water boils at 100°C.' Would you call this a fact by discovery or a fact by definition?

Encyclopaedias are full of facts that are well established; but daily discourse is full of **factual claims** that *look* like facts—the authors want us to think that they are facts—but they never could be facts because they remain (and always will remain) open to disagreement. Here is one such:

> The human world was irrevocably changed by Borromini, Bach and Braque, even if many people are unable to notice the fact.
>
> ROGER SCRUTON, *Modern Philosophy*, London: Sinclair-Stevenson, 1994

Because there will be others who claim that the world was changed by three artists whose names began with A, C, or D, Scruton's claim can only ever be a factual claim, and never a fact. Critics are particularly given to making claims that they would like us to think were facts; they make them forcefully, as if to warn us against contradicting them:

> *Wuthering Heights* is the most remarkable novel in English. It is perfect. There is nothing that one can compare it to.
>
> WALTER ALLEN, *The English Novel*, London: Phoenix House, 1954

> *The Thin Red Line*, the greatest American war-movie ever made.
>
> MICHAEL NEWTON, *The Guardian*, July 2011

> Sibelius's Seventh is the greatest symphony of the 20th Century. It says it all.
>
> ROB COWAN, BBC Radio 3 presenter, November 2012

> [I was told] nothing was known or could be found out about Matisse's youth in Bohain. This kind of ignorance in the place that had shaped the greatest French painter of the 20th century was hard to credit.
>
> HILARY SPURLING, *Guardian Review*, February 2005.
> © Guardian News & Media

One might suggest an alternative 'best' novel in English, American war movie, 20th-century symphony, French painter, but no suggestion of this kind could ever be a fact. Military men make factual claims more forcefully than most, especially when they imagine they speak for God:

110. Perpetual peace is a dream—and not even a beautiful dream—and war is an integral part of God's ordering of the universe. In war, man's noblest virtues come into play: courage and renunciation, fidelity to duty and a readiness for sacrifice that does not stop at giving up life itself. Without war the world would be swamped in materialism.

HELMUTH VON MOLTKE, German field marshal, 1880

It is a claim similar to that made by Mussolini (Argument 23 in Chapter 2), 50 years later—and it had not become a fact by then, either.

Sometimes, of course, a factual claim is simply false, either in a small way, as in Argument 111 (from a book about Hungary), or in a big way, as in Argument 112. We will allow both authors (and their editors) to remain anonymous:

111. I have acted as a consultant to PhD students, fired by an interest in Renaissance masques or the novels of William James, who feel that they cannot pursue research into what interests them until they can view it through the lens of a ready-made literary theory. It seems not to occur to them (or to their teachers) that theory is what might issue from, not pre-determine, a study of Renaissance masques or the novels of William James. When theory comes first, it clouds the lens.

*A Country Full of Aliens: A Briton in Hungary*,
Budapest: Corvina Books, 2010

112. Historical context can be very important in interpreting and evaluating an argument. For example, in 1798, Thomas Malthus famously argued that population growth inevitably meant that it was impossible to have a society 'all the members of which should live in ease, happiness and comparative leisure and feel no anxiety about providing the means of subsistence for themselves and families'. To understand and evaluate this famous argument you need to take account of its historical context. Following the French Revolution there was much discussion about whether it was possible to establish a society based on social and economic equality. Malthus argued against that possibility, and he did this in the context of a society which was very unequal, which was very influenced by the thinking of Charles Darwin (on natural selection and evolution).

An introductory text on critical thinking, 2001

**5d.** What is factually wrong with these two arguments? Do the mistakes made weaken the conclusions the authors come to?

When factual claims are made that appear to contradict those made by others, it may be far from clear which claim is the weightier. In May 2010, the Holocaust survivor Elie Wiesel made a claim in an open letter to US President Obama, about the city of Jerusalem; Wiesel lives in the United States. His factual claim was countered by that of 100 residents of Jerusalem. Does the fact that there are one hundred of them, or the fact that they live in the city, make their evidence weightier than Wiesel's, winner of the Nobel Peace Prize? (Notice Wiesel's forceful capitals):

113. For me, the Jew that I am, Jerusalem is above politics. Today, for the first time in history, Jews, Christians and Muslims all may freely worship at their shrines. And, contrary to certain media reports, Jews, Christians and Muslims ARE allowed to build their homes anywhere in the city. The anguish over Jerusalem is not about real estate but about memory.

Extract from an open letter to Barack Obama, from Elie Wiesel

We invite you to our city to view with your own eyes the catastrophic effects of the frenzy of construction. You will witness that, contrary to some media reports, Arabs are not allowed to build their homes anywhere in Jerusalem. You will see the gross inequality in allocation of municipal resources and services between east and west.

Extract from letter, from 100 Jewish residents of Jerusalem to Elie Wiesel

Perhaps it is only Wiesel who is presenting an argument here; the 100 residents supply what they take to be 'facts on the ground'. Their claims seem to be well based but, apart from the wonderful roundedness of their number, they do not present figures of a sort that might strengthen their case.

When you present what you take to be evidence, take care to distinguish between facts and factual claims, and offer neither too forcefully.

# Statistical evidence

Evidence is not always easy to come by; it is not always clear what might count as evidence; and even when there is evidence, what can be inferred from it may be disputed. In July 2010, a haul of flints was found in Norfolk, England, that seemed to testify to human life in Britain 800,000 years ago. Experts disagreed about what the findings tell us about these Britons:

> They lived out in the open, but we don't know if they had basic clothing, were building primitive shelters, or even had the use of fire.
>
> CHRIS STRINGER, Natural History Museum, London

> Surely they must have worn some clothing and made artificial shelters. Perhaps, even, they had mastered the use of fire (charcoal was found at the dig).
>
> MIKE PITTS, Editor *British Archaeology*

We speak of 'hard' evidence as evidence that is plain for all to see: it can scarcely be disputed. Is charcoal 'hard' evidence? It would seem so. Numbers, though, are harder still. One may drive in Britain with up to 80mg of alcohol in 100ml of blood. In 2004, the then Transport Minister, David Jamieson, was asked in Parliament whether the government had plans to reduce the limit to the European norm—50mg:

114. The Government thought about lowering the limit, but the vast majority of drivers involved in road accidents are 'way over' the legal limit and there is 'no great evidence' of drivers with 50–80mg being the cause of accidents. I think the line we have drawn is a good line. What we must do is to give the police better powers to enforce it and carry on driving down the figures.

> Adapted from an article in *The Times*, July 2004

It would have strengthened the government's case if Mr Jamieson had been able to say how 'large' the majority of drivers over the limit was; and how far 'way over' that limit they were. It might have been useful, in addition, to know just how few drivers were involved in accidents whose alcohol intake gave a reading of between 50mg and 80mg. Perhaps an MP, dissatisfied with the minister's answer, submitted a 'freedom of information' request to find out.

Figures are not always very instructive. The following notice was posted above the ready-prepared meals in a big supermarket:

> All the recipes for our prepared meals
> are created by top chefs with over
> 100 years combined experience.

The shopper was expected to be impressed. The critical shopper, though, might have wondered how many chefs were involved (two 70-year-old chefs with 51 years' experience each? Or 51 chefs with two years' experience each?), and how many chefs there are at the top—perhaps as many as the books that bear the label:

The No. 1 International Best-Seller

(as if there could be more than one 'best'). Numbers may deceive, and they are not least deceptive when they are in the form of percentages. The following two factual claims were made by two journalists on consecutive days in *The Guardian* newspaper:

> Many Spaniards are still religious. A recent survey showed 17.5% in Spain had some contact with churches during the previous 12 months.
>
> POLLY TOYNBEE, 30 March 2011

> Only 15% of Spanish Catholics attend mass every week. More than 60% rarely step foot inside a church.
>
> GILES TREMLETT, 31 March 2011

It is likely that the figures are accurate, in both cases. Neither writer is wrong; but they do draw different conclusions from the numbers at their disposal. Toynbee's figure relates to the entire **population** of Spain, which, at the time of writing, is 47.27 million; elsewhere in his article, Tremlett states that three-quarters of Spaniards call themselves Catholics—so *his* population is approximately 36 million. It is important, in any survey, to be sure about the nature and size of the population that is being surveyed:

115. You mentioned research that found that 11 per cent of the population is left-handed. Did the researchers mean people who write with their left hand? Or did they include people who are right-handed when they write, but left-handed when they play ball games? Lots of tennis-players, for example, are left-handed on the court, but right-handed when they write. Certain African ethnic groups are almost entirely left-handed; and it has been shown that something like 38 per cent of native Australians throw a boomerang with their left hands. And half the Stone Age tools that we've found were designed to be used by left-handers.

Adapted from a letter to the *Daily Mail*, September 2007

How big was 'the population' here: all the human beings who have ever lived; the present population of the world; or the present population of Great Britain?

Because few researchers can hope to survey an entire population, they have to study a **sample** of that population—ideally, a sample that **represents** the population. If it is not a **representative sample**, we cannot infer anything useful from it about the population at large. If the population is big, the sample has to be big.

Whether the sample is big or not, we do need to know something about it, and about the population which it is supposed to represent. The manufacturers of a loaf of organic rye bread boasted on the packet:

MORE THAN

# 80%

AGREE

Rye leaves you less bloated, fuller for longer
and more energetic

Eighty per cent of what?; 80 per cent of the population at large?; 80 per cent of a sample of bread-eaters? No, it can only be 80 per cent of those who already eat rye bread (otherwise, most of those questioned would have said: 'I don't know. I don't eat it')—but we do not know how many rye bread-eaters were asked: 1,000? 100? 10? It matters. It also matters whether or not they were presented with the words with which they were asked to agree.

At the time of writing, the combined population of France (65.4 million), Germany (81.8 million), and the UK (63.2 million), is pretty big, at about 210 million. Women (aged 15–64) will account for rather less than half of this total. An attitude survey was conducted of a sample of 40,000 women in France, Germany, and the UK, and the results were reported in *The Times*, in November 2006. The women were asked to agree (or not) with four statements. Here are the results (expressed as percentages):

|  | France | Germany | UK |
|---|---|---|---|
| I like to look elegant | 74.1 | 62.4 | 49.1 |
| It's important to be attractive to the opposite sex | 71.4 | 59.8 | 45.1 |
| It's important to keep looking youthful | 65.8 | 55.3 | 41.8 |
| I have a very good sense of style | 62.5 | 36.9 | 42.9 |

Just as it is vital that we know what population is being talked about, and how big it is, so we need clear information about the sample. In this case, the sample is a very large one (the minimum statistically respectable sample would have been *c*.1,000 women for each country); but we do not know who the women were, and how they were chosen. Was the age, socio-economic, educational, regional composition of the sample representative in these respects of the female population in these three countries? In such a large sample, it is likely that it was broadly representative.

Until we know how big the pie is, and how it was made, we cannot make sense of the slices into which it is cut:

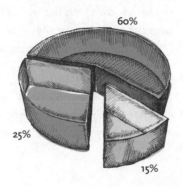

There are many ways of ensuring that a sample is (adequately) representative, but it is enough for present purposes to mention four:

- *random sampling*, where subjects are chosen 'blind', and any one person has as much chance of being chosen as anyone else;
- *systematic sampling*, where, for example, every 5th or 10th person in a population (a college year group, perhaps) is chosen;
- *stratified sampling*, where subjects are grouped by age, or other criterion, so as to reflect the proportions of these groups (or strata) in the population;
- *convenience sampling*, where subjects are chosen who happen to be available.

> **5e.** If you wanted to find out what proportion of the population of your country, or region, write with their left hand, how would you select a representative sample?

If you conduct a survey, and your population is small (e.g. students of social sciences at a provincial university), then your sample can be (relatively) small—but it still needs to be as big as you can make it. The following extract is from a popular 'social science' text (that, for the author's sake, I shall refrain from identifying):

> In our survey, when asked where they would like to be in ten years' time, nearly three quarters (72 per cent) of young people chose the safe, sensible options of being 'settled down' or 'successful at work', compared with just 38 per cent of the older generation. Only 20 per cent of 16–24 year-olds chose the more adventurous option of 'travelling the world/living abroad', compared with 28 per cent of 45–54 year-olds. The older age group was also *twice* as likely as the youngsters to want to be 'footloose and fancy-free'.

It is understandable that an author would not want to burden a popular text with too much 'academic' apparatus—but if we are to take the survey seriously, we need to know how many 16–24-year-olds and how many 45–54-year-olds were questioned. The sample appears to have been *stratified* (perhaps for the purposes of this survey it was not necessary to question 25–44-year-olds), but we do not know how the subjects in each stratum were chosen. Were they stopped in the street by researchers with clipboards? Or were they unlucky enough to have been at home when the telephone rang, and a researcher said: 'This is not a sales call. We're conducting a survey. Would you be kind enough to answer a few questions? It'll only take a few minutes'?

A Word of Advice

If you conduct a survey of fewer than 50 people, don't convert raw numbers into percentages at all. If 19 people out of 30 agree with a statement, you cannot safely infer that 63.3 people in every hundred would agree with it.

Here is one further piece of 'research' done by a private health-insurance company in the UK which appears to explain why more and more people are taking out such insurance:

116. People are accustomed to having access to services when they want and need them. This is why eight out of ten Britons tell us that they think the 18 weeks that they might have to wait for an operation under the National Health Service is still too long. Private insurance also guarantees that people will receive the treatment that they need where and when it is most convenient for them. Thus, even if the NHS was to hit all its targets, eight out of ten people say that they would not give up their private cover. Reports of 'superbugs' in state hospitals are another factor: hospital cleanliness is the main reason why people take out private medical insurance: two out of three people take it out because they want to be sure that they will be treated in a superbug-free hospital.

Adapted from a letter from the MD of a private health-insurance company to *The Times*, January 2009

**5f.** The writer refers to 'eight out of ten Britons', and 'two out of three people'. How does the company appear to have chosen the sample, and how representative of the population of (all) Britons is it likely to be?

# Credibility and corroboration

'All genuine knowledge originates in direct experience': so said Mao Zedong (Argument 106). A judge does not have direct experience of the circumstances he is judging, so is reliant on eyewitness evidence. This is *primary* evidence. You may have access to primary evidence, but it is more likely that you will use *secondary* sources of evidence, at one or more removes from eyewitness testimony. Primary or secondary, it needs to be **credible**, believable, in accordance with our experience and common sense.

For centuries, Jews and Christians accepted it as a fact that the Earth was corrupt, and full of violence; that Noah was a righteous man; that God decided to destroy what he had made; that there was a Great Flood and that Noah and his family and pairs of sinless animals were saved. It was a 'fact' because the account of the flood was to be found in the Bible (Genesis 6–9). It was all the evidence that was needed—and to some, it still is:

117. The Great Flood happened more than 4,000 years ago; so there are no eyewitnesses remaining to give us an account of it. There is, though, a written record of that cataclysm, which informs us that the flood-waters overtopped the tallest of all the mountains. Some ask themselves whether the story of the whole world being flooded is a myth or possibly an exaggeration. Believers in the Bible as the Word of God, however, know that the Great Flood is no mere possibility. It is a fact.

Adapted from an article in an evangelical tract, June 2008

'Scientist' was a word first used in 1840 to define one who sought to systematize knowledge and its acquisition. This was at a time when growing numbers of thinkers were asking searching, 'scientific' questions, even about the books of the Bible: who wrote these books; when; in what circumstances; and with what motives? There were those who shuddered at the blasphemy; but there were those who rejoiced because they found stories of the 'supernatural' were no longer credible.

In 1872, an assistant in the British Museum, George Smith, deciphered a 7th-century BCE tablet from Nineveh:

118. He found that it told the story of Utnapishtim, who had been warned by the gods that there would be a great flood that would destroy the world. He built a boat and loaded it with everything he could find. He survived the flood for six days while mankind was destroyed. At the end of the flood he sent a dove and a swallow out and they came back because they could not find dry land. Then he sent a raven, which did not return, and he knew the floods had subsided. This was proof positive that the Biblical story of Noah was not unique. A different man in a different place was told by a different god, or, even more alarmingly several gods, to take his precautions. None of this proved or disproved any historical fact, nor indeed any religious creed. But this kind of comparative religious study changed the status of all claims to exclusive truth of whatever kind.

NEIL MACGREGOR, Director of the British Museum, 2004.
© Guardian News & Media

If the story of Utnapishtim was a myth, so might the story of Noah be a myth: the Nineveh tablet proved nothing, perhaps, but it **corroborated**—it agreed with, it backed up—what many 'scientists' had come to think. It gave support to the view that the story of Noah and the Great Flood was a myth—and it lent **credibility** to the inference that many, perhaps most, of the stories in the Old Testament (and the New Testament, too?) were myths.

Science is what it is because its results are tested in use: the findings of Heinrich Hertz, and John von Neumann, and Albert Einstein, and Linus Pauling, and Dorothy Hodgkin, and countless other scientists, are corroborated on a daily basis.

119. Scientists have the ability to pose questions and resolve them in a way that critics, philosophers, historians cannot. Theories are tested experimentally, compared to reality, and those found wanting are rejected. The power of science cannot be denied; it has given us computers and jets, vaccines and thermonuclear bombs,

technologies that, for better or worse, have altered the course of history. Science, more than any other mode of knowledge—literary criticism, philosophy, art, religion—yields durable insights into the nature of things. It gets us somewhere.

JOHN HORGAN, US science writer, The End of Science, Boston, MA:<br>Addison-Wesley, 1996

Though, perhaps there are few if any facts to be had in criticism, philosophy, and art, surely MacGregor (Argument 118) is justified when he refers to 'historical fact'?

> **5g.** Can you think of events or circumstances in history that are established facts, beyond all disagreement?

Politicians and military leaders assume that we can learn from history, even when there is disagreement among historians. The politician here was speaking in Afghanistan:

120. In the debate that we inevitably have in Britain about whether it's right to be spending money on aid, I would say this is a great example of a country that, if we walk away from, and if we ignore and forget about, the problems come visited back on our doorstep.

    How do we know this? Because we've done it before. We walked away from Afghanistan in the past. The problem of drugs got worse. The problem of terrorism got worse. The problem of extremism got worse. The problem of asylum and immigration got worse.

DAVID CAMERON, UK Prime Minister,<br>in a speech in Kabul, July 2011

Cameron **justified** the aid given to Afghanistan (at a time when it seemed to many voters back home that nothing was being achieved) by appealing to history: previous experience appeared to corroborate his (political) judgement that it was not time to quit Afghanistan. Historians may, or may not, agree with him, as evidence accumulates one way or the other. Cameron's claim is, at least, credible as it stands; it remains to be corroborated by researchers less politically involved.

Science, then, and history offer us evidence that can be tested. In spite of what Scruton, Allen, Newton, Cowan, and Spurling had to say earlier in this chapter, it is Horgan's view that art does not—and nor does religion. Here is a writer who wonders whether the 650 or so religious houses of medieval England were 'good for the country':

121. Were they of much use, all these monks and nuns? Well, without undertaking to show exactly what beneficial effect they had on many departments of life—as learning, art, agriculture—I do not hesitate to say that, not only in such ways, but in the way which they primarily had at heart, the monks and nuns of the earlier period were of immense use. That way was the worship of God. Whatever lower motives in later ages induced some men and women to take monastic vows, the original object was that high purpose; and, whatever view one may take of the particular means chosen to achieve it, I do not think it can be denied that the mere presence of a number of companies of people devoted to living the best life they could conceive of was good for the country in which they lived.

M.R. JAMES, English medieval scholar, 1926

How credible is this argument? James makes (at least) three factual claims:

- monks and nuns had beneficial effects in many departments of life;
- their primary purpose was to worship God;
- in doing so, in such numbers, they were good for the country.

> **5h.** How might one corroborate the first two claims? What sort of evidence might corroborate the third?

Perhaps Horgan was right about art, religion, philosophy—and criticism. In these domains, it is all too likely that the only corroboration for a factual claim will be another factual claim. Still, even rival factual claims can be weighed in the balance and one be found wanting. UK journalist David Aaronovitch considered the claim made by conspiracy theorists that the 1969 Apollo Moon landings were a fraud, and that the photographic 'evidence' had been manufactured. Aaronovitch thought this claim would have to be:

attested to by an army of photographic experts and scientists who had done years of research and whose conclusions were practically irrefutable. If the pictures were fake then, it followed, the moon landings themselves must have been counterfeited.

Then he thought about all the people who would have had to be party to the fraud, and he came to this conclusion:

> It is far more likely that men did actually land on the moon in 1969 than that thousands of people were enlisted to fabricate a deception that they did.
>
> DAVID AARONOVITCH, *Voodoo Histories*, London: Vintage, 2010

'Criterion' comes from the same root word as 'criticism': it is a standard or test for reaching a judgement. We have already identified some criteria for testing the credibility of claims, your own and those of others:

- the reliability of sources;
- the assumptions that appear to be made;
- the expertise and reputation of 'authorities' appealed to.

Others are to consider the **consequences** of accepting the claims, as Aaronovitch did, and the historical **context** of those claims, as the author of Argument 112 did not. This is what any judge has to do.

In this chapter, then, we have considered the evidence that you might present in support of your **Argument B**.

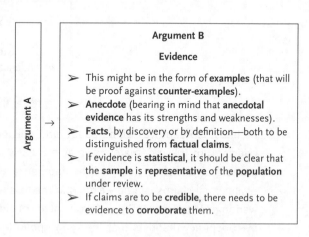

We have thought about when it is that facts are facts, and when claims are credible or not, in this chapter. It is time now to consider how far you can be sure of your case, and when you might risk using the words 'true' and 'truth'.

# 6 How much can you be sure about?

I shall aim in this chapter to explain:

- why certainty may be hard to come by;
- and why this makes deductive argument unsafe;
- why 'if...then' claims might be unsafe, too;
- and why logic may not get us very far.

## Certainty and plausibility

The distinction was made in Chapter 5 between facts and factual claims. Facts are, so to speak, the raw material of knowledge—but it is generally agreed that there is more to knowledge than facts. A lot of philosophy has been about how much we know; what we can know; and what it is to know. Socrates knew what he knew (or he thought he did):

> It is perfectly certain that the soul is immortal and imperishable, and our souls will actually exist in another world.
>
> SOCRATES, Greek philosopher, 5th century BCE

Few would want to say such a thing with **certainty** now, however much they might believe in the soul and its immortality. On the other hand, few would be quite as downright as Mill:

> There is no such thing as absolute certainty, but there is assurance sufficient for the purposes of human life.
>
> JOHN STUART MILL, *On Liberty*, 1859

Is there nothing about which we can be absolutely certain? I made a distinction in Chapter 5 between facts by discovery and facts by definition, and I said that (as long as we speak English) we can be absolutely certain that if New Year's Eve falls on a Saturday, New Year's Day must fall on a Sunday. Facts by definition are certain until we are minded to change the definition. Can we ever be certain about facts by discovery? This philosopher thinks not:

122. The interior angles of a plane triangle are equal to 180°—we know with certainty that this is true. Some cats are black—we also know with certainty that this is true. So it seems [these statements] are in that respect alike. But some people used to think they knew with certainty that the Earth is flat; and they were mistaken. Now, no doubt we are not mistaken when we say some cats are black, but it at least makes sense to say we *could* be mistaken.

GEOFFREY J. WARNOCK, *English Philosophy Since 1900*,
Oxford: Oxford University Press, 1969.
By permission of Oxford University Press

That 'some cats are black' is a fact by discovery (once we have defined 'cat' and 'black'); and, as long as black cats do not fall prey to a catastrophic disease, we can go on being certain about it—even *absolutely* certain.

But it is, perhaps, only trivial things like this that we can be absolutely certain about (and we shall look, in the next section, at the kind of argument—deductive argument—that concerns itself with such things). Here, it is worth considering what we might mean when we say we *know* something. Montaigne, the French essayist, considered it:

123. The difficulties and challenges in any field of learning are understood only by those who have entered it. For one needs to have some knowledge to know how ignorant one is; one has to push at a door before finding out that it is locked. Hence, Plato's paradox that those who know already have no need to find out; and they have no need to inquire who do not know, since, in order to inquire, one needs to know what it is one wishes to find out about. The fact that everyone seems certain that they know themselves pretty well and seem so self-satisfied, just shows that no-one knows anything about themselves.

MICHEL DE MONTAIGNE, 'On Experience', 1580

Plato made the mistake of supposing that 'those who know' know everything and those 'who do not know' know nothing; and, perhaps, Montaigne overstates his final claim. Surely we know more in the 21st century, and how we come to know it, than Montaigne could in 1580.

Donald Rumsfeld was taxed at a press conference, in 2002, about whether there was any evidence to suggest that Iraq was supplying weapons of mass destruction (WMD) to terrorist groups. His answer was mocked for its seeming clumsiness—but he could hardly have expressed himself more clearly:

> There are known knowns; there are things we know that we know. There are known unknowns; that is to say, there are things that we now know we don't know. But there are also unknown unknowns—there are things we do not know we don't know.
>
> DONALD RUMSFELD, US Secretary of Defense, February 2002

No one could be **certain** that Iraq possessed or supplied WMD; but Rumsfeld (among others equally under-informed) thought that it was, at least, **probable**. Only the probability that Iraq was passing, for example, sarin nerve agents to al Qaida could have justified the invasion in 2003. Whether or not this was a 'known unknown', or an 'unknown unknown', the fact is that no one *knew*.

Leaving aside trivial facts by definition (e.g. that the interior angles of a plane triangle are equal to 180°), much of what we say we know is rather probable than certain. We may calculate probabilities mathematically, but we can judge what is probable and what is not, without resorting to numbers, as Pascal the mathematician did (surely) with his tongue in his cheek:

124. Let us weigh up the gain and loss involved in calling heads that God exists. Let us assess the two cases: if you win you win everything, if you lose you lose nothing. Do not hesitate then; wager that he does exist.

       BLAISE PASCAL, French mathematician and philosopher, c.1660

Had Pascal been certain that God existed he would not have needed to place the bet. How certain can we be about the future? (How certain about the future were Harold Nicholson, in Argument 78, and Jesús María Yepes, in Argument 81 in Chapter 4?):

125. Over the next ten years the world we inhabit will change massively. Technology will change out of recognition, millions more will go to university, the number of low-skilled jobs will fall, with more reward for those with good qualifications. *So, we need to have an education system equipped for that world—one which equips young people for all its challenges and opportunities.*

       MICHAEL GOVE, UK Education Secretary, March 2012

Mr Gove's conclusion (italicized) might be called a safe bet.

**6a.** Michael Gove bases his conclusion on five predictions. How *probable* would you say it is that each of these predictions will come to pass?

If to be *probable*, a claim has to be highly likely, we might say that for a claim to be **plausible** it is still likely, but rather less so. That some cats are black is (presently) certain; that black cats account for fewer than half of all cats is probable; and that black cats are declining in number is, at least, plausible—it would be a credible claim, especially if it was made by a zoologist.

How plausible is this argument?

126. It is a part of the destiny of the human race, in its gradual improve-
ment, to leave off eating animals, as surely as the savage tribes
have left off eating each other when they come in contact with the
more civilized.

    HENRY DAVID THOREAU, US essayist and poet, 1854

To be sure, cannibalism (as Thoreau defines it) has come to an end—
whether or not in deference to missionaries; but is it as sure that we
shall all be vegetarians one day? It is far from certain (is anything
inevitable?); environmentalists may think it probable; but—given
what we (think we) know about future food resources and land avail-
ability—it is at least plausible.

Here is a rather more developed argument which we may think
makes plausible claims:

127. In the more than two decades that I have traded in coffee, prices
have risen and fallen dramatically. Over-supply and various environmental factors have generally been to blame. Early in 2011,
when there was plenty of coffee about, prices were nevertheless
the highest on record. Commentators this time blamed rising
demand in the BRIC countries, Brazil, Russia, India, and China.

    This wasn't the reason at all: the high prices were the direct
result of shiny new financial instruments devised by corporate
investors, disappointed by the returns on traditional stock
markets. Now they were investing in the future supply of staple
food products—and forcing up the prices of these products

on supermarket shelves. The price of coffee is not one more consequence of climate change; it's a consequence of heartless gambling by big investors.

Adapted from a letter to *The Observer*, 28 July 2013

To those of us who are not in the coffee business, any one of the four reasons given for the fluctuation in coffee prices might seem plausible: over-supply; environmental factors; demand in the BRIC countries; and investment activity—but, perhaps, the fourth reason is the most plausible, when there is plenty of coffee about, *and* prices are at record levels.

It is plausible that black cats are declining in number; it is less likely still, but it is at least **possible**, that they will become extinct.

Andrew Carnegie was a Scotsman who emigrated to the United States, where he invested not in coffee, but in railways, bridges, oil wells, ironworks, and steel:

128. While the law [of competition] may be sometimes hard for the individual, it is best for the race, because it ensures the survival of the fittest in every department. We accept and welcome, therefore, as conditions to which we must accommodate ourselves, great inequality of environment, the concentration of business, industrial and commercial, in the hands of a few, and the law of competition between these, as being not only beneficial, but essential for the future progress of the race.

ANDREW CARNEGIE, Scottish-American industrialist
and philanthropist, 1889

It was acceptable, in 1889, to talk about the 'law' of competition, of 'the race', of the 'survival of the fittest', and of 'progress', without irony. Could the boss of a major company, nowadays, *plausibly* claim that 'great inequality' is 'essential' to progress, and that we should not only accept it, but welcome it? Perhaps not; nevertheless, it is *possible* that big business always will be in 'the hands of a few'.

J.M. Keynes probably did not have the philanthropic Carnegie in his sights when he wrote the following:

129. The love of money as a possession—as distinguished from the love of money as a means to the enjoyments and realities of life—will be recognized for what it is, a somewhat disgusting morbidity, one of those semi-criminal, semi-pathological propensities which one hands over with a shudder to the specialists in mental disease.

JOHN MAYNARD KEYNES, English economist, 1931

It is a little difficult to guess who might have been in his sights, in fact—misers, perhaps. It is possible that the lover of money for its own sake will one day be thought of as a suitable case for treatment; but is it likely?

We can put the terms that I have highlighted so far on a continuum of knowledge:

**Knowledge**

Certain    Probable    Plausible    Possible    Unlikely

> **6b.** Following are six claims. Which if any of them do you consider to be certain, which probable, which plausible, and which only possible, or unlikely?

a. Any woman who understands the problems of running a home will be nearer to understanding the problems of running a country.

MARGARET THATCHER, UK Prime Minister, 1979

b. The sound of the flute will cure epilepsy and sciatic gout.

THEOPHRASTUS, Greek philosopher, *c.*300 BCE

c. We are of course a nation of differences. Those differences don't make us weak. They're the source of our strength.

JIMMY CARTER, US President, 1976

d. Treaties, you see, they are like roses and like young girls: they last for just as long as they last.

CHARLES DE GAULLE, French President, 1963

e. We learn wisdom in three ways: first, by imitation, which is easiest; second by reflection, which is noblest; and third, by experience, which is the bitterest.

CONFUCIUS, Chinese philosopher, *c.*500 BCE

f. Normally speaking, it may be said that the forces of a capitalist society, if left unchecked, tend to make the rich richer and the poor poorer and thus increase the gap between them.

JAWAHARLAL NEHRU, Indian statesman, 1960

It is worth adding that there is a way, or degree, of knowing that it is not easy to place on the continuum mentioned previously—one that might be illustrated by the following claim:

An exaggeration is a truth that has lost its temper.

KALIL GIBRAN, Syrian artist and writer, 1926

Just as there must be room for an appeal to feeling in argument, so must there be room for poetry on the continuum of knowledge.

# Deductive argument

It was Aristotle who devised rules for coming to a certain conclusion from certain claims (or reasons, or premises, or propositions). His aim was to put a conclusion beyond doubt. If the claims were facts, then the conclusion drawn from them must be a fact. He **deduced** the conclusion from two premises, the major premise and the minor premise; and the resulting deduction was a **syllogism**.

We saw in Chapter 1 that a claim makes an association between two objects, or terms, which I called **P** and **Q**. A syllogism associates three terms, so I shall use the letters **A**, **B**, and **C**.

Major premise: All living things (**A**) are bound to die (**B**).
Minor premise: I (**C**) am a living thing (**A**).
Conclusion: Therefore, I (**C**) am bound to die (**B**).

The major premise is a *general* claim: all **A** are **B**. The minor premise is a *specific* claim: **C** is **A**. The conclusion is the only possible one: **C** is **B**. The inference is *necessary*; if the premises are 'true' the conclusion must be true; and therefore the argument is a **valid** argument.

Reasoning of this deductive (or *rationalist*) kind was the norm from late classical, through medieval, to early modern times. John Wycliffe reasoned deductively—and dangerously:

130. Christ during His life upon earth was of all men the poorest, casting from Him all worldly authority. I deduce from these premises that the Pope should surrender all temporal\* authority to the civil power and advise his clergy to do the same.

JOHN WYCLIFFE, English Bible translator, 1384

\* Temporal—worldly, non-spiritual.

It is a fair deduction, if we accept that the Pope ought to imitate Christ; but it is not a valid one, unless it is accepted that Christ and the Pope are one and the same: are both **A**—which, of course, they are not. Twenty years later, Jean de Valois (dubbed John the Fearless for his exploits against the Turks) argued deductively in an even more explicit fashion. He had had Louis, Duke of Orleans assassinated in 1407, and he justified himself in a syllogism:

131. The deed that has been done was perpetrated, as I now proceed to explain, for the safety of the king's person and that of his children, and for the general good of the realm. My thesis is the following syllogism:

| The major: | It is permissible and meritorious to kill a tyrant. |
| The minor: | The Duke of Orleans was a tyrant. |
| The conclusion: | Therefore the Duke of Burgundy did well to kill him. |

JOHN THE FEARLESS, Duke of Burgundy, 1408

Jean de Valois, John the Fearless, and the Duke of Burgundy *were* all one and the same—but is it always permissible to kill a tyrant? And was Louis of Orleans a tyrant? (It seems he was less a tyrant than a womanizer, killed by a wronged husband with Fearless John's blessing.) Still, if (and only if) we accept John's premises, the argument is a valid one; the conclusion is inescapable. An argument is valid when the conclusion is a necessary consequence of accepting the premises—whether those premises are 'true' or not. It is **invalid** when the conclusion cannot be inferred from the premises. A **sound** argument is one where premises and conclusion are all credible, or 'true'. An argument may be valid, yet be unsafe or **unsound**—as is this one.

The problem with deductive reasoning lies, principally, with the major premise: either it is not a certain, well-established fact by discovery; or it is a trivial fact by definition, and we learn nothing new, as in:

All mammals suckle their young; cats are mammals; therefore, cats suckle their young.

**6c.** How might you complete a deductive argument, whose major premise is: 'All EU member countries subscribe to the rule of law'?

Though he was not the first to do so, Francis Bacon is famous for proposing that deductive argument got things the wrong way round:

132. There are and can be only two ways of searching into and discovering truth. The one (leaving aside the senses and specific things) starts from general axioms, and from these—the truth of which it assumes is fixed and immovable—proceeds to a minor premise and a conclusion. This is the accepted way of thinking. The other starts from the senses and from specific things, rising by gradual stages, and arriving at the most general axioms last of all. This is the true way, but it is as yet untried.

FRANCIS BACON, Lord Chancellor of England, 1620

By an 'axiom' Bacon meant an established fact, an accepted, *general* truth: deductive thinkers supposed that this was where an argument began. Bacon proposed that one should argue by **induction** (or *empirically*) from a *specific* observation (or, rather, many specific observations) to a *general* conclusion. Only when one had observed this animal suckling its young; and this one; and this one (and black cats, and other cats); and given the name 'mammals' to all these animals—only then could one state the general 'truth' that 'all mammals suckle their young'.

Bacon claimed that there were two ways of discovering truth. It would, perhaps, be more accurate to say that there is one way, having two stages: first one observes *specific* things, coming to a general conclusion **inductively**; then that conclusion is the major premise of a deductive argument, from which one can make a *specific* inference. (The weakness of inductive argument—and therefore of deductive argument—of course, is that one might just find a black cat in some far-flung wilderness unable to suckle its young. Is it a cat? Is it a mammal? Must we change our definition of a 'mammal'? Is this why, as Warnock supposes, in Argument 122, we might be 'mistaken' about black cats?)

I suggested at the end of Chapter 2 that in Western Europe we think inductively (from a specific cat to cats in general), whereas Eastern

European thinking is deductive (from general to specific). Stalin bears out this generalization:

133. In our country there are no longer any landlords and kulaks,* merchants and usurers who could exploit the peasants. Consequently our peasantry is a peasantry emancipated from exploitation.

> JOSEPH STALIN, Soviet Communist Party General Secretary, 1936

\* Kulak—relatively wealthy peasant.

If this argument was laid out as a syllogism, it might look something like this:

| | |
|---|---|
| Major premise: | Landlords, kulaks, merchants and usurers exploited the peasantry. |
| Minor premise: | There are no longer such people in our country. |
| Conclusion: | Consequently our peasantry is emancipated from exploitation. |

We might accept Stalin's major premise (though there must, surely, have been some landlords who were not exploitative); and it may be that they had been effectively purged—but few peasants, following 'dekulakization' in 1929, would have felt wonderfully emancipated. The argument is deductive, but is both unsound and invalid. Here's another 'Eastern' thinker and communist:

134. The main task of socialism is to develop the productive forces, steadily improve the life of the people, and keep increasing the material wealth of the society. Therefore, there can be no communism with pauperism, or socialism with pauperism. So to get rich is no sin.

> DENG XIAOPING, Chinese communist politician, 1986

Perhaps these men thought deductively—and downrightly—because they were communists as much as because they were 'Easterners'. This Hungarian-American was an 'Easterner', now a 'Westerner', and no communist (he refers here to the time, before 1920, when the present-day Romanian province of Transylvania was part of the Austro-Hungarian Empire):

135. The Hungarians deny the accusation that they oppressed the Rumanians. It is well known that the Hungarians belong to the Turanian group of people. In their state organization, the Turanian peoples never practised oppression of conquered peoples. They simply demanded obedience and loyalty.

> LÁSZLÓ BOTOS, The Road to the Dictated Peace,
> Cleveland, OH: Árpád Publishing Co, 1999

The major premise here is, in effect, that all Hungarians **(A)** are Turanians **(B)**; given that Turanians did not oppress conquered peoples **(C)**, Hungarians did not oppress the Romanians—or Rumanians—who might have been mistaken and thought otherwise.

Freud was no communist either, though Vienna is to the east of Prague:

136. Criticisms which stem from some psychological need of those making them don't deserve a rational answer. When people complain that psychoanalysis makes wild and arbitrary assertions about infantile sexuality, this criticism stems from a certain psychological need of these people. Therefore, the criticism that psychoanalysis makes wild and arbitrary assertions about infantile sexuality doesn't deserve a rational answer.

SIGMUND FREUD, Austrian neurologist
and pioneer of psychiatry, 1933

> **6d.** Which of Freud's claims seems to you to be the major premise of his argument? Is it a 'fact' from which he can safely draw the conclusion that he does?

If 'Easterners' tend to think deductively, and communists do so (or did so) for ideological reasons, it is fair to add that deductive thinking comes naturally to anyone who argues from a fixed position—it may be a conservative interpreter of the US Constitution (Argument 14 in Chapter 2); it may be anyone who appeals to tradition (Argument 79 in Chapter 4), or to authority, or to 'fundamentals' (Argument 83 in Chapter 4 and Argument 117 in Chapter 5); or it may be a Roman Catholic for whom the teachings of the Church are sacrosanct (Argument 32 in Chapter 2 and Argument 137 which follows).

When the contraceptive pill was introduced (in the UK) in 1961, liberal Catholics hoped that the Church would soften its stand against contraception. In 1968, the then Pope issued an encyclical that dashed these hopes:

137. [We affirm] the inseparable connection, willed by God and incapable of being broken by man on his own initiative, between the two meanings of the conjugal act: the unitive meaning and the procreative meaning. Indeed, by its intimate structure, the conjugal

act, while most closely uniting husband and wife, enables them to generate new lives, according to laws inscribed in the very being of man and of woman. Contraception deliberately deprives the conjugal act of its openness to procreation and in this way brings about a voluntary dissociation of the ends of marriage.

POPE PAUL VI, *Humanae Vitae*, 1968

A Word of Advice

When you can speak for God, you can argue with utter conviction. The rest of us, if we are to argue deductively at all, must ensure that our premises are watertight.

# Conditional claims

A major premise might be affirmative ('All living things are bound to die'), or negative ('No living thing lives for ever'). Alternatively, it may be conditional: 'If a thing is living, it is bound to die'. We have already noted the difference between *necessary* and *sufficient* conditions (in Chapter 4). As *soundness* will be of greater interest to us than *validity*, so it is of more importance to us that a claim is *credible* (or 'true') than that it is conditional. But it is worth thinking, briefly, about 'If...then...' claims.

An atheist campaign placed this slogan on London buses, in January 2009:

> ## THERE'S PROBABLY NO GOD
> ### NOW STOP WORRYING AND ENJOY YOUR LIFE

A *Times* reader recalled Pascal's Wager (Argument 124):

138. If it is at least possible that God exists, then you would do well to believe, since you have nothing to lose. It's hardly likely that you'll be unhappier. But if you don't believe, and you find that he does exist, you'll find yourself in a tight corner on Judgment Day.

Adapted from a letter to *The Times*, January 2009

A believer objected that atheists had no documentary evidence that 'there is probably no God'; and this provoked a second 'if…then…' letter:

> If atheists are called upon to supply documentary evidence that there is probably no God, then surely those posters outside churches and chapels which claim 'Jesus Saves' must do the same.

I have not numbered this second letter since its two parts—'if…' and 'then…'—are the two halves of a single claim. By itself, it is not an argument. And nor is this claim:

> If men were angels, no government would be necessary.
> JAMES MADISON, 4th US President, 1788

Such a claim might be made in a number of ways:

- No government would be necessary if men were angels.
- Either men are angels, or government isn't necessary.
- Unless men are angels, government is necessary.
- Only when men are angels is government unnecessary.

But perhaps the 'If…then…' form is the most usual. Conditional claims like this might otherwise be called **hypothetical**. They float a possibility; they say: 'let's suppose…'. The first half of the condition ('If…'), or *antecedent*, is one half of the possibility; and the second half ('then…'), the *consequent*, is the other—though 'consequent' may be a misleading term since the second half of the claim is no more probable than the first.

In an important sense, when an argument contains a condition—when it is a piece of **hypothetical reasoning**—the whole argument, and not least the conclusion, is conditional. As readers, we must consider whether we think the reasoning is, at least, *plausible*; and as writers, we must not even imply that hypothetical reasoning can lead to a *probable*—much less a *certain*—conclusion.

Here's a piece of hypothetical reasoning from a lawyer:

139. If for four centuries there had been a very widely extended franchise and a very large electoral body in this country, there would have been no reformation of religion, no change of dynasty, no toleration of Dissent, not even an accurate Calendar. The threshing-machine, the power-loom, the spinning-jenny, and possibly the steam engine, would have been prohibited.
      SIR HENRY MAINE, English historian,
      and professor of international law, 1885

Maine was no friend of the popular vote: in 1884, Gladstone had extended the franchise to 60 per cent of males in Britain. How would the other 40 per cent (to say nothing of women) have countered Maine's argument? Where to start? It is *possible* that if every working man had had the vote, machines that put them out of their jobs might have been delayed; but what evidence might Sir Henry have offered to support his claim that workers would have voted against the Reformation? There was nothing wrong with his reasoning—his claims were not 'false'; but nothing could make them 'true'.

The same goes for this argument:

140. Had every Christian in Hitler's Europe followed the example of the King of Denmark and decided to put on the yellow star, there would be today neither despair in the church nor talk of the death of God.

> EMIL L. FACKENHEIM, *Quest for Past and Future*,
> Bloomington, IN: Indiana University Press, 1968

It is an interesting hypothesis—but an hypothesis is all it is, and all it ever could be.

The fact that hypothetical reasoning is the art of the (only) possible does not mean that it cannot be very persuasive. Here is a soldier reasoning hypothetically with men of the Third Army, on the eve of D-Day, 5 June 1944:

141. Every single man in this army plays a vital role. Don't ever let up. Don't ever think that your job is unimportant. Every man has a job to do and he must do it. Every man is a vital link in the great chain. What if every truck driver suddenly decided that he didn't like the whine of those shells overhead, turned yellow, and jumped headlong into a ditch? The cowardly bastard could say, 'Hell, they won't miss me, just one man in thousands.' But, what if every man thought that way? Where in the hell would we be now? What would our country, our loved ones, our homes, even the world, be like? No, goddammit, Americans don't think like that. Every man does his job. Every man serves the whole. Every department, every unit, is important in the vast scheme of this war.

> GENERAL GEORGE S. PATTON, US army commander, 1944

How many adults have asked 'What if everyone did that?' when children have dropped litter, or started a fight? (And how many children have answered: 'But everyone doesn't'?)

Maine's and Fackenheim's 'if' claims concerned the past, where what *did* happen supersedes what *might* have happened. Patton's 'what if' question concerned the immediate future. The whole insurance industry profits by persuading us that anything might happen:

142. We are the UK's largest independent provider of service agreements for Sky TV systems. We understand the initial manufacturer's warranty on your digital satellite system has now expired and unless you have already taken out extended cover this leaves you open to expensive call-out charges and repair costs should anything go wrong! So, fill out the enclosed form now, or call us for immediate peace of mind.

And the costly confidence trick that is nuclear deterrence is based on a 'what if' hypothesis:

What if free people could live secure in the knowledge that if their security did not rest upon the threat of instant US retaliation to deter a Soviet attack, that we could intercept and destroy strategic ballistic missiles before they reached our soil or that of our allies?

RONALD REAGAN, US President, 1983

Reagan (at least in this extract) left it to his audience to answer his question: he supplied the premises—the antecedent 'if...'; it was for the rest of us to supply the consequent, the 'then...', and a conclusion.

> **6e.** What consequent (what 'then...'), and what conclusion might Reagan have wanted his audience to supply?

Perhaps the most famous and most radical of all published conditional claims was this one by J.S. Mill, whom we met at the beginning of this chapter:

> If all mankind minus one were of one opinion, and only one person were of the contrary opinion, mankind would no more be justified in silencing that one person than he, if he had the power, would be justified in silencing mankind.
>
> JOHN STUART MILL, *On Liberty*, 1859

It is a bold claim—a wonderfully humane claim—that is so hypothetical (and yet so imaginable) that it seems to transcend all talk of what is, or might be, certain, probable, plausible, possible, false, or 'true'.

# Logic and truth

A Word of Advice

If you have limited time, or limited patience with philosophizing, you might go straight from here to the summary at the end of this chapter.

I have put 'true' in kid-glove quotation marks until now because much of philosophy has been about trying to define it. The problem (for philosophers) was that language is inexact. Aristotle's propositions were too vague for the expression of watertight truths: words like 'and', 'or', 'if', 'then', 'some', 'all' could not do the work that a mathematician like Frege (1848–1925) wanted them to do. Scientists, philosophers—all searchers after truth—needed a new language, a new **logic** that would express meanings without ambiguity:

> To discover truths is the task of all sciences; it falls to logic to discern the laws of truth.
>
> GOTTLOB FREGE, German mathematician and logician, 1879

There was an important drawback to this passion for exactness, however: the sort of logic that Frege had in mind was based on the assumption that each and every sentence is either **true** or **false**:

This posed no problems for many philosophers: they were perfectly happy to accept that propositions were either true or false. What else could they be?

143. It would seem that a judgment is, strictly speaking, always either true or false and cannot be more or less true; and it is surely obvious that '2 + 2 = 4' and 'Washington is the capital of the United States' are absolutely true.

A.C. EWING, *The Fundamental Questions of Philosophy*, London: Routledge, 1951

These truths, indeed, as we have seen, are 'absolutely true' inasmuch as they are truths, or facts, by definition—but they are not **judgements**, a word we generally use to mean a carefully considered point of view. We can say that:

- *facts by definition* (such as '2 + 2 = 4') are either true or false because we determine whether they are or not;
- *facts by discovery* (such as 'hot air rises') may be true or false, depending upon whether they have stood up to repeated testing—they are 'facts' only when they have done so;
- *factual claims* (such as 'this is the greatest symphony of the 20th century') cannot be true or false, since there is no test that could put the claim beyond dispute.

Here is a mathematician, and logician, who acknowledged that logic has its limits (and who by 'declarative sentence' meant 'statement' or 'proposition'):

144. Logicians say that the *truth-value* of a declarative sentence is Truth when the sentence is true, and Falsehood when it is false. In any situation, a declarative sentence has just one truth-value; either Truth or Falsehood. There is something in this to catch the imagination. Life seems full of half-truths, grey areas, borderline cases, but Logic stands with sword uplifted to divide the world cleanly into the True and the False.

Many people have been attracted to logic by some such feeling. But an honest thinker must ask himself whether this clean and absolute division into Truth and Falsehood is perhaps no more than a verbal illusion. Maybe Truth itself has degrees and blurred edges.

WILFRID HODGES, *Logic*, London: Penguin Books, 1977, 2001.
Reproduced by permission of Penguin Books Ltd

> **6f.** Do you share the view of logicians who hold that a sentence expresses either truth or falsehood?

Hodges came to this conclusion early on in his book (the italics are his):

> We are forced to admit that *where borderline cases may arise, logic is not an exact science.*

He wrote the rest of the book, nevertheless, as if classical logic still had a job to do.

Philosopher and mathematician Bertrand Russell seized on Frege's ideas: he, too, despaired of ordinary language as a vehicle for exact meaning. He turned to Aristotle for three 'laws of thought' that had been singled out by tradition:

(1) *The law of identity*: 'Whatever is, is'

(2) *The law of contradiction:* 'Nothing can both be and not be'

(3) *The law of excluded middle:* 'Everything must either be or not be'.

BERTRAND RUSSELL, *The Problems of Philosophy*, 1912.
By permission of Oxford University Press

Russell called all three laws 'self-evident principles'. You might agree with him about the first two: but the third? According to this third 'law' (otherwise called the 'principle of bivalence') there is no middle way between the two 'values' truth and falsehood. There are no borderline cases. You are either tall or short, thin or fat.

It was a Frege scholar, an English professor of logic, who laid this law to rest, and he did for classical logic while he was about it:

> We must reject the law of excluded middle as a universally valid logical law. With it, we must also reject classical logic, normally taken as resting on the two-valued semantics that embodies the principle of bivalence.

SIR MICHAEL DUMMETT, *Thought and Reality*, Oxford: Oxford University Press, 2006. By permission of Oxford University Press

Logic/mathematics is, doubtless, a vital tool in the exact sciences, and in computer programming; it was a pioneer of artificial intelligence, though, who said:

> Logic doesn't apply to the real world.
>
> MARVIN MINSKY, US computer scientist, 1981

We argue in the real world; (in the unreal world where logic does apply, everything is certain, so there is no need for argument-as-persuasion). In 'the real world', 'borderline cases' do arise. Indeed, when there is no vertical line drawn between what is said to be TRUE and what is said to be FALSE, there is no 'borderline': most cases stand somewhere on the continuum between these two terms. They arise whenever we are concerned not with what is certain, but with what is probable, plausible, possible; whenever what we think we 'know' is, really, a matter of *judgement*.

Philosophy's search for The Truth was, perhaps, a long and forlorn search for a lost god; and the hope was that logic would be 'The Word'.

We tend to use the word 'true' when we merely want to affirm or lend extra weight to a claim. If we were to say: 'It's true that a third world war is possible', the words 'it's true' add nothing: they do not make what is only possible more likely. William James put it thus:

> 'The true' to put it very briefly, is only the expedient in the way of our thinking, just as 'the right' is only the expedient in the way of our behaving.
>
> WILLIAM JAMES, US philosopher and psychologist, 1907

By 'the expedient' James meant what gives us confidence; what we can believe; what works for us. What is 'true' may simply boil down to what we can **trust**, and whom we can trust—whether or not they are 'experts' (Chapter 3):

> Truth, and specifically the virtues of truth, are connected with trust. The connections are to be seen in the English language.
>
> BERNARD WILLIAMS, *Truth and Truthfulness*,
> Princeton, NJ: Princeton University Press, 2002

Perhaps, indeed, 'truth' is less a philosophical, than a psychological issue: trust, after all, is the very basis of a baby's attachment to its mother.

Whether you are assessing someone else's argument, then, or advancing an argument of your own, you would do well to:

> ➤ Avoid using the word **certain**, other than when stating facts by definition.
>
> ➤ Refer instead—and discriminatingly—to what is **probable**, what is **plausible**, and what is merely **possible**.
>
> ➤ Engage in **deductive reasoning** with care, if you do so at all.
>
> ➤ Be aware that **conditional**, or **hypothetical**, argument will generally yield a conditional conclusion.
>
> ➤ Speak of what is **true** only to the extent that you can trust the evidence, the author who adduces it, and the conclusion he or she draws from it.

Having considered how much we can claim to *know*, it is worth giving thought to what we may *believe*, or think we believe.

# 7 How much is a matter of belief?

I shall aim in this chapter to explain:

- that we all look at the world from our own angle;
- why this might influence the opinions we hold;
- why absolute objectivity may not be possible;
- why argument from principle may be risky.

## Point of view

Every one of us sees the world from a particular **point of view**. This is what I meant when I said, in Chapter 2, that in your opening **Statement**, you might make it clear where you stand. You occupy a certain *position*: you live in a certain time, in a certain place, and you see the world at this time, in and from this place. You cannot do otherwise.

Consider what it is that makes you what you are:

- your genetic inheritance;
- the attachments you formed in infancy;
- your family background;
- the schooling you received;
- the 'significant others' in your life;
- what you have seen, heard, and done.

You are unique. You see the world from a unique *angle*: no one else frames the world in the same viewfinder, and commits it to long-term memory, from where you are standing, and when.

Your point of view, your angle, will influence your claims, your choice of evidence, and the conclusion you come to. If you want to earn your reader's trust, you will need to be honest about your point of view.

145. The significance of man is that he is that part of the universe that asks the question, 'What is the significance of Man?' He alone can stand apart imaginatively and, regarding himself and the universe in their eternal aspects, pronounce a judgment: The significance of man is that he is insignificant and is aware of it.

CARL BECKER, US historian, 1936

'Man' may scan the universe where cats cannot; and 'man' may indeed be insignificant—but each man and woman is insignificant in his or her own way. If you are not 'man', but a man, you see the world from a man's point of view. In Argument 21 (Chapter 2) Sir Almroth Wright scoffed at the idea of giving women the vote; he was a man, and he was a man writing in 1913.

Montaigne (whom we last met in Argument 123 in Chapter 6), a man writing in 1580, spoke highly of friendship. In doing so, he spoke lowly of marriage—and of women:

146. As for marriage, whilst it is a contract entered into freely enough, but escape from which is impossible whatever our wishes in the matter, it is a contract that is often entered into for ulterior motives. Marriage involves an encounter with all sorts of unnecessary complications that threaten to break the delicate thread of the mutual attraction that set it off. Friendship, on the other hand, is untroubled by any consideration beyond the benefits that friendship brings. What is more, women simply do not have what it takes to meet the demands made on them by the married state. Their temperament is not firm enough to withstand the strains of such a commitment.

MICHEL DE MONTAIGNE, 'On Friendship', 1580

> **7a.** Montaigne came under pressure from his family to marry Françoise de la Cassaigne. Does this justify his point of view, as expressed here?

Edward Fitzgerald might have been a fine poet (he is actually best known as the translator of *The Rubaiyat of Omar Khayyam*) but his point of view was infected by an unpoetic male chauvinism—and what might have been professional jealousy (Elizabeth Barrett Browning's poem *Aurora Leigh* was published in 1857; she died in June 1861 at the age of 55):

> 147. Mrs Browning's death is rather a relief to me, I must say: no more *Aurora Leighs*, thank God! A woman of real genius, I know; but what is the upshot of it all? She and her sex had better mind the kitchen and their children; and perhaps the poor: except in such things as little novels, they only devote themselves to what men do much better, leaving that which men do worse, or not at all.
>
> EDWARD FITZGERALD, English poet, 1861

Robert Browning, her poet husband would have seen things from an altogether different point of view—as many (but not all) women would have done.

The American journalist H.L. Mencken married in 1930: he was 50, his wife 32; she died five years later, and he outlived her by 21 years:

> 148. Men have a better time of it than women. For one thing, they marry later. For another thing, they die earlier.
>
> H.L. MENCKEN, US journalist and critic, 1949

This was a point of view that could be justified in general, if only half of it was borne out in his own case. Abigail Adams (Argument 9 in Chapter 1) did not see the world as her husband saw it; and no man could have made these claims:

> It is well within the order of things | that man should listen when his mate sings; | But the true male never yet walked | who liked to listen when his mate talked.
>
> ANNE WICKHAM, English poet, 1915

> This is an important book, the critic assumes, because it deals with war. This is an insignificant book because it deals with the feelings of women in a drawing room.
>
> VIRGINIA WOOLF, *A Room of One's Own*, 1929

When one is writing may influence one's point of view as much as, or more than, whether one is a man or a woman. The Marquis de Condorcet wrote the following when he had cause to be optimistic about the course of the French Revolution:

Have we not arrived at the point when we no longer need fear, either what new errors may bring, or what old ones might be repeated; when hypocrisy cannot introduce some new corrupt institution, to be taken up by ignorance or enthusiasm, and when no malevolent group can spoil the happiness of a great people?

NICOLAS DE CONDORCET, French mathematician
and political theorist, 1794

Within a matter of months, the Marquis was dead in his cell, one more of Robespierre's victims.

Swedish chemist Alfred Nobel invented dynamite in 1867. Five years later, Irish American Patrick Ford suggested a use for it:

149. I believe in all things for the liberation of Ireland. If dynamite is necessary to the redemption of Ireland, then dynamite is a blessed agent and should be availed of by the Irish people in their holy war. Every creature of God is good and nothing is to be rejected when it can be made to subserve a good cause; speaking in all soberness, I do not know how dynamite could be put to better use than in blowing up the British Empire.

PATRICK FORD, Owner and editor of *Irish World*, *c.*1872

(Had he waited three years, Ford might have recommended the use of gelignite—again, invented by Nobel, in 1875.) He was safe as long as he expressed this point of view in New York; he might not have been had he done so in Ireland, or in England. It was, of course, the point of view of an Irishman.

Joseph Chamberlain was an Englishman, who would happily have dynamited the offices of *Irish World*:

I believe in this race, the greatest governing race the world has ever seen; in this Anglo-Saxon race, so proud, tenacious, self-confident and determined, this race which neither climate nor change can degenerate, which will infallibly be the predominant force of future history and universal civilisation.

JOSEPH CHAMBERLAIN, British Colonial Secretary, 1895

It is doubtful whether Chamberlain thought of the Irish, or the Americans, as of 'the Anglo-Saxon race'. His point of view was often at variance with that of the mainstream political parties—but it was shared by many a late-Victorian, empire-minded Briton.

Andrew Jackson, seventh president of the United States, was another political maverick. He was a slave-owner and instigator of the Indian Removal Act: he defied Congress by having the Cherokee removed from their homeland in Georgia to present-day Oklahoma:

150. Philanthropy could not wish to see this continent restored to the condition in which it was found by our forefathers. What good man would prefer a country covered with forests and ranged by a few thousand savages to our extensive Republic, studded with cities, towns, and prosperous farms, embellished with all the improvements which art can devise or industry execute, occupied by more than 12,000,000 happy people, and filled with all the blessings of liberty, civilization, and religion?

ANDREW JACKSON, 7th US President, 1830

This would certainly not have been the point of view of the Cherokee; and it would not have been the point of view of Tecumseh, Chief of the Shawnees, whom we met in Argument 80 (Chapter 4). It might have been a point of view with which this American might have agreed, though, writing five years after Chamberlain:

151. God has not been preparing the English-speaking and Teutonic peoples for a thousand years for nothing but vain and idle self-contemplation and self-admiration. No! He has made us the master organizers of the world to establish system where chaos reigns. And of all our race He has marked the American people as His chosen nation to finally lead in the regeneration of the world. This is the divine mission of America.

ALBERT BEVERIDGE, US historian and senator, 1900

Adolf Hitler might have seconded the first two sentences; only an American—and perhaps only an American at the beginning of the 'American century'—could have authored the third (though, perhaps, on reflection, the view of George W. Bush, expressed in Argument 82 in Chapter 4, is not so very different).

> **7b.** Let us suppose that you are presented with this question: 'Did America "regenerate the world" in the 20th century?' What *point of view* might you need to declare in your opening **Statement?**

# Belief and opinion

Notice that Patrick Ford and Joseph Chamberlain both began with the words 'I believe'. Though we might well say: 'I believe it's going to rain later', we tend to use the word 'believe' when the view we have is of some significance, whether it is believing *in* something, or believing *that* something. Beveridge, in Argument 151, plainly believed *in* God, and he just as plainly believed *that* God had chosen America. When **belief** is as firm as this, one can seem not only to be making **factual claims**, but to be announcing **facts**.

Is religious belief different in kind from other sorts of belief? Dr Johnson seemed to think so:

152. It is wonderful that five thousand years have now elapsed since the creation of the world, and still it is undecided whether or not there has ever been an instance of the spirit of any person appearing after death. All argument is against it, but all belief is for it.

DR SAMUEL JOHNSON, English writer, critic, lexicographer 1778

He drew a contrast between argument (knowledge-based reasoning) and belief, where 'belief' meant something like 'faith' or 'trust' or, maybe 'hope'. Cardinal J.H. Newman seems to have had a similar contrast in mind when he said:

It is as absurd to argue men, as to torture them, into believing.

JOHN HENRY NEWMAN, Roman Catholic churchman, 1831

Argument is one thing; belief another. What, then, is the relationship between *knowledge* and belief—between knowing and believing? In 2006, when Rowan Williams, then Archbishop of Canterbury, was asked (oddly, on the face of it) whether or not he believed in God, he said:

I *believe* in God, yes. I don't know that he exists in the sense in which you are sitting opposite me now.

He laid great stress on the word 'believe', and he went on to say that he believed in God with all the faith and trust at his command. When the Swiss psychologist Carl Jung was asked the same question, he said:

I don't *believe* that God exists, I *know* he does.

Are 'belief' and 'knowledge' one and the same thing? Or is belief a kind of knowledge? We say that we *know* facts; we do not say that we believe facts. When we *know*, we do not have to ask ourselves whether or not we *believe*. It does seem that when we say: 'I believe', we are simply making a factual claim—a fact-sounding claim.

153. Only reason can convince us of those three fundamental truths without a recognition of which there can be no effective liberty: that what we believe is not necessarily true; that what we like is not necessarily good; and that all questions are open.

CLIVE BELL, English art critic, 1928

> **7c.** How far would you agree with Bell that 'what we believe is not necessarily true' is a 'fundamental truth'?

Are belief and **opinion** one and the same thing? The word 'opinion' is one to which we sometimes attach a positive (see Mill's bold claim in Chapter 6, on p 118) and sometimes a negative meaning ('Well, that's only *your* opinion!'). Physicians seek a 'second opinion', when they are not sure about a diagnosis; lawyers are asked for their 'legal opinion' when there is uncertainty about points of law; and a judge's decision—his or her considered opinion—is final:

154. Where there is much to learn, there of necessity will be much arguing, much writing, many opinions; for opinion in good men is but knowledge in the making.

JOHN MILTON, *Areopagitica*, 1644

In this positive sense, an opinion is something like a working hypothesis, or a sort of interim **judgement**. A judgement requires time, deliberation, and a certain expertise. Lawyers and physicians, in this respect, would qualify as 'good men' to whom we would go for an 'expert opinion'—but not a final one, if Milton is to be believed.

And then there is the sense in which we speak of an opinion as if it was a fleeting idea, worth little, as Hazlitt (whose opinion of Nelson and Davy we heard in Argument 103 in Chapter 5) does here:

155. There is a kind of conversation made up entirely of scraps and hearsay, as there are a kind of books made up entirely of references to other books. This may account for the frequent contradictions which abound in the discourse of persons educated and disciplined wholly in coffee-houses. They hear a remark at the Globe which they do not know what to make of; another at the Rainbow in direct opposition to it; and not having time to reconcile them, vent both at the Mitre. In the course of half an hour, if they are not more than ordinarily dull, you are sure to find them on opposite sides of the question. This is the sickening part of it. People do not seem to talk for the sake of expressing their opinions, but maintain an opinion for the sake of talking.

    WILLIAM HAZLITT, English essayist, 1822

It is the sense in which Butler uses the word:

156. The public buys its opinions as it buys its meat, or takes in its milk, on the principle that it is cheaper to do this than to keep a cow. So it is, but the milk is more likely to be watered.

    SAMUEL BUTLER, English novelist and critic, 1912

Opinions of this sort—some more 'watered' than others—fill the correspondence columns of newspapers and magazines. Here are a couple of examples:

157. Your cover story on 'teen depression' was a blatant advertisement for the pharmaceutical industry. America is a great country to grow up in, so what's all this about being 'young and depressed'? We drug our children with Ritalin and Paxil and heaven knows what else to support an antidepressant industry worth 12.5 billion dollars. The parents who didn't give their children the attention they needed when they were young compound this child abuse by conspiring with 'big pharma' to pin the label 'depressed' on them when they're in their teens. Teen depression is a cruel myth. What kids need is a bit of self-esteem and lots of exercise.

    Adapted from a letter to *Newsweek*, August 2002

158. Let us give a thought, in the run-up to Christmas, to all those millions of farm-animals due to be slaughtered, often in hideous conditions. How many of us consider for a moment the suffering of these animals and their basic rights? Instead of subjecting the food industry to intense scrutiny, and radical reform, we demand ever cheaper meat and more of it, and animal welfare goes by the board. It is high time we paid attention to how farm-animals are treated, and to what is done to satisfy our appetite for meat and meat-products. After all, these animals are sentient beings, closer to us genetically than many of us would care to think.

Adapted from a letter to The Irish Times, December 2010

A medical diagnosis, a point of law, would seem either to be right or wrong—though there is, perhaps, more room for interpretation in law than there is in medicine. Would we turn to an artist or an art critic for an 'expert opinion'? I quoted the judgements—or the opinions—of four critics in Chapter 5: they appeared to be making factual claims, like 'believers'; but their claims fell a long way short of fact.

This claim was, at least, made tentatively:

159. The best subjects for artists, surely, are animals and plants, grasses and trees; these they can represent, but human beings they ought to leave to poets.

WILHELM HEINSE, German art critic, 1787

This one was not:

160. There is nothing ugly; I never saw an ugly thing in my life: for let the form of an object be what it may—light, shade and perspective will always make it beautiful.

JOHN CONSTABLE, English landscape painter, 1843

In 1913, Marcel Duchamp mounted a bicycle wheel on a stool and called it *Bicycle Wheel*; in 1917, he inscribed a gents' urinal 'R. Mutt', and called it *Fountain*. In 1973, Michael Craig-Martin exhibited a glass of water on a bathroom shelf and called it *An Oak Tree*. All were called 'art'. Joseph Beuys (see Argument 27 in Chapter 2) said that anything could be 'art'.

The British sculptor Anthony Caro said what he thought about such 'art':

161. Some of the stuff that's called art is just damned stupid. I mean, 'That glass of water's an oak tree' kind of thing. I think that Marcel Duchamp, and later Joseph Beuys, did a great deal of harm. Duchamp was having a joke and it's been taken seriously.

ANTHONY CARO, quoted in The Guardian,<br>January 2005. © Guardian News & Media

In the same week (in January 2005), it was announced that a piece of street art by German sculptor Michael Beutler, consisting of yellow plastic sheets, had been mistaken for rubbish by Frankfurt refuse collectors, and incinerated. When it was realized that they had made a 'mistake' 30 of them were sent on a course, entitled 'Check your art sense'. This gave rise to a deluge of letters to the press: here are adapted extracts from three, sent to *The Guardian*:

> Could we not interpret what the binmen did as a piece of performance art, and give them a grant to repeat it elsewhere?
>
> The binmen were misunderstood: if a load of rubbish is valid as art, incinerating it is valid as art criticism.
>
> So, the Frankfurt binmen are to be sent back to school to learn the difference between art and rubbish. I suggest, to be fair, that artists should attend the same course.

> **7d.** Would you say that Caro and the three letter-writers were expressing a belief; making a judgement; or asserting an opinion? And what would you say about Pater's Argument 162?

For Constable, the beholder is able to see beauty in anything. Until the turn of the 20th century, artists, and art critics, seemed to agree that art was about 'beauty': it was the subject matter of 'aesthetics'. Walter Pater was an aesthete if anyone was, yet he went far to endorse the view that 'beauty is in the eye of the beholder'—that it was **relative** to the observer, not some **absolute** quality in what was observed:

162. What is this song or picture, this engaging personality presented in life or in a book, to *me*? What effect does it really produce on me? Does it give me pleasure, and, if so, what sort of degree of pleasure? How is my nature modified by its presence, and under its influence? The answers to these questions are the original facts with which the aesthetic critic has to do; and, as in the study of light, of morals, of number, one must realise such primary data for one's self, or not at all. And he who experiences these impressions strongly, and drives directly at the discrimination and analysis of them, has no need to trouble himself with the abstract question what beauty is in itself.

WALTER PATER, English art critic, 1873

Students are often wary of expressing their opinions. It is wise to be wary, and to avoid too much 'I think...I think...'; but you are expected to answer the question, and to do this you must make a *judgement*. To have an opinion is not the same as being 'opinionated'. Making a judgement is not being 'judgemental'—but it *is* being careful, considered, reflective, and as objective as possible.

# Bias and neutrality

We accept that we see the world from a certain point of view; we are less willing to accept, perhaps, that this lends a **bias** to the way we see it—it tilts our view to one side. We do not like to think that our judgements, our opinions, may be **biased**. If there is a continuum between being **objective** (or entirely unbiased, impartial) and being **subjective** (or hopelessly biased, partial), we like to think that we are at the objective end of it.

Objective                                                     Subjective

←——————————————————————————————→

Queen Victoria's husband was German and most of her family was German. It was understandable, therefore, that she should have raised this complaint with Prime Minister Palmerston in October 1861:

> The Queen has long seen with deep regret the persevering efforts made by the *Times*, which leads the rest of our Press, in attacking, vilifying, and abusing everything German, and particularly everything Prussian. That journal [has] since years shown the same bias...which could not fail to produce the deepest indignation amongst the people of Germany, and by degrees estrange the feelings of the people of this country from Germany.

Her husband Albert died in December of that year, and Victoria set about marrying her elder son Edward to Alexandra Princess of Denmark. At the time of the marriage, in March 1863, Germany and Denmark were at loggerheads as to the future of the duchies of Schleswig and Holstein. Victoria spoke sternly to her son:

A Danish partisan you must never be, or you put yourself against your whole family and against your Mother and Sovereign—who (God knows!) has been as impartial as anyone ever was!

That is to say: not very impartial at all. Victoria was as subjective as any of her subjects, to the point, it might be said, of **prejudice**. She had a tendency, that is, to prejudge: to form an opinion, and to express it, before giving a matter serious thought. English essayist Charles Lamb did think about things—yet still admitted to being prejudiced:

163. I have, in the abstract, no disrespect for the Jews. They are a piece of stubborn antiquity compared with which Stonehenge is in its nonage.* They date beyond the pyramids. But I should not care to be in the habits of familiar discourse with any of that nation. I confess that I have not the nerves to enter their synagogues. Old prejudices die hard.

CHARLES LAMB, 'Imperfect Sympathies', 1821

\* Infancy (non-agedness).

> **7e.** In the same essay, Lamb admitted to being prejudiced against the Scots. Where might such 'old prejudices' have come from, do you suppose?

Ferdinand Lassalle was unashamedly biased; he wore his prejudice on his sleeve:

164. I do not like the Jews at all—I even detest them in general. I see in them nothing but the very much degenerated sons of a great but vanished past. As a result of centuries of slavery, these people have acquired servile characteristics, and that is why I am so unfavourably disposed to them. Besides, I have no contact with them. There is scarcely a single Jew among my friends and in the society which surrounds me.

FERDINAND LASSALLE, German political thinker, 1878

Perhaps, after all, Lassalle's problem was precisely that he *was* ashamed: he was born Ferdinand Lassal, of a Silesian Jewish family (though, like Engels, he helped to sustain the German-Jewish Karl Marx and his family in London).

We probably think of science and scientists as operating at the objective end of the continuum.

Max Planck, born in the duchy of Holstein, doubted whether scientists were any more qualified to be objective than the rest of us:

165. Science cannot solve the ultimate mystery of nature. And that is because, in the last analysis, we ourselves are part of nature and therefore part of the mystery that we are trying to solve.

   MAX PLANCK, German theoretical physicist, 1932

Scientists are 'only human', and therefore will have their own points of view, their own biases, and even, perhaps, their own prejudices—and we saw in Chapter 3 that scientists might have a vested interest in what their findings 'prove'.

The rather longer argument that follows has it that, if scientists, like the rest of us, have mixed motives, this is nothing to be ashamed of:

166. There are many highly respectable motives which may lead men to prosecute research, but three which are much more important than the rest. The first (without which the rest must come to nothing) is intellectual curiosity, desire to know the truth. Then, professional pride, anxiety to be satisfied with one's performance, the shame that overcomes any self-respecting craftsman when his work is unworthy of his talent. Finally, ambition, desire for reputation, and the position, even the power or the money which it brings. It may be fine to feel, when you have done your work, that you have added to the happiness or alleviated the sufferings of others, but that will not be why you did it. So if a mathematician, or a chemist, or even a physiologist, were to tell me that the driving force in his work had been the desire to benefit humanity, then I should not believe him (nor should I think the better of him if I did). His dominant motives have been those which I have stated,

and in which, surely, there is nothing of which any decent man need be ashamed.

G.H. HARDY, A Mathematician's Apology, Cambridge: Cambridge University Press, 1940

An Oxford anaesthetist wrote to *The Guardian* in a similar, but more incisive, vein:

167. Scientists are human beings and are driven by the same selfish desires as the rest of us. The altruistic scientist, driven only by 'the search for truth' is a media fabrication. Fame and influence inflate egos. Hubris, arrogance and a woeful lack of self-awareness is common in both scientific and medical communities. In my experience many scientists cannot see beyond their limited horizons and only the most remarkable individuals are able to see the big picture.

DR M. TARIQ ALI, The Guardian, June 2010

Does this mean that **neutrality** is impossible; that if even scientists are driven by money, fame, power to do what they do, it is vain to hope that historians, economists, sociologists will be **neutral** observers of the world? Perhaps it is unreasonable to expect that they will be 100 per cent objective, 100 per cent of the time—but authors will earn our trust who declare an interest when there is one, and who admit to a bias when they have one.

> **7f.** Does what Tariq Ali has to say in any way contradict what John Horgan said in Argument 119 in Chapter 5?

The three authors of *The Science of Life* (a survey of the field of biology in the late 1920s; see Argument 89 in Chapter 4), worked hard to earn their readers' trust (H.G. Wells had written *The Outline of History*, in 1919; G.P. Wells was his son):

168. The triplex author claims to be wedded to no creed, associated with no propaganda; he is telling what he believes to be the truth about life, as far as it is known now. He is doing exactly what the author of *The Outline of History* attempted for history. But no-one can get outside himself, and this book, like its predecessor, will surely be saturated with the personality of its writers. The reader

has to allow for that, just as a juryman has to allow for the possible bias in the evidence of an expert witness or in the charge of a judge. This book is written with a strenuous effort to be clear, complete, and correct; each member of the trinity has been closely watched by his two associates with these qualities in view. But they cannot escape or even pretend to want to escape from their common preoccupations. The reader of this book will not have made the best use of it, unless, instead of accepting its judgments, he uses them to form his own.

H.G. WELLS, JULIAN HUXLEY, and G.P. WELLS,
*The Science of Life*, 1931

> **7g.** Why might H.G. Wells have been more successful in his attempt to be 'truthful' in *The Science of Life*, than he had been in *The Outline of History*?

We might try putting terms used so far in this chapter on a continuum of knowledge similar to that drawn in Chapter 6, combining it with that already drawn in this chapter:

**Knowledge**

| Fact | Factual Claim/Belief | Judgement | Opinion | Prejudice |
| --- | --- | --- | --- | --- |

← Objectivity                                                    Subjectivity →

(I have not included bias on the continuum since this might be said to begin as soon as we leave facts behind and to gain in strength as we move from left to right—and, of course, one's choice of facts may be biased.)

# Values and principles

The terms 'belief' and 'value' are similar in meaning: they both have to do with what we attach importance to, with what we stand for. We might distinguish between two sets of **values**:

- *aesthetic* values (where we speak of what is 'good' and 'bad'), and
- *ethical*—or moral—values (where we speak of what is 'right' and 'wrong').

I used the phrase 'beauty is in the eye of the beholder' in connection with Walter Pater's art criticism (Argument 162). His opinion was that beauty is *relative* to the observer; it is not something *absolute* in art or nature. No one can say of an artwork that it is *absolutely* 'beautiful' or 'ugly', 'good' or 'bad'; other critics will have other opinions.

Ethical values, on the other hand, are thought by some to be absolute and not matters of opinion. They are spoken of as fundamental; as first **principles** (or 'categorical imperatives' in Kant's phrase) from which all rules guiding moral conduct ultimately spring. Philosopher Roger Scruton, for instance, wrote:

> Moral principles produce their beneficial effects only when regarded as absolutely binding.
>
> ROGER SCRUTON, *Modern Philosophy*, London:
> Sinclair-Stevenson, 1994

In Argument 87 (Chapter 4), Chris Patten calls certain principles 'hard as flint and clear as crystal'; and he gave 'political freedom and economic liberty' as two examples of such principles. Few would disagree with him, at least in respect of political freedom.

Jefferson went back to first principles when he drafted the US Declaration of Independence; he was not shy to use the word 'truths':

> We hold these truths to be sacred and undeniable; that all men are created equal and independent, that from that equal creation they derive rights inherent and inalienable, among which are the preservation of life, and liberty, and the pursuit of happiness.
>
> THOMAS JEFFERSON, rough draft of
> Declaration of Independence, 1776

Thomas Paine wrote in a similar vein. When he wrote 'I believe', he supposed that everyone would join him in that belief—that he was stating principles:

> I believe in one God and no more, and I hope for happiness beyond this life. I believe in the equality of man; and I believe that religious duties consist in doing justice, loving mercy, and endeavouring to make our fellow creatures happy.
>
> THOMAS PAINE, English-born political
> theorist and campaigner, 1793

We have seen how bold John Stuart Mill could be in his pronouncements. Perhaps the most famous statement of principle, referred to as 'absolute' (there is no 'I believe' here), is this one, from the same essay:

169. The object of this essay is to assert one very simple principle, as entitled to govern absolutely the dealings of society with the individual in the way of compulsion and control, whether the means used be physical force in the form of legal penalties or the moral coercion of public opinion. That principle is that the sole end for which mankind are warranted, individually or collectively, in interfering with the liberty of action of any of their number is self-protection. That the only purpose for which power can be rightfully exercised over any member of a civilized community, against his will, is to prevent harm to others. His own good, either physical or moral, is not a sufficient warrant.

JOHN STUART MILL, *On Liberty*, 1859

Mill's principle applied to society's treatment of the individual. Woodrow Wilson applied it to the dealings of nations with each other, at a time when European nations were at war with each other:

170. Nations should with one accord adopt the doctrine of President Monroe as the doctrine of the world: that every people should be left free to determine its own policy, its own way of development, unhindered, unthreatened, unafraid—the little along with the great and powerful. These are American principles, American policies. We could stand for no others. They are also the principles of mankind, and must prevail.

WOODROW WILSON, US President, 1917

> **7h.** This might have sounded like a principle as 'hard as flint' in 1917; is it a principle that we could still invoke now, do you think?

Other principles have been invoked of a less fundamental kind (the following one, by the man who revived the Olympic Games, in 1896, is not an argument; it is a claim made three times):

The most important thing in the Olympic Games is not winning but taking part—just as the most important thing in life is not the triumph but the struggle. The essential thing in life is not conquering but fighting well.

BARON PIERRE DE COUBERTIN, French academic, 1908

> Legal aid is a service which the modern state owes to its citizens as a matter of principle.
>
> E.J. COHN, German academic, 1943

171. The issue is not how to stop globalization. The issue is how we use the power of community to combine it with justice. If globalization works only for the benefit of the few, then it will fail and will deserve to fail. But if we follow the principles that have served us so well at home—that power, wealth and opportunity must be in the hands of the many, not the few—if we make that our guiding light for the global economy, then it will be a force for good and an international movement that we should take pride in leading. Because the alternative to globalization is isolation.

TONY BLAIR, UK Prime Minister, 2001

Even 'fundamental' principles, though, might be in conflict with each other. Thomas Modyford was a sugar-plantation owner, later governor of Barbados; Richard Ligon wrote what he called a 'True and Exact History of the Island of Barbados':

**RL:** Sir, one of your slaves, an honest and good-natured poor soul named Sambo asked me to help him to become a Christian.

**TM:** Under the laws of England, a Christian cannot be made a slave.

**RL:** But why should a slave not be made a Christian?

**TM:** It is true, there is a great difference in that, but being once a Christian, I could no longer count him a slave, so we slave-owners would lose the hold we have over them as slaves and by so doing open up such a gap that all the planters in Barbados would curse me.

RICHARD LIGON, English chronicler, 1657

Jefferson found himself in the same bind: he could write 'all men are created equal' and yet keep hundreds of slaves.

Here are two, more modern, instances of a clash of principles:

172. It isn't stem-cell research that is the problem: scarcely anyone opposes that. What President George W. Bush did was to place restrictions on *embryonic* stem-cell research. It's this that is open to question. It was Bush's belief, indeed, it was a firm principle of his—and many inside and outside his administration agreed with him—that life begins at conception. The restrictions that were imposed led to the discovery of the potential of other types of stem cells.

Adapted from a letter to *Time* magazine, March 2009

173. Take freedom of information: there is not a journalist worthy of the title who doesn't hold dear to this principle. But should it be applied whatever the potential damage?...Consider how many more deaths would have resulted from the Troubles if journalists had exposed everything they knew. Rigorous, unthinking freedom of information would have killed any notion of a peace process, and made the Northern Ireland situation infinitely worse.

DAVID ADAMS, *The Irish Times*, December 2010

Is there a clash of aesthetic and ethical values in this claim of Faulkner's, or should it not be taken too seriously?

If a writer has to rob his mother, he will not hesitate; the *Ode on a Grecian Urn* is worth any number of old ladies.

WILLIAM FAULKNER, US novelist, 1956

It has been said that there is nothing more eloquent than a vested interest disguised as a point of principle. It is easy to invoke a principle when one simply hopes to silence objection to one's claims. To do something on principle is not always to do the 'right' thing; it may be to do the 'wrong' thing domineeringly:

174. There is nothing so bad or so good that you will not find Englishmen doing it; but you will never find an Englishman in the wrong. He does everything on principle. He fights you on patriotic principles; he robs you on business principles; he enslaves you on imperial principles; he bullies you on manly principles; he supports his king on loyal principles and cuts off his head on republican principles.

GEORGE BERNARD SHAW, Irish-born playwright, 1897

It should be said in his defence that it is nowhere recorded that Faulkner did actually rob his mother either on business or aesthetic principles.

> **7i.** I have twice quoted parts of this passage by Darwin: 'I must begin with a good body of facts and not from a principle (in which I always suspect some fallacy) and then as much deduction as you please'. What do you think he meant?

To summarize this chapter, in your

---

### Statement

Be clear about **your point of view**.

---

When you assess the strengths and weaknesses of

---

### Argument A

Be alert to when an author is declaring a **belief** that may **bias** the argument; and note where this may lead to the expression of ill-considered and **subjective opinion**.

---

And in drafting your own counter-argument

---

### Argument B

➤ Be aware of **bias** in your own position.
➤ Aim to be **objective** (without feeling that you have to strive for a possibly inappropriate **neutrality**).
➤ When expressing your **opinion**, do so after you have marshalled your evidence, when it is more likely to be a considered **judgement** than a **prejudice**.
➤ Avoid committing yourself to a **principle** of an **absolute** kind unless it meets with near-universal consent.

---

Your counter-argument needs to be stronger than the argument you are countering. Just as you should take **Argument A** seriously, so you should recognize that the issues you are discussing may be *complex*—most issues worth writing about are complex. Chapter 8 will look at how you might avoid over-simplifying them in your **Argument B**.

# 8 Are you over-simplifying the issue?

I shall aim in this chapter to explain:
- why it is unwise to resort to personal attack;
- and to make a too-easy either/or distinction;
- why it is wiser to speak of 'some' rather than 'all';
- and why a parallel case might not work.

## *Ad hominem* and *tu quoque* ploys

These Latin tags are the names we give to two ways in which writers and speakers may try to get the better of their opponents. In the first, they do not address the argument; they address the author of the argument. They make fun of a personal characteristic of the author—especially, it seems, when that author is a prominent politician. In 1940, George Orwell insulted Stanley Baldwin, three times UK Conservative Prime Minister between 1923 and 1937:

> As for Baldwin, one could not even dignify him with the name of stuffed shirt. He was simply a hole in the air.

Three times, according to Orwell, the British people elected a non-entity to the highest office in the land. Might the insult tell us as much about Orwell as it does about Baldwin?

This sort of argument-by-cheap-shot we call ***ad hominem*** argument (which means: 'to the man'). Instead of engaging with the way in which the politician (or whoever it may be) has reasoned, and reached his or her conclusion, the critic goes on the *ad hominem* attack: he makes personal remarks about his opponent, as if wounding the man will wound his argument (or, of course, the woman, and *her* argument).

In 1950, Senator Joseph McCarthy referred to the then US Secretary of State, Dean Acheson, as:

> this pompous diplomat in striped pants, with a phony British accent.

The writer Keith Waterhouse said of UK Prime Minister Margaret Thatcher:

> I cannot bring myself to vote for a woman who has been voice-trained to speak to me as though my dog had just died.

And in 2009, Jeremy Clarkson, presenter of BBC2's *Top Gear*, said this of then UK Prime Minister Gordon Brown, at a press conference in Australia:

> We have this one-eyed Scottish idiot who keeps telling us everything's fine and he's saved the world, and we know he's lying but he's smooth at telling us.

None of these claims (taken out of context) is an argument at all, which is why I have not numbered them. Let me restore McCarthy's quip to the argument from which I wrenched it (the 'traitor' referred to was the alleged Soviet spy, Alger Hiss):

175. As you know, very recently, the Secretary of State proclaimed his loyalty to a man guilty of what has always been considered as the most abominable of all crimes—of being a traitor to the people who gave him a position of great trust. The Secretary of State in attempting to justify his continued devotion to the man who sold out the Christian world, referred to Christ's Sermon on the Mount as a justification and reason there for, and the reaction of the American people to this would have made the heart of Abraham Lincoln happy.

      **When this pompous diplomat in striped pants, with a phony British accent,** proclaimed to the American people that Christ on the Mount endorsed communism, high treason and betrayal of a sacred trust, the blasphemy was so great that it awakened the dormant indignation of the American people.

      JOSEPH MCCARTHY, US senator, 1950

> **8a.** Why might it be said that McCarthy's *ad hominem* description of Dean Acheson weakened his overall argument?

Here is another blast from the past; men have no monopoly of direct speech:

176. His incompleteness as a thinker, his shallow and vulgar view of many human relationships—the lack of a sterner kind of humour which would show him the dreariness of his farce and the total absence of proportion and inadequateness of some of his ideas—all these defects came largely from the flippant and worthless self-complacency brought about by the worship of rather second-rate women.

> BEATRICE WEBB, English socialist and social reformer, 1897

Webb was writing about the playwright and fellow Fabian socialist George Bernard Shaw. Shaw left it to H.G. Wells to lampoon Beatrice and her husband Sidney Webb; Shaw himself was forgiving: in 1948, he campaigned to have the couple's ashes interred in Westminster Abbey.

This was one way of neutralizing an *ad hominem* attack: having the last laugh is another. The then deputy leader of the UK Labour Party, Harriet Harman, thought to have a laugh at the expense of the Scot, ginger-haired Danny Alexander, Liberal Democrat Chief Secretary to the Treasury in the 2010 coalition government; Alexander turned the gibe to his advantage in this exchange:

HH: Many of us in the Labour Party are conservationists and we all love the red squirrel. But there's one ginger rodent we never want to see in the Highlands of Scotland—Danny Alexander.

DA: I am proud to be ginger and rodents do valuable work clearing up the mess others leave behind.

> As reported in *The Observer*, 31 October 2010

It (almost) goes without saying that going on the offensive in this fashion has no place in a serious argument. You will recognize the ploy when you see it in other people's arguments, and you will do well to deny yourself the pleasure of indulging the *ad hominem* ploy in arguments of your own.

> **8b.** Can *ad hominem* claims really have *no* place in 'serious argument'? Do any of Beatrice Webb's potshots at Shaw, for instance, make an important point?

Less offensive, but scarcely more subtle, is a style of argument to which we give another Latin name: **Tu quoque** (You, too!). It takes a kind of tit-for-tat line:

177. The burning of widows is your custom. Prepare the funeral pyre. But my nation also has a custom. When men burn women alive, we hang them and confiscate all their property. My carpenters shall therefore erect gibbets on which to hang all concerned when the widow is consumed. Let us all act according to national customs.

       SIR CHARLES NAPIER, British administrator in India, *c*.1844

Napier did not *argue* against killing by burning; his answer to it was killing by hanging.

178. *Newsweek* welcomed the approach of Easter with the headline 'The Decline and Fall of Christian America', printed in red in the shape of a cross, on its black front cover. It was still more explicit inside: 'The end of Christian America' it shouted, and all because the magazine found that the number of people declaring themselves to be Christians had fallen by ten per cent since 1990 ... And what has been the percentage drop in *Newsweek*'s circulation in that time? Since 2007, by its own admission, its circulation has dropped by 52%. It would be more appropriate to announce 'The End of *Newsweek*'.

       Adapted from a US blog-post, 2009

The fact that *Newsweek*'s circulation dropped rather a lot does not mean that the numbers of self-declared Christians were not dropping, too. *Newsweek* overstated its case; but a 10 per cent fall in numbers suggests it did have a case. The blogger who shouted 'You, too!' had nothing to say about whether 'Christian America' was in decline or not. She did not engage with the argument; she simply threw it back in *Newsweek*'s face.

A smoker wrote to *The Guardian*, in November 2004, to challenge the anti-smoking lobby:

179. I'm sure that the majority of these anti-smoking worthies drive or use motorised vehicles. What do they imagine comes out of their exhaust pipes? These individuals seem to be hypocritically oblivious to the fact that they are liable for significantly more atmospheric pollution than your average smoker.

And a gay reader wrote to the *Irish Independent*, in February 2010, to berate the Roman Catholic Church:

180. The Catholic Church has set out its stall on homosexuality, and most gay people and their families and friends are either disgusted or bewildered by its constant barrage against gay people. Given its track record on child sex-abuse cover-ups, it's high time the Catholic Church did some repentance of its own.

It may, sometimes, be legitimate to call out *tu quoque*—and to advance a you're-no-better-than-I-am style of argument. It is tempting, when we are accused of bad grammar in our own writing, to draw attention to a spelling mistake in our accuser's, and to shout: **Touché!**

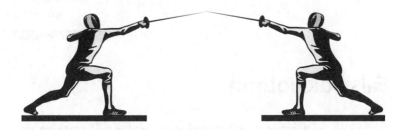

But arguing is not fencing: the objective is not to touch your 'opponent' with the tip of your foil—it is not to touch your opponent at all; it is to come to grips with his argument.

There is an element of 'a tooth for a tooth' about *tu quoque* argument. The following is a composite of the many letters that were written to the press when the Libyan Abdelbaset al-Megrahi was released from a Scottish prison, in August 2009:

181. The Scottish Justice Secretary freed the Libyan terrorist Abdelbaset al-Megrahi on 'compassionate' grounds. His doctors said that Megrahi was suffering from terminal prostate cancer, and that he had only three months to live at the most.

Megrahi was the only man convicted of the bombing of Pan Am Flight 103, in December 1988, killing everyone on the plane and many residents of Lockerbie, the Scottish town on which the doomed airliner fell—270 people altogether. It was the worst terrorist attack ever to have been carried out in the UK.

Did Abdelbaset al-Megrahi show any compassion to his victims in 1988? Why therefore, when Megrahi had served only 11 years of his life sentence, did the Scottish government think that he deserved to be shown compassion?

Following his release, Megrahi lived not for a further three months, but for a further three years. The *tu quoque* reasoning of the letter-writers seems to have been: 'He didn't show compassion; why should compassion be shown to him?' In response, the Scottish government might have offered the cliché: 'two wrongs don't make a right'.

> **8c.** What would you say is the conclusion of this argument (it is implied rather than made explicit)? What alternative conclusion might the letter-writers have come to?

# False dichotomy

What is a **dichotomy**? It is a cutting of anything into two. A false dichotomy is a take-it-or-leave-it choice of opposites, presented as if there was no alternative: black and white, for instance, when there might be several shades of grey. We often think in false dichotomies, and when we do so we over-simplify—not always, but often. In Chapter 6 we saw how the true/false dichotomy is more often than not an over-simplification. Genesis Chapter 1 is full of dichotomies:

> In the beginning God created heaven and earth. And the earth was waste and empty; and the darkness was on the face of the deep; and the spirit of God moved on the face of the waters. And God said, Let there be light; and there was light. And God saw the light, that it was good: and God divided the light from the darkness. And God called the light Day, and the darkness he called Night. And there was evening and there was morning, one day.
>
> THE BIBLE (Revised Version), Genesis 1:1–5

In five verses, four dichotomies:

| | |
|---|---|
| heaven | earth |
| light | darkness |
| day | night |
| evening | morning |

Is it light one moment, and dark the next? When does day end and night begin? It depends where you live, or whether you are on a plane flying east or west.

What God was supposed to have begun, man was only too happy to continue: the good Abel and the wicked Cain; sacred and profane; clean and unclean; circumcised and uncircumcised; priest and people; Jew and Gentile... Who was man to join together what God himself had put asunder? There are dichotomies in the New Testament, too; we saw one in Argument 75 in Chapter 4: here is another:

> 182.  A man cannot be a servant to two masters, for either he will hate the one and love the other, or he will be loyal to the first, and despise the second. One cannot serve God and Money.
>
> THE BIBLE, MATTHEW 6:24

Are love and hate the only options? Whatever happened to indifference? Where theologians had divided the world in two, philosophers divided the way we *see* the world in two (some of these dichotomies we have seen already):

| | |
|---|---|
| Absolute | Relative |
| Appearance | Reality |
| Deduction | Induction |
| Mind | Matter |
| Rationalism | Empiricism |
| True | False |

And there have been many, many more, some proposed by writers whom we might call philosophers, and some by others whom we probably would not:

> 183.  Is it better to be loved than feared, or the other way round? The answer is that it is desirable to be both, but because it is difficult to combine them together, it is much safer for a prince to be feared than loved if he is likely to fail in one or the other.
>
> NICCOLÒ MACHIAVELLI, *The Prince*, 1513

> There are only two types of people: the virtuous who believe themselves to be sinners and the sinners who believe themselves to be virtuous.
>
> BLAISE PASCAL, *Pensées*, 1654–62

All books are divided into two classes: the books of the hour, and the books of all time.

JOHN RUSKIN, English art critic, 1865

Everything made by man's hands has a form, which must be either beautiful or ugly; beautiful if it is in accordance with Nature, and helps her; ugly if it is discordant with Nature, and thwarts her; it cannot be indifferent.

WILLIAM MORRIS, English designer and writer, 1877

So long as the state exists there is no freedom. When there is freedom, there will be no state.

VLADIMIR LENIN, Russian revolutionary and politician, 1918

Would you rather have butter or guns? Preparedness makes us powerful. Butter merely makes us fat.

HERMANN GOERING, German Nazi leader, 1936

Not only in China but also in the world without exception, one either leans to the side of imperialism or to the side of socialism. Neutrality is mere camouflage and a third road does not exist.

MAO ZEDONG, Chairman of the People's Republic of China, 1949

Aristotle (and his so-called 'law of excluded middle') has a lot to answer for. In what Marvin Minsky called 'the real world', a third road often does exist—and a fourth, and a fifth.

> **8d.** Can you identify a 'third road' in the previous claims— an alternative that is not covered by either of the two on offer?

Gibbon identified a third road in this claim:

The various modes of worship which prevailed in the Roman world were all considered by the people as equally true; by the philosopher as equally false; and by the magistrate as equally useful.

EDWARD GIBBON, *The Decline and Fall of the Roman Empire*, 1776–88

We have to classify if we are to make sense of the world; but a division of the world into two is often—not so much 'false' as—simply unconvincing. Life seldom presents us with a simple **either/or**, but most people in 1914, asked whether or not they were pleased that Europe was at war, would have answered no. The novelist D.H. Lawrence answered yes (Compton Mackenzie was a fellow novelist, and *Sinister Street*, a long semi-autobiographical novel):

> I am glad of this war. It kicks the pasteboard bottom in of the usual 'good' popular novel. People have felt much more deeply and strongly these last few months, and they are not going to let themselves be taken in by 'serious' works whose feeling is shallower than that of the official army reports. Mackenzie was a fool not to know that the times are too serious to bother about his *Sinister Street* frippery. Folk will either read sheer rubbish, or something that has in it as much or more emotional force than in today's newspaper. I am glad of the war. It will put a stop to trifling.
>
> D.H. LAWRENCE, from a letter written 5 December 1914

Leaving aside Lawrence's gladness about a war that had already seen the First Battle of the Marne and the beginnings of trench warfare, the distinction between 'sheer rubbish' on the one hand, and works that outdid the newspapers in 'emotional force' on the other, is surely an over-simplification.

Not all dichotomies are 'false', though, any more than they might be 'true'; the question is whether they *exhaust the possibilities* or not. Lawrence's did not; but perhaps Johnson's did:

> Knowledge is of two kinds. We know a subject ourselves, or we know where we can find information upon it.
>
> DR SAMUEL JOHNSON, 1775

Is there a third kind of knowledge? Perhaps one really does either know what 'egregious' means or one does not. Jefferson offered a choice that seems to exhaust the possibilities, though it was a hypothetical one:

> 184. The basis of our government being the opinion of the people, the very first object should be to keep that right; and were it left to me to decide whether we should have a government without newspapers, or newspapers without a government, I should not hesitate a moment to prefer the latter.
>
> THOMAS JEFFERSON, 1787

One might hope, of course, to have both—and this is often the answer to what appears to be an either/or choice.

Here are two rather more extended arguments that contain dichotomies, published in consecutive years. We have met both philosopher Susan Stebbing, and the mathematician G.H. Hardy before (in Arguments 17 and 166, Chapters 2 and 7, respectively):

185. The vast majority of English people want to be governed peaceably, and want to be free to pursue their own unpolitical interests. I, for my part, am not politically minded. I am thoroughly English; I do not want to accept political responsibilities. Unfortunately, I cannot avoid them. Neither can you. We are confronted, I believe, with only two alternatives: **either** we must freely decide to support (or to oppose) this or that political measure **or** we must acquiesce in the decisions made by those who control us.

SUSAN STEBBING, *Thinking to Some Purpose*, 1939

186. It is useful to be tolerably quick at common arithmetic (and that, of course, is pure mathematics). It is useful to know a little French or German, a little history and geography, perhaps even a little economics. But a little chemistry, physics, or physiology has no value at all in ordinary life. We know that the gas will burn without knowing its constitution; when our cars break down we take them to a garage; when our stomach is out of order, we go to a doctor or a drugstore. We live **either** by rule of thumb **or** on other people's professional knowledge.

G.H. HARDY, *A Mathematician's Apology*, Cambridge: Cambridge University Press, 1940

By 'rule of thumb' Hardy means a rough-and-ready, practical, commonsense method. His argument is not unlike Dr Johnson's.

> **8e.** Do Stebbing and Hardy, in their dichotomies, exhaust the possibilities? Are there just two in each case, or can you think of others?

A Word of Advice

Sometimes things do divide neatly into two (or three); but it is probably more 'realistic' to place things on a *continuum*—a horizontal line—rather than on either side of a *dichotomy*—a vertical line. Most things are a matter of degree.

# Over-generalization

A false dichotomy over-simplifies what may be complex. Any sort of classification or grouping of individual things or people will over-simplify matters; but we have to classify if we are to make sense of the world—and we have to generalize. If we did not, we would be condemned to study single events, and individual people and things—and we should not learn much that we could apply to other events, people, and things.

It is doubtful whether, in the study of history, though, we *can* learn much from single events and individual people, yet these are what an historian studies:

187. Men wiser and more learned than I have discerned in history a plot, a rhythm, a predetermined pattern. Those harmonies are concealed from me. I can see only one emergency following upon another, as wave follows upon wave; only one real fact with respect to which, since it is unique, there can be no generalizations.

H.A.L. FISHER, English historian and politician, 1936

Fisher was modestly understating the case: what he really meant was that there are no patterns, no harmonies, to be discerned in history—but he did not want to **over-generalize**. Generalization is one thing—and there are *some* generalizations that even historians can safely make (Andrew Marr thought so, in Argument 5 in Chapter 1). Social scientists generalize from representative samples; physical scientists generalize from the results of experiments to the extent of establishing laws. **Over-generalization**, though, is something else.

We saw, in Chapter 6, that it is not easy to devise major premises of the 'all living things are bound to die' sort—and yet it is all too easy to think we can. Ruskin thought he could when he talked about 'all books'; but 'all' is just one of the **quantifiers** that we use when we over-generalize:

All men would be tyrants if they could.

DANIEL DEFOE, English journalist and novelist, 1713

All generalizations are dangerous, even this one.

ALEXANDRE DUMAS, French novelist, 1824–95 (attributed)

A Frenchman must be **always** talking, whether he knows anything of the matter or not; an Englishman is content to say **nothing** when he has nothing to say.

DR SAMUEL JOHNSON, 1780

A work, known and acknowledged as the product of mere intelligence, will **never** be accepted as a work of art, however perfect be its adaptation to its end.

HERMANN VON HELMHOLTZ,
German physiologist and physicist, 1862

[There was] a little girl aged four, whose nurse objected to her table manners. 'Emily', said the nurse, '**nobody** eats soup with a fork.' 'But', replied Emily, 'I do, and I am somebody'.

Quoted in SUSAN STEBBING, *Thinking to Some Purpose*, 1939

Emily's answer was an ingenuously pointed caution against making 'sweeping' generalizations. Quantifiers, like much else, can be placed on a continuum:

| All/Every | Most | Many | Some | Several | Few | No/None |
|---|---|---|---|---|---|---|

◄────────────────────────────────────────────────►

| Always | Often | Sometimes | Seldom/Rarely | Never |
|---|---|---|---|---|

If most things are a matter of degree, then most of the time, it is wise not to stray too far to either end of the continuum. Of course, it is not necessary to use explicit quantifiers like 'all' and 'never' to over-generalize. It is of such over-generalizations as those that follow that *stereotypes* are made:

188. Because they cannot straight away assess the social status of those they meet, Englishmen are careful not to have anything to do with them. They fear that if they do them a kindness they will be drawn unwillingly into a tiresome relationship; they shun common courtesies, and thus avoid the gushing thanks of a stranger as surely as they escape his contempt.

ALEXIS DE TOCQUEVILLE, French historian and politician, 1835–40

189. [The Americans] are really a strange people. Perhaps the mistake we make is to continue to regard them as an Anglo-Saxon people. That blood is very much watered down now; they are a Latin-Slav mixture, with a fair amount of German and Irish. They are impatient, mercurial, panicky. But, while capable of terribly narrow views and incredible breaches of decency and decorum, they are also capable of broad and generous sentiments and really big-hearted generosity.

HAROLD MACMILLAN, *The Macmillan Diaries: the Cabinet Years 1950–1957*, London: Macmillan Publishers, 2003

Is there really *anything* that *everyone* who lives in this or that country has in common? Is there any characteristic that we all have in common? These two writers thought that there was something useful that could be said about *homo economicus*:

190. **Every** individual intends only his own gain, and he is in this, as in **many** other cases, led by an invisible hand to promote an end which was **no** part of his intention. By pursuing his own interest he **frequently** promotes that of the society more effectively than when he really intends to promote it. I have **never** known much good done by those who affected to trade for the public good.

     ADAM SMITH, *The Wealth of Nations*, 1776

191. The impulse to acquisition, pursuit of gain, of money, of the greatest possible amount of money, has in itself **nothing** to do with capitalism. This impulse exists among waiters, physicians, coachmen, artists, prostitutes, dishonest officials, soldiers, nobles, crusaders, gamblers and beggars. One may say that it has been common to **all** sorts and conditions of men at **all** times and in **all** cultures of the Earth, **wherever** the objective possibility of it is or has been given.

     MAX WEBER, German sociologist, 1904–5

Were these two writers as careful as they might have been about the quantifiers they used? And are their (over)generalizations justified? Or might we be tempted to say: 'Speak for yourself!' But perhaps Smith was really only talking about tradespeople; and perhaps in referring to 'dishonest officials', Weber implied that there are honest officials who do not lust after riches. Are there no honest, satisfied physicians? Are there no artists at work for whom art is its own reward? The 'artist' in Argument 192 is George Sand, and the 'you' is Prince Napoléon Jérôme:

192. I am and **always** have been an artist before **all** else; I know that **all** men who are politicians **only**, have a great contempt for artists because they judge them by certain idiotic types who are a dishonour to the name of art. But you, my friend, must know that the true artist is as useful as the priest or warrior, and that when the

artist respects the true and the good, he is on a road which God will bless without ceasing. Art is of all nationalities and of all periods; its particular quality is precisely that of being able to survive when all else must perish.

GEORGE SAND, French novelist, socialite,<br>and progressive thinker, 1854

Most of George Sand's contemporaries would have thought of her as a novelist before 'all else' (when they did not merely think her scandalous); Jean Cocteau was another French socialite and friend of the famous—he was a lot of things:

193. Art produces ugly things which **frequently** become beautiful things with time. Fashion, on the other hand, produces beautiful things which **always** become ugly with time.

JEAN COCTEAU, French writer, artist,<br>film director, and critic, 1960

He was more careful in his choice of quantifier in respect of art than he was in respect of fashion.

> **8g.** Can you think of any 'ugly' artwork that has become 'beautiful'? Can you think of any 'beautiful' product of fashion that has *not* become 'ugly'?

Was Cocteau's art/fashion dichotomy a 'false' one because it failed to exhaust the possibilities? What might he have had to say about craft, or design; and might we not talk meaningfully of fashionable art, and of artistic fashion? Perhaps the real difficulty here is that we think of art (*positively*) as lasting, and of fashion (*negatively*) as passing.

Abraham Lincoln may or may not have uttered the following lines; but if he did, he was prodigal with his quantifiers—yet his words have been quoted often enough to convince many people much of the time that they are 'true':

194. If you forfeit the confidence of your fellow citizens, you can **never** regain their respect and esteem. It is true that you may fool all the people **some** of the time; you can even fool **some** of the people all the time; but you can't fool **all** the people all the time.

ABRAHAM LINCOLN, 1858 (attributed)

The problem with using quantifiers at the extremes of the continuum (as we saw in Chapter 6, in respect of deductive argument) is that it only needs one exception to an over-generalization to falsify it: one citizen whose respect and esteem was not forfeited; and one stalwart individual who refused to be fooled at any time. 'Some' is (nearly) always a safer bet than 'all' or 'none'. 'Many' or 'few' would be safe, too, if you had the numbers to support them.

# Analogy and slippery slope

When we struggle to make a point, a rather *abstract* point, perhaps, we might make a comparison with something more *concrete*. We look for a **parallel case**. A politician who gives offence to his constituents? He is rather like a shopkeeper who insults his customers.

A campaigner for a ban on selling arms to oppressive regimes argued thus:

> Saying that if Britain doesn't sell arms to regimes like Saudi Arabia, Libya, Indonesia, then other countries will is no different from saying 'If I don't steal your car and go for a joyride in it, someone else is sure to steal it.'
>
> Adapted from an article in *The Observer*, July 1994

It is only necessary for the two cases to be similar in some way; if one was 'no different from' the other, they would be the same. When a child died following infection from dog faeces, a columnist proposed that all dogs be put down; a pet lover objected:

> If we follow the logic of that proposal, we would ban cars: don't they kill, too? Don't they pollute the air we breathe? Aren't they a much bigger problem than pet dogs?
>
> Adapted from a letter to *The Times*, February 2009

When it was suggested that retail banking should be separated from investment banking to reduce the risk to current accounts, a leading banker said:

> [That's] a bit like a debate about having better seatbelts on passenger planes—it's hard to argue against better seatbelts, but when the plane crashes it's sort of irrelevant.
>
> As reported in *The Guardian*, January 2011

When a senior member of a police drugs squad retired and he reflected on his more than 20 years in the service, he wrote:

I got tired of seeing otherwise innocent young kids from all walks of life getting criminal records for, in effect, doing nothing more than millions of other people in society were doing with alcohol.

As reported in *The Independent on Sunday*, September 1997

UK Prime Minister Margaret Thatcher was famous for her homely comparisons: in 1979 she invited journalists to look inside her larder, and said:

Any woman who understands the problems of running a home, will be able to understand the problems of running a country.

A parallel case can give telling support to a claim as long as the two objects being compared are alike in some significant way.

> **8h.** How persuasive do you find the comparison made by Mrs Thatcher?

To make use of a parallel case in argument is to argue by **analogy**. I have not numbered the claims; but, in a sense, an analogy is an implicit argument—in likening one thing with another, an author is trying to persuade an audience that there is a lesson to be learnt in the comparison. What is time? It is an abstract idea; and rivers are the concrete analogy that most often comes to mind to 'explain' it:

**Time is like a river** made up of the events which happen, and its current is strong; no sooner does anything appear than it is swept away and another comes in its place, and will be swept away too.

MARCUS AURELIUS, Roman emperor, CE 170–80

**Time seems to be like a river** which carries down to us things that are light and airy, and that drowns things weighty and solid.

FRANCIS BACON, English philosopher and statesman, 1605

Government is pretty abstract, too:

A **monarchy is a merchantman** which sails well, but will sometimes strike on a rock, and go to the bottom; a **republic is a raft** which will never sink, but then your feet are always in the water.

FISHER AMES, US congressman, 1795

Government, even in its best state, is but a necessary evil; in its worst an intolerable one. **Government, like dress**, is the badge of lost innocence.

THOMAS PAINE, *Common Sense*, 1776

> Government is like a big baby—an alimentary canal with a big appetite at one end and no responsibility at the other.
>
> RONALD REAGAN, US politician and statesman, 1965

What are some of the strengths and weaknesses of arguing by analogy?

> Analogies decide nothing, that is true, but they can make one feel more at home.
>
> SIGMUND FREUD, Austrian psychoanalyst, 1933

The strengths of argument by analogy are a mirror image of their weaknesses. I will use Ronald Reagan's analogy as an example:

| Strengths | Weaknesses |
|---|---|
| A big baby is familiar | It is too different from government |
| The image has a definite impact | It distorts what it tries to explain |
| There is insight in the comparison | It is a superficial insight |

Much will depend on what parallel is chosen—whether it is intended to cast a *positive* light on the object to be illuminated, or a *negative* one. The time/river analogy is, perhaps, a neutral one: time is not being mocked by its being compared with a river. Reagan was not running for president in 1965; he might not have compared government with a big baby when he campaigned for the White House.

Let us look at a few examples of where an analogy is used in slightly more developed arguments:

195. Science is facts. Just as houses are made of stones, so science is made of facts. But a pile of stones is not a house and a collection of facts is not necessarily a science.

    HENRI POINCARÉ, French mathematician, 1905

> **8i.** Is this an effective analogy, in terms of the table of strengths and weaknesses?

196. Many politicians of our time are in the habit of laying it down as a self-evident proposition that no people ought to be free till they are fit to use their freedom. The maxim is worthy of the fool in the old story who resolved not to go into the water till he had learnt to

swim. If men are to wait for liberty till they become wise and good in slavery, they may indeed wait for ever.

THOMAS BABINGTON MACAULAY, English historian and politician, 1843

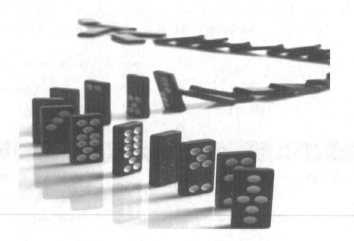

197. You have a row of dominoes set up, you knock over the first one, and what will happen to the last one is the certainty that it will go over very quickly. So you could have a beginning of a disintegration that would have the most profound influences.

DWIGHT D. EISENHOWER, US President, 1954

This 'domino' analogy proved to be extremely persuasive to American policy-makers as they watched the advance of communism in South East Asia in the 1950s and 1960s. They might have asked themselves whether there was enough in common between countries and dominoes.

Chess is another game that has often been invoked to explain 'life, the universe, and everything':

198. The chess-board is the world; the pieces are the phenomena of the universe; the rules of the game are what we call the laws of nature. The player on the other side is hidden from us. We know that his play is always fair, just, and patient. But we also know, to our cost, that he never overlooks a mistake, or makes the smallest allowance for ignorance.

THOMAS HENRY HUXLEY, English biologist, 1870

Did Huxley over-extend his analogy? Who was the 'player' on the other side, and where was that other side? He can hardly have been God in His Heaven, since, the year before, Huxley had coined the word 'agnostic' to describe himself. The longer an analogy is sustained, and the more likenesses between (for example) 'life' and 'chess' there are said to be, the more likely it is that the analogy will come to grief.

The following argument by analogy is grossly over-extended—a not uncommon tendency in 19th-century sermons and 'how to' books:

199. After the general superintendence of her servants, the mistress, if the mother of a young family, may devote herself to the instruction of some of its younger members, or to the examination of the state of their wardrobe, leaving the latter portion of the morning for reading, or for some amusing recreation. 'Recreation', says Bishop Hall, 'is intended to the mind as whetting is to the scythe, to sharpen the edge of it, which would otherwise grow dull and blunt. He, therefore, that spends his whole time in recreation is ever whetting, never mowing; his grass may grow and his steed starve; as contrarily, he that always toils, and never recreates, is ever mowing, never whetting, labouring much to little purpose. As good no scythe as no edge. Then only doth the work go forward when the scythe is so seasonably and moderately whetted that it may cut, and so cut, that it may have the help of sharpening'.

MRS ISABELLA BEETON, *The Book of Household Management*, 1861

By the end of the paragraph, our attention is rather focused on the scythe, than on recreation. This is an analogy that does not so much over-simplify the issue, perhaps, as over-complicate it.

A Word of Advice

It is difficult to come up with an analogy that offers a truly enlightening parallel case; it is probably wise, therefore, to leave this device to poets.

If I do not over-complicate the issue myself, it is worth mentioning a particular analogy to describe a further sort of over-simplification: the **slippery slope**. Put one foot on the slope, and there is no stopping you sliding down it. The domino theory is a kind of slippery slope: one thing leading to another, seemingly *inexorably*. Here is a classic case:

A little neglect may breed mischief...for want of a nail, the shoe was lost; for want of a shoe, the horse was lost; and for want of a horse, the rider was lost.

BENJAMIN FRANKLIN, US statesman and scientist, 1758

A little later, Jefferson argued in this Washingtonian way:

200. He who permits himself to tell a lie once finds it much easier to do it a second and third time, till at length it becomes habitual; he tells lies without attending to it, and truths without the world's believing him. This falsehood of the tongue leads to that of the heart and in time depraves all its good dispositions.

THOMAS JEFFERSON, when US Minister to France, 1785

One lie and the liar is on a moral slippery slope to hell.

Here is a British version of the domino theory (Colonel Gretton objected to the British government's talks with Irish 'rebels'):

201. If we have a British government terrorised, and a British government submitting to negotiations with a gang of murderers, what a vista is opened? A British government brought to heel here may be brought to heel elsewhere than in Ireland by methods of this kind. They are beginning in India. We hear of something in Egypt.

JOHN GRETTON, Olympic medallist and Conservative MP, 1921

For want of a nail, the empire would be lost—and it was lost, of course, though not because killings in Ireland gave way to talking in 1921. Technological progress has often been likened to a slippery slope:

One has to look out for engineers—they begin with sewing machines and end up with the atomic bomb.

MARCEL PAGNOL, French writer and film director, 1949

When it was suggested that goal-line technology be used in professional football to settle disputes about whether the ball had gone over the line or not, soccer's international body objected:

If we approved goal-line technology what would prevent the approval of technology for other aspects of the game? Every decision in every area of the pitch would soon be questioned.

SEPP BLATTER, President of FIFA, 2010

And there was anxiety about where it might lead, when, for the first time in the UK, an embryo was screened for a genetic disease:

202. Where in future will the threshold be set for determining when to screen an embryo? How serious will a condition need to be? The

birth, this week, of the first baby to have been screened justifies us in marvelling at modern science; but it must not be the first step on what may prove to be a very slippery slope.

Adapted from an editorial in the *Daily Mail*, January 2009

This writer made fun of such reasoning by turning the slope round and making it go uphill:

If once a man indulges himself in murder, very soon he comes to think little of robbing; and from robbing he comes next to drinking and Sabbath-breaking, and from that to incivility and procrastination.

THOMAS DE QUINCEY, English writer, 1839

And this advertisement did the same, in that it starts big and comes to something of an anticlimax:

203. History shows that gradual erosions of liberty can lead to its total loss. Which is why any democracy must be very careful about imposing restrictions on freedom of expression. This includes private, religious, political and commercial expression.

In July a Canadian court confirmed that advertising was a form of commercial speech. As a result, it ruled that banning tobacco advertising was 'a form of censorship and social engineering which is incompatible with the very essence of a free and democratic society'. It struck down Canada's advertising ban.

Yet Brussels is still trying to ban tobacco advertising in Europe. It makes you wonder what's next on Brussels' list.

Adapted from an advertisement of the
Tobacco Advisory Council, 1991

8j. The Tobacco Advisory Council suggests that if tobacco advertising is banned, freedom of expression is at risk. Do you find this argument persuasive?

We should not be intimidated by the slippery-slope analogy: the thing to do when standing at the top of a slippery slope is to throw sand or salt on it.

Here is a short summary of what has been a rather long chapter:

As you review **Argument A**, see if you can spot any of these over-simplifying ploys, and try not to give way to them in your own **Argument B**:

> ➤ making cheap-shot (**ad hominem**) personal comments about an 'opponent';
> ➤ indulging in tit-for-tat (**tu quoque**) duelling;
> ➤ setting up **'false' dichotomies**, when the issue is more likely to be a matter of degree;
> ➤ **over-generalizing** by using quantifiers at the extremes of the continuum;
> ➤ using an unsuitable, or over-extended **analogy**, and arguing as if once on a **slippery slope** the end is nigh.

There is one further set of precautions to take as you gather together the points that you will make in your argument: you will need to ensure that you are consistent and that you avoid contradicting yourself, changing the subject, and begging the question. And, of course, once again, you might be alert to whether the writer (or writers) of **Argument A** does any of these things.

# 9 Does your argument hang together?

I shall aim in this chapter to explain:

• and illustrate the perils of contradicting oneself;
• as well as of making incompatible claims;
• how one claim might not follow from another;
• and how one might find oneself arguing in a circle.

## Contradiction

I quoted Aristotle's three so-called 'laws of thought' in Chapter 6, as represented by Bertrand Russell. The second of these 'laws' was:

*The law of contradiction*: 'Nothing can both be and not be'

What could be more obvious; more reasonable? I was sceptical about the either/or dichotomy in Chapter 8: life rarely offers us two possibilities only. 'Either it is morning, or it is afternoon' are not necessarily cut-and-dried opposites, when you are still at your desk at 12.45 pm, and you have not had lunch.

Ordinarily, though, when a piece of music is by Nielsen, it cannot be by Gershwin; when a football is round, it cannot be square; and when there is a BMW in your parking space, it cannot at the same time not be there. We can establish facts, and we do—or we try to. When we think people have got their facts wrong, we write to the newspaper editor to say so:

(a) In his comment about Coleridge's play *Remorse*, Ben Cushman wrote that: 'neither this nor any other English Romantic play survives in the modern theatre'. I saw Shelley's *The Cenci* at the Almeida Theatre, in London, in 1985.

(b)     Jane Mumford is mistaken when she says that James II tried
to return England to the Roman Catholic Church. What he
actually wanted was for everyone to worship as they pleased.
It was William of Orange who peddled the lie about James.

Adapted from letters to *The Guardian*, 2008

The writer of (a) **contradicts** Cushman, whose factual claim is an
over-generalization; and the writer of (b) contradicts Mumford by
making an alternative factual claim. Claim is met by counter-claim.
Were Cushman and Mumford 'wrong' and the letter-writers right?
Cushman does appear to have been wrong if writer (a)'s memory can
be relied on; but it might need a third (expert) opinion to corroborate
writer (b)'s counter-claim.

It is customary for newspapers to print **contradictory** opinions, in
the interests of balance. When the Mayor of London, Boris Johnson
introduced bicycles for hire ('Boris bikes') on to London's streets, in
September 2012, one user wrote:

> It feels like riding a bull-dozer. It's incredibly slow and wobbly. It's
> fun, though.

And another wrote:

> It's very stately. It's so absurdly stable that you could signal with
> both arms.

Both writers could not have been 'right': a bike cannot be both
'wobbly' and 'stable' any more than it can both be and not be. Still,
we can put such contradiction down to the different experiences of
two different people.

It may be that two different people wrote the leader columns in the
*Daily Mail* on 25 March 2005 and 8 March 2006. The first began:

> In this nation of laws, some things should be beyond question.
> We may go to war on the basis of dubious politics and dodgy dos-
> siers. We may witness the outrageous exaggeration of intelligence
> to manipulate Parliament and the public. We may see the BBC
> hounded for telling the truth.

and the second (in which 'The Corporation' is the British Broadcasting
Corporation—the BBC) ended:

> The Corporation may offer wonderful things to Britain. Sadly, good
> journalism isn't one of them.

The second comment does not exactly contradict the first; one does not say that something is, and the other that it is not; and, of course, a writer might change his mind from one year to the next. It is when one person says that something both is and is not in the space of a few pages that we might wonder whether she is not contradicting herself. On one page of her introduction to a book on critical thinking, an author writes:

Nobody is an absolute beginner when it comes to critical thinking.

Just two pages later, the same author writes:

Many people find critical thinking to be a challenging activity when they begin.

> **9a.** Does the author contradict herself here, in your view? Or is there simply a change of emphasis?

I have preserved this author's anonymity, and I shall do the same in respect of the quotations that follow. I shall not charge the authors with contradicting themselves; rather I shall question whether the claims they make are perfectly compatible.

A Word of Advice

In so doing I am applying what is sometimes called the 'principle of charity'. It is wiser to question than to accuse; to be tentative than to be downright. It may be that you have misunderstood an author's intention, rather than that the author has got it wrong.

Sometimes, though, the conclusion that an author, or editor, has simply slipped up is unavoidable. In a book about the London of Oscar Wilde's time, we are told on page 81 that:

The printed word was all over London, from the 'yellow press' to esoteric literary magazines. Most of the bookstores were concentrated along the Strand.

On page 83 of the same book, we are told that:

> Most London bookstores were located along Charing Cross Road.

It is not necessary to know much about London, whether in the 1880s/90s or now, to know that the Strand (the A4) and Charing Cross Road (the A400) are not one and the same. (They leave Trafalgar Square at right angles to each other.) Perhaps it would not be uncharitable to wonder whether this is not a straightforward factual contradiction.

In a book about body language, the author refers to a survey of men's preferences concerning the ways in which women sit. On one page (226) we are told:

> Men voted Parallel-Legs as their number one favourite position in women who are seated. (Over 86% of male participants in our leg-rating surveys voted this the most attractive female sitting-position).

Apparently, men cannot sit like this, so the position may be taken to be a powerful token of femininity. On a later page (303), under the subtitle 'Courtship displays and Attraction Signals', we are told:

> Most men agree that the Leg Twine is the most appealing sitting position a woman can take.

Are these two claims compatible? Even over a span of 77 pages, such a disparity seems odd—but two apparently incompatible claims made on a single page is odder:

> Almost every study into attraction conducted over the last 60 years reached the same conclusions as the painters, poets and writers over the past 6,000 years—a woman's appearance and body and what she can do with it is more attractive to men than her intelligence or assets, even in the politically-correct 21st Century.
>
> ...
>
> Most people are tempted to believe that physical appearance is the key to attracting a potential partner, but this is largely an idea promoted by television, films and the media.

A woman could be forgiven for not knowing what to believe. It goes without saying (but I will say it) that when two claims in an argument are contradictory, they are both compromised, and the argument is weakened.

Finally, on one page of a biography of the English Liberal Prime Minister William Gladstone (1809–98), the author writes:

[Gladstone] told John Bright (10 December 1867) that he had hesitated for a long time to attack the Irish Church because it was a subject which 'may again lead the Liberal Party to martyrdom'.

Just five pages later, the author writes:

When [Gladstone] formed his government in 1868 he had no experience and no real knowledge of the Irish problem, and his ignorance was shared by the whole of his cabinet and by the mass of the British people. He had no suspicion that in the cause of Ireland he was destined to lead the Liberal Party to martyrdom, or that the whole of the rest of his life was to be devoted to that cause.

> **9b.** On what grounds might you suspect that the author has contradicted himself here—or that, at least, it is difficult to reconcile the two claims?

# Consistency and coherence

A contradiction is fairly easy to spot, and to avoid. If you write: 'Napoleon was a Corsican through and through' on one page, and then 'Napoleon might as well have been from Caen as from Corsica' on the next, you have simply slipped up—you cannot hold both opinions at the same time.

Whether or not your claims are **consistent** with each other is a little more subtle. Being consistent is being able to make two claims that are different but compatible. Being **inconsistent** is making claims that may not contradict each other, but that cannot be easily reconciled. Is there inconsistency in the following argument?

204. To my taste there is nothing so fascinating as spending a night out in an African forest, or plantation; but I beg you to note I do not advise anyone to follow the practice. Nor indeed do I recommend African forest life to anyone. Unless you are interested in it and fall under its charm, it is the most awful life in death imaginable. It is like being shut up in a library whose books you cannot read, all the while tormented, terrified, and bored. And if you do fall under its spell, it takes all the colour out of other kinds of living.

MARY KINGLSEY, English traveller, 1895

Kingsley does not exactly contradict herself; but she makes these two claims:

1. There is nothing more fascinating than spending a night out in an African forest.
2. It is the most awful life in death imaginable.

Are these claims consistent with each other? She does open the first claim with the words: 'to my taste', but then implies that spending a night in an African forest is not likely to be to anyone else's. She claims to be the exception that proves the rule. But can spending a night in an African forest—can anything at all—be both 'terrifying' and 'boring'?

A well-known science-fiction writer made this complaint, not uncommon among science-fiction writers, and readers:

> My work is rather neglected, along with that of many others, simply because so-called 'high culture' snobs have decided that science fiction isn't literature.

Later, in the same quite long article, he wrote this:

> Orchestral music is one of the great features of a civilised society: when the members of an orchestra come together to make music, they raise our culture to a higher level. And then it's pulled down again by rock'n'roll, and noisy boy-bands.

Can one consistently complain that snobs elevate 'literature' above 'science fiction', and then—snobbishly?—elevate 'high-culture' orchestral music over 'low-culture' rock 'n' roll?

Queen Victoria was not better known for consistency than for impartiality. (The 'Lady Amberley' referred to in this tirade was a suffragette and early advocate of birth control; she was also the mother of the philosopher Bertrand Russell.)

> This mad, wicked folly of 'women's rights' with all its attendant horrors, on which her poor sex is bent, forgetting every sense of womanly feeling and propriety. Lady Amberley ought to get a good whipping.
>
> QUEEN VICTORIA, 1870

Victoria was the most powerful woman (if not the most powerful person) in Britain; was she well placed to refuse a little empowerment to other women; and did she display 'womanly feeling' in recommending that a lady be whipped?

We do not expect travel agents or estate agents to be consistent, perhaps:

# Undiscovered Provence

Immortalised by Cézanne and Van Gogh, Provence possesses a history as long as time. The Greeks visited, the Phoenicians traded, the Saracens looted, but most of all the Romans settled—all have left their legacies.

How can so many people have visited Provence—even 'immortalised' it—without its having been discovered? Perhaps by 'undiscovered' the advertiser meant 'unspoilt'—in which case one might ask whether it is consistent to celebrate Provence as it is, and to arrange that it be besieged by holidaymakers.

An estate agent put this leaflet through my door:

**205.**

## Fed Up With Estate Agents Putting Leaflets Through Your Door?

## Why Not Move!

We are currently experiencing a huge demand for all types of properties in this area and urgently need more to satisfy the current demand

Was it consistent of this estate agent to acknowledge that I might be fed up with leaflets through my door, and then to annoy me with yet one more? And if I had moved, would I have been spared the further attentions of this estate agent, or of others? Perhaps I would have done if I had moved to a slum.

We do expect writers of books about critical thinking, of all people, to be consistent (though you might, earlier in this chapter, have charged the writer of one such book with inconsistency). Here, the writers of a standard UK text are referring to 'appeals' of the sort that we met in Chapter 4 (appeals to pity, to fear, to patriotism); they ask their readers to 'remember' that:

206. Appeals often give weak support to a conclusion, because an argument requires logical support and appeals arouse our feelings rather than engage us in logical thinking. But an appeal can be strong. Our feelings of concern for the survivors of a natural disaster can be a good reason to offer help.

> **9c.** Would you convict the writers of this short argument of inconsistency?

Here, another writer almost convicts himself of contradiction: he is writing about principles of the sort that we considered in Chapter 7:

207. Principles are general claims about the way things should be. They are inflexible—they cannot be adjusted to suit the circumstances.

Most of us would concede that bribery is immoral—but consider this example: in the course of the Balkan War of 1992–95, in Bosnia-Herzegovina, aid agencies had to bribe local warlords to let them through roadblocks to reach civilians with the medical supplies that they needed. Bribery in this case appears to have been justified.

In acknowledging this we are going against the definition of a principle that I have just given you, that they are inflexible. But, in practice, we have to accept that there will be exceptions to every principle.

Why does a writer define a principle so forcibly in the first place, when he knows that within seconds he will blow his definition apart?

Something similar, if perhaps less obvious, happens in this next example. Two American authors of a book on critical thinking make the following claim on page 4 of the book:

We shall show that there are good reasons for finding that these two claims are false:

- There's no such thing as objective truth; we construct our own truth.
- There's no such thing as objective reality; we construct our own reality.

Then on page 39, they offer the following argument:

208. The notion that our everyday perceptions correspond exactly, one-to-one, to the real world—that they are, as it were photographic representations of that world—is plain wrong. Researchers have found that perception *constructs* what we make of reality: our minds re-create what we see and hear and touch and taste and feel out of materials supplied by our experience. What that experience leads us to expect we shall see and hear, and so on; what we believe; and how we feel physiologically—all this feeds into how we perceive the world. That our minds construct reality in this way has helped us to adapt ourselves to the world, and to adapt the world to our needs—indeed, it has helped us to survive as a species.

> **9d.** Would you say the research findings reported on page 39 by these two writers are consistent with the claim that they make on page 4 of their book?

One contradiction, or one example of inconsistency, in a piece of writing is not a mortal sin; it might not even be noticed if you are writing at some length. An argument can survive an inconsistency many pages apart, or a minor contradiction, and still hang together, still be **coherent**. It is when claims-as-reasons are inconsistent—claims intended to support the main conclusion—that an argument begins to come apart.

**Incoherence** is about the most unfriendly judgement that can be made against any argument, which is why I do not make it against this one. Moore was, after all, a professor of philosophy at the University of Cambridge, noted for his common sense:

209. I am inclined to think that 'right', in all ethical uses, and, of course, 'wrong', 'ought', 'duty', also are not the names of characteristics

at all, they have merely 'emotive meaning' and no 'cognitive meaning' at all; and, if this is true of them, it must also be true of 'good', in the sense I have been most concerned with. I am *inclined* to think that this is so, but I am also inclined to think that it is not so; and I do not know which way I am inclined most strongly. If these words, in their ethical uses, have only emotive meaning, then it would seem that all else I am going to say about them must be either nonsense or false (I don't know which).

G.E. MOORE, 'A Reply to My Critics' in
Philippa Foot (ed.), *Theories of Ethics*, Oxford:
Oxford University Press, 1967.
By permission of Oxford University Press

One must be patient when a philosopher 'thinks out loud', even in print. Philosophy is a serious business. Moore's inclinations are not incoherent, perhaps (and there might have been a 'third road' out of his final dichotomy), but to a non-philosopher, they may seem to come pretty close.

The sentimental Stevenson might also appear to succumb to well-meaning incoherence in this extract:

210. From the mind of childhood there is more history and more philosophy to be fished up than from all the printed volumes in a library. The child is conscious of an interest, not in literature but in life. A taste for the precise, the adroit, or the comely in the use of words, comes late; but long before that he has enjoyed in books a delightful dress rehearsal of experience.

ROBERT LOUIS STEVENSON, 'Random Memories', 1888

What is the sequence here? Children give voice to wisdom of a sort not found in books; life comes first, literature is for later; but there is a foretaste of life in the enjoyment of books. Does this make sense? Stevenson the romantic hymns the child's unlettered mind; but Stevenson the writer for children has high hopes of the power of books to feed the child's imagination. It seems he wants to have his cake, and he wants to eat it, too.

# Changing the subject

Sequence is important (and I shall say more about ordering claims in an argument, in Chapter 10). Ideally, one point in an argument should *lead* to another—one claim should *follow* another—flowingly, like numbers. There is some impact, and amusement, in a disjunction of points:

> The French will only be united under the threat of danger. How else can one govern a country that produces 246 different types of cheese?
>
> CHARLES DE GAULLE, French soldier and statesman, 1951

It does not follow from the fact that France makes lots of different cheeses that, unless it is in danger, it is ungovernable. When two claims are linked in this way, yet the one does not in the least imply the other, we say (using another Latin tag) that the second is a **non sequitur**—it does not follow. (Of course, it would be heavy-handed to accuse de Gaulle of committing a non sequitur; his question is a tongue-in-cheek, cheesy comment on French liberties.)

This conditional claim, on the face of it, looks like a non sequitur; it was made by novelist Jenny Diski in a recent literary review:

> If writing weren't ordered in some way, no one would be able to read it, and all books would be 60–100,000 words in alphabetical order.

She is quite right about the need for order; but the consequent ('and/then...') does not follow logically from the antecedent ('if...').

The authorities responsible for putting up this notice probably did not intend a non sequitur (South Stack is a rocky island with a lighthouse on it, just off the coast of Anglesey, north Wales):

---

**Anglesey County Council and Trinity House are responsible for South Stack, therefore EVERYONE has to pay to go onto the island.**

---

The word 'therefore' is usually a reliable argument indicator, linking a reason with a conclusion (see Chapter 2); here, though, the second claim does not follow from the first—and the threat, in the capitalized EVERYONE, is empty.

The word 'so' is another conclusion-indicator: does it link the first claim with the second in the following 'argument' (from yet another writer on critical thinking, whose anonymity we shall preserve)?

> It's often said that critical thinking is all about the study of arguments. So, you'll find some people (teachers of the subject, and others) fretting right at the start of proceedings about the difference between arguments in critical thinking and other sorts of arguments.

The second sentence does not follow from the first. It is a quite separate point (and, incidentally, one might wonder what 'other sorts of arguments' there might be than those that interest critical thinkers).

Is there any logical, or otherwise meaningful, connection between the claims made in this argument?

211. If I had to reply to the following question: *What is slavery?* with the simple reply: *It is murder*, my thinking would immediately be understood. I would not need to make a long argument to show that the power to take away a man's thought, will, personality, is a power of life and death, and that to enslave a man is to kill him. Why then to this other question: *What is property?* might I not answer equally: *It is theft!*

    PIERRE-JOSEPH PROUDHON, French socialist thinker, 1840

As a matter of legal fact, slavery is not murder (any more than abortion or execution is); it cannot then, 'equally', be the case that property is theft. Proudhon does not show how the two pairs of concepts are linked; he just asserts it.

Nietzsche appears to do something similar (and, once again, the reason indicator 'since' is not the link that it pretends to be):

212. No act of violence, rape, exploitation, destruction, is intrinsically 'unjust', since life is violent, rapacious, exploitative, and destructive and cannot be conceived otherwise.

    FRIEDRICH NIETZSCHE, German philosopher, 1887

It is reasonable to claim that no act is *intrinsically* (or essentially) anything: it is what we collectively say it is. Thus, we say that slavery is one thing and murder is something else. But does it follow from the sour observation that life is violent that rape is not unjust? It might even be thought of as intrinsically unjust once we have defined the offence in law.

In a sense, both Proudhon and Nietzsche are drawing a **red herring** across our path, as one might try to put the hounds off the scent of a fox by introducing a more powerful scent to distract them from that of the fox.

'Slavery is murder', 'life is violent'—these are the red herrings. We are lured by the apparent 'truth' of these claims into accepting the claims that 'follow'—except that they do not.

213. The sum of human happiness would not necessarily be reduced if for ten years every physical and chemical laboratory were closed and the patient and resourceful energy displayed in them transferred to the lost art of getting on together and finding the formula for making both ends meet in the scale of human life.

EDWARD BURROUGHS, Bishop of Ripon, Yorkshire, 1927

> **9e.** What is the red herring that Bishop Burroughs draws across our path here?

Just as an analogy might lead us astray—perhaps down a slippery slope (see Chapter 8)—so a red herring might be a rather particular way in which a writer simply **changes the subject**. Here are two writers to the *Daily Mail*, in March 2005: are they setting up a parallel case, or changing the subject (both letters are adapted)?

214. Are there limits to our compassion? People always respond magnificently to appeals for help when disaster strikes on the other side of the world. But those same people, without thinking twice, buy cheap battery-farmed chickens at their local supermarket. I'm not suggesting that animals should be privileged over humans; but we should not so casually connive at the cruel treatment of our fellow creatures.

215. The government is planning to place cannabis in the same class as more addictive substances, demonstrating just how little most people know about cannabis and its effects. Alcohol, for some reason, is a more socially acceptable drug, advertised as bringing happiness in good company, whilst cannabis is presented as having dire effects for mental health. Yet the effects of alcohol on those who are predisposed to mental health problems are far greater.

Does it help the campaign for compassion in farming to draw attention to people's generosity towards the disaster-prone? Does it strengthen the hand of the cannabis-user to point to the problems associated with alcohol? Shifting the focus may distract, and so weaken the main case. This is what seems to happen here:

216. As soon as I had power, I immediately established religion. I made it the groundwork and foundation upon which I built. I considered it as the support of sound principle and good morality, both in doctrine and in practice. Besides, such is the restlessness of man that his mind requires that something undefined and marvellous which religion offers; and it is better for him to find it there, than to seek it of fortune-tellers and impostors.

NAPOLEON BONAPARTE, one-time Emperor of France, 1816

(Napoleon was looking back from exile on St Helena, a prisoner of the British.) The word 'besides' is where Napoleon changes the subject, from what might have been a case founded on high principle, to one based on cynical calculation.

In changing the subject you may introduce an issue that is simply not **relevant** to the main point that you seek to make. On the other hand, to distract attention away from the main issue in a debate may be precisely what a writer intends to do. We have seen what Proudhon thought of slavery, and what James Boswell and what Erasmus Darwin (Arguments 90 and 91 in Chapter 4) thought of it. The following writer defended the slave trade in the same year as Boswell:

217. Some gentlemen may, indeed, object to the slave trade as inhuman and impious; let us consider that if our colonies are to be maintained and cultivated, which can only be done by African Negroes, it is surely better to supply ourselves with those labourers in British boats, than to purchase them through the medium of French, Dutch or Danish agents.

TEMPLE LUTTRELL, British MP, and
grandson of the Governor of Jamaica, 1777

To distract the reader's attention away from the inhumanity and impiety of slavery, Luttrell changes the subject: he wants his reader not to dwell on principle but to view with horror the prospect of handing a lucrative trade to Britain's enemies.

A British government minister argued in a similar fashion when he made the case for development aid, and for seeking to achieve the UN target of 0.7 per cent of GDP:

218. This is a moral issue. In a hundred years, people will look back on our generation in much the same way as we look back on the slave trade and they will marvel at the fact that we allowed 25,000, mainly children, to die every single day of diseases we had the

power to prevent. But if you don't buy that argument, it is in our national self-interest too.

ANDREW MITCHELL, UK Minister for Overseas Development, 2010

British self-interest *ought* to be **irrelevant**: just as Napoleon appealed to 'good morality', so Mitchell called development aid a 'moral issue'. He cited a shocking statistic. Then he changed the subject.

> **9f.** What is the (implicit?) conclusion of Mitchell's argument? Does he, in your view, weaken or strengthen the argument by introducing his final point?

# Begging the question

Consider this brief argument, attributed to a Roman-Catholic Frenchman, turned Quaker missionary in the United States:

219. I expect to pass through the world but once; any good thing, therefore, that I can do, or any kindness that I can show to any fellow-creature, let me do it now: let me not defer or neglect it, for I shall not pass this way again.

STEPHEN GRELLET, 1773–1855

Grellet passed through more of the world than most people. Is he merely repeating himself in these lines, giving the same reason for his conclusion ('therefore...') twice? Is he arguing in a circle $(P \rightarrow Q \rightarrow P)$?

And which is the novelist Salman Rushdie doing here?

> I would suggest that Peter Jackson's *Lord of the Rings* films surpass Tolkien's originals, because, to be blunt, Jackson makes films better than Tolkien writes.
>
> SALMAN RUSHDIE, Indian novelist, 2009

The 'explanation' following the word 'because' seems not to add anything to the first claim. Perhaps repeating oneself and arguing in a circle amount to pretty much the same thing. If one is sure of oneself, all one needs to do is to say the same thing again, in other, more emphatic words. There were few men more self-assured than Mussolini, the fascist leader of Italy for 21 years:

220. Opposition is not necessary for the working of a healthy political regime. Opposition is senseless, superfluous in a totalitarian regime like the fascist regime. So, let no-one hope, after this speech, to see anti-fascist journalists appear—no. Or that the resurrection of anti-fascist organizations will be allowed: not that either.

> BENITO MUSSOLINI, Italian head of government, 1927

> **9g.** Is Mussolini arguing in a circle here? Is he, indeed, arguing at all? (Note that word 'so'.)

Aristotle appears to have been rather given to arguing in what appears to be a circular way:

221. For man, therefore, the life according to reason is best and pleasantest, **since** reason more than anything else *is* man.

> ...
>
> Every art and every investigation, and likewise every practical pursuit or undertaking seems to aim at some good: **hence** it has been well said that the Good is that at which all things aim.
>
> ARISTOTLE (384–322 BCE), *The Nicomachean Ethics*

The life of reason is best for man because man lives by reason. Everything aims at the good because the good is what everything aims at. The (emboldened) argument indicators do not link a reason and a conclusion: they link two statements of the same claim. (I have numbered Aristotle's two aphorisms, but they can only loosely be called arguments.)

You may find Argument 222 so antagonistic to common sense that you would prefer not to trouble with it. If you are confident that you will avoid begging the question on this scale, you could even be forgiven for going straight to the summary at the end of the chapter.

Theologians and philosophers have been particularly given to arguing in a circle. The most famous example, perhaps, of such an argument is Anselm's so-called Ontological Argument for the Existence of God. The archbishop sought to counter the Fool, in Psalm 14, who 'says in his heart, there is no God':

> 222. God is a being, by definition, than which no greater being can be conceived. This being exists so truly that God cannot be conceived not to exist. So, by definition, God exists as an idea in the mind. Yet if we can conceive of a God who exists also in reality, that God would be greater than the God in our minds than whom no greater being can be conceived. But this is a logical contradiction. Therefore, there truly exists in reality a being than which no greater being can be conceived, and that is God.
>
> ANSELM (1033–1109), Archbishop of Canterbury, *Proslogium*

There are two versions of Anselm's argument, and numerous ways of translating them—and the arguments attacking and defending the argument have been just as numerous. But no matter how one interprets the meanings of terms like 'being', and 'exist', and no matter whether or not one thinks the premises are 'true' and the argument 'valid', the fact is that only those who believe in God already find Anselm's argument convincing.

Descartes advanced a similar argument in a tighter circle (and, again, this 'exists' in a number of forms):

> 223. I could not possibly exist with the nature I actually have, that is, one endowed with the idea of God, unless there is a God; the very God, I mean, of whom I have an idea.
>
> RENÉ DESCARTES, French philosopher, 1641

What both Anselm and Descartes do, in effect, is to **beg the question**: this is an antique way of saying they *assume* that the central question has already been dealt with; they assume precisely what it is (the existence of God) that they are trying to prove. In effect, they argue: $P \to P$, which does not help us much. The phrase 'beg the question' is used quite a lot, and often rather loosely, as in this newspaper comment piece (the name is changed):

---

### Divided Loyalties

His mother is English, his father is American, which begs the question: who is **Martin Berryman** going to support in Saturday's World Cup match between the two countries?

---

All the writer meant was: 'which *raises* the question'. (Though the question that the writer was begging, perhaps, was that Martin Berryman cared enough to support either team.)

Articles in religious tracts often beg the question:

> Do you long to live in a better world? You can take comfort from the well-known story of Noah and the Flood, in Genesis Chapters 6–9. Did the Flood really happen? You can be sure that it did, for the Word of God leaves no room for doubt. The Genesis account tells us the exact year, month, and day when the Flood rose, and when it abated.

How do we know that what it says in the Bible is true? The Bible is 'the Word of God', so it must be true.

Those who argued against women clergy in the Church of England were inclined to beg the question:

> 224. I believe [the proposal to ordain women clergy] undermines and questions the way in which God himself has taught us how to speak of Him and know Him. I do not believe that it was by accident, but by God's deliberate choice, that He chose to reveal Himself in a patriarchal society and become man in Christ as a male.
>
> GRAHAM LEONARD, Bishop of London, 1986

There is a sense in which the bishop turns to the Bible to justify a belief that came from the Bible in the first place. Here is a Polish philosopher who appears to argue much as Anselm and Descartes did:

225. Is it not reasonable to suspect that if existence were pointless and the universe devoid of meaning, we would never have achieved not only the ability to imagine otherwise, but even the ability to entertain this very thought—to wit, that existence is pointless and the universe devoid of meaning?

LESZEK KOŁAKOWSKI, *Metaphysical Horror*,
London: Blackwell, 1988

What Kołakowski appears to be saying is that there must be meaning in the universe for us to have the very idea that there is, or is not, meaning in the universe. He seems to be trying to persuade us of the existence of something by appealing to our idea of that something—just as Anselm and Descartes did when they thought to prove the existence of God.

> **9h.** Does the author of Argument 226 argue in a circle, or beg the question, or neither of these things?

226. Like many philosophers, I have long been impressed by the failure of attempts to find a correct analysis of the notion of knowledge in terms of supposedly more basic notions, such as belief, truth, and justification. One natural explanation of the failure is that knowledge has no such analysis. If so, I wondered, what follows? At first, I was tempted to draw the conclusion that the notion of knowledge did not matter very much, because we could use those other notions instead. Around 1986, however, I began to notice points at which philosophers had gone wrong through using combinations of those other notions when the notion of knowledge was what their purposes really called for. That raised the question: why did they not use the notion of knowledge when it was just what they needed?

TIMOTHY WILLIAMSON, *Knowledge and its Limits*,
Oxford: Oxford University Press, 2000.
By permission of Oxford University Press

What might this chapter have prepared you to look out for in your review of the arguments of others and in writing an argument of your own? I hope it has alerted you to when:

> ➤ one claim might **contradict** another;
> ➤ there is a danger of being **inconsistent** and, indeed of an argument becoming **incoherent**;
> ➤ one claim does not follow from another— is a **non sequitur**;
> ➤ an **irrelevant** point is made that may perhaps be a **red herring** and that may **change the subject** rather abruptly;
> ➤ an argument might be **circular**, and when a premise may **beg the question**.

Now that you know from (a close or selective, or skimmed acquaintance with) the foregoing nine chapters what you might observe happening in other people's arguments, and what you might guard against in writing your own, it is time for a brief look at how you might lay out your case: how you might order your points; how you might come to a safe conclusion, and how you should acknowledge the sources of information and ideas that you have used.

# 10 How will you lay out your case?

I shall aim in this chapter to explain:

- how you might best order your reasons;
- and draw more than one conclusion;
- how evidence might point in more than one direction;
- how to acknowledge your sources of information.

## Structure of reasoning

In an argument of any length, you will present a number of reasons for coming to the overall conclusion. The question is: how to place these reasons in the most effective order—so that:

1. one reason **flows** naturally from the one before;
2. the reasons **lead** the reader to the overall conclusion; and
3. the conclusion seems to **follow** almost inescapably.

An argument that flows is more likely to persuade than one that jumps haphazardly from one point to another. The following argument flows—until the waterspout at the end:

227. Considering the care and anxiety a woman must have about a child before it comes into the world, it seems to me, by a *natural right*, to belong to her. When men get immersed in the world, they seem to lose all sensations, excepting those necessary to continue or produce life! Are these the privileges of reason? Amongst the feathered race, whilst the hen keeps the young warm, her mate stays by to cheer her; but it is sufficient for a man to condescend to get a child, in order to claim it. A man is a tyrant!

MARY WOLLSTONECRAFT, pioneer English feminist, 1794

Wollstonecraft was writing to her absentee (common-law) husband, the American Gilbert Imlay. Her conclusion seems to be that 'when a child is born it belongs to the mother'. She gives two reasons to support this conclusion:

[R1] A woman has care and anxiety about a child before it comes into the world.

[R2] A man begets a child, but then (unlike a bird) he loses all feeling for it, and gets on with his life.

---

[C] When a child is born it belongs to the mother.

The two reasons are separate, **independent** reasons: they complement each other; but each could stand alone, and be a sufficient support for the conclusion without the other.

Here is an argument advanced by the UK Prime Minister, in which he gave three reasons for claiming that the 500-year-old King James Bible of 1611 (the 'Authorised Version') was as relevant in 2011 as at any point in its history:

228. First, the King James Bible has bequeathed a body of language that permeates every aspect of our culture and heritage. Second, just as our language and culture is steeped in the Bible, so too is our politics.

   Third, we are a Christian country. And we should not be afraid to say so. Let me be clear: I am not in any way saying that to have another faith—or no faith—is somehow wrong. I know and fully respect that many people in this country do not have a religion. And I am also incredibly proud that Britain is home to many different faith communities, who do so much to make our country stronger. But what I am saying is that the Bible has helped to give Britain a set of values and morals which make Britain what it is today.

   DAVID CAMERON, in a speech to Church of
   England clergy, Oxford, 17 December 2011

Simply put, the argument can be set out as follows:

[R1] The 1611 Bible gave us language that permeates our culture and heritage.

[R2] Our political life is steeped in the King James Bible.

[R3] It has helped to give us a set of values and morals which make Britain what it is today.

---

[C] The King James Bible is as relevant in 2011 as at any point in its history.

Cameron had to be careful what he said to justify his third reason (as the Queen was, in Argument 44 in Chapter 3); and it might have helped his argument if he had explained what he meant by his second reason—nevertheless, each of the three reasons is independent of the others and could support the conclusion by itself. (Reasons 1 and 3 could, anyway.) All three together give strong support to the conclusion—strong enough, in Cameron's view, to justify placing a copy of the King James Bible in every school in the country.

The *order* in which he placed the three reasons is a reasonable one.

A Word of Advice

There is no 'right' order of claims-as-reasons in an argument, but you might bear in mind the suggestions for informing your order that I listed at the end of Chapter 2:

Specific → General
Small → Big
Simple → Complex
Less significant → More significant
Early → Late (chronological order)

Cameron hangs his second claim on the first which does have a certain priority. Of the three reasons, though, the third is the 'biggest', the most 'complex' and 'significant', so there is much to be said for leaving this one until last.

The American novelist Jonathan Franzen expresses his preference for the printed book over the computer-screen version, in this argument:

229. 'When I read a book, I'm handling a specific object in a specific time and place. The fact that when I take the book off the shelf it still says the same thing—that is reassuring. Someone worked really hard to make the language just right, just the way they wanted it. They were so sure of it that they printed it in ink, on paper. A screen always feels like we could delete that, change that, move it around. So for a literature-crazed person like me, it's just not permanent enough.'

JONATHAN FRANZEN, in a speech at a literature festival, Colombia, January 2012

Franzen gives five reasons for coming to his conclusion, each of which might have been a paragraph in a more developed argument:

[R1] A book is a specific object in a specific time and place.

[R2] It is reassuring that a book says the same thing each time it is read.

[R3] The writer worked hard to make the language just right.

[R4] The result was pleasing enough to be given permanence in print.

[R5] We feel that we could edit what we read on a screen.

[C] A lover of literature will prefer a real book to an e-book.

The reasons here are rather **interdependent** than independent of each other; they make a **joint** case. Each reason runs into the next, so that the first four (about the permanence of the book) lead naturally to the fifth—which is the one explicitly negative reason (about the seeming *im*permanence of an e-book) that prompts the conclusion.

Let us look at one more, rather longer, argument to see how the claims-as-reasons are ordered. It is taken from a report presented to US President Eisenhower in 1960 by his Science Advisory Committee.

230. What are the principal reasons for undertaking a national space program? What can we expect to gain from space science and exploration?

It is useful to distinguish among four factors which give importance, urgency, and inevitability to the advancement of space technology.

The first of these factors is the compelling urge of man to explore and to discover, the thrust of curiosity that leads men to try to go where no-one has gone before. Most of the surface of the Earth has now been explored, and men now turn to the exploration of outer space as their next objective.

Second, there is the defensive objective for the development of space technology. We wish to be sure that space is not used to endanger our security. If space is to be used for military purposes, we must be prepared to use space to defend ourselves.

Third, there is the factor of national prestige. To be strong and bold in space technology will enhance the prestige of the United States among the people of the world and create added confidence in our scientific, technological, industrial, and military strength.

Fourth, space technology affords new opportunities for scientific observation and experiment which will add to our knowledge and understanding of the Earth, the solar system and the universe.

In fact, it has been the military quest for ultra-long-range rockets that has provided man with new machinery so powerful that it can readily put satellites in orbit, and send instruments out to explore the Moon and nearby planets. In this way, what was at first a purely military enterprise has opened up an exciting era of exploration that few men, even a decade ago, dreamed would come in this century.

JAMES R. KILLIAN, Chair of the President's
Advisory Committee, 1960

At a time when Soviet Russia had already put three Earth satellites into orbit, and fired three successful Moon shots, President Eisenhower needed to persuade the American people of the need for the United States to embark on an expensive space programme. The Committee was called upon to make the President's case for him—and for his successor, John F. Kennedy.

> **10a.** Are the four claims *independent* or *joint* reasons, in your view?
> And are they set out in what you take to be a reasonable order?

Let us suppose that you face this question: Should 16-year-olds be given the vote? Let us further suppose that you think they should. You have examined the argument for *not* giving them the vote in **Argument A**; now you are going to argue for doing so. Your reasons—in random order—are these (they apply in the UK, but not necessarily elsewhere):

a. A 16-year-old can drink alcohol on licensed premises if with an adult.

b. Young people at 16 know as much about politics as many adults.

c. A young person can choose to leave school at 16 and embark on an apprenticeship or training programme.

d. 16–18-year-olds are directly affected by policies concerning university entrance, tuition fees, and employment.

e. 16 is the legal age of consent to sex and 16-year-olds can marry with their parents' permission.

f. Young people mature earlier now than a generation or two ago.

> **10b.** What would you consider to be the most suitable order in which to place these reasons, so that they have maximum impact?
> Are there others that you can think of?

# Intermediate conclusion

You might have been impressed by one or more of the reasons in **Argument A** for *not* giving 16-year-olds the vote: you might, for instance, agree with Zoe (Argument 22 in Chapter 2) that politics should be on the curriculum in schools so that young people are better prepared to vote. Nevertheless, you believe, on balance, that your **Argument B** (thanks to the evidence that you have presented in support of one or more of the reasons, perhaps) is stronger than **Argument A** overall.

So as not to sound too one-sided—or too sure of yourself—you may want to bring your case to something like the following *pair* of conclusions:

It may be that if young people are to feel confident to vote at the age of 16, they need to have been taught the essential differences between the major parties and their policies as a part of the normal school curriculum.

Once such teaching is in place, there would seem to be no good reason for extending certain rights to 16-year-olds, yet depriving them of the right to vote for or against the politicians who make the decisions in such matters.

We call the first of these two conclusions an **intermediate conclusion**. It prepares the ground for the main conclusion, perhaps saving that conclusion from being too hasty an inference, or over-generalization.

We can see something of this sort happening in the following argument: Prince Bernhard was the first president of what was the World Wildlife Fund that became the World Wide Fund for Nature:

> 231. We are poisoning the air over our cities; we are poisoning the rivers and seas; we are poisoning the soil itself. Some of this may be inevitable. But if we don't get together in a real and mighty effort to stop these attacks upon Mother Earth, wherever possible, **we may find ourselves one day—one day soon, maybe—in a world that will be only a desert full of plastic, concrete and electronic robots.** In that world there will be no more 'nature'; in that world man and a few domestic animals will be the only living creatures.
>
> And yet, *man cannot live without some measure of contact with nature.* It is essential to his happiness.
>
> PRINCE BERNHARD OF THE NETHERLANDS, 1962

I have italicized what I think is his main conclusion (it might otherwise be expressed as that: 'some measure of contact with nature is essential to man's happiness'). The nightmare vision of the lines that I have emboldened is an intermediate conclusion giving us (literally) a concrete illustration of the abstract and generalizing (but not over-generalizing) main conclusion. The intermediate conclusion adds to the credibility, and therefore to the persuasiveness, of the main conclusion.

An intermediate conclusion may play a more significant role in an argument than this, however: it might serve as the conclusion to one part of the argument, and as an introduction to the next. The six reasons for giving the vote to 16-year-olds might be divided into the personal (reasons: a, c, e, and f) and the political (reasons: b and d). **Argument B**, in very skeletal form, might look something like this:

> In a number of ways we treat 16-year-olds as grown-ups. For example, a young person can drink alcohol on licensed premises if with an adult. A young person can choose to leave school at 16 and embark on an apprenticeship or training programme. Furthermore, 16 is the legal age of consent to sex and 16-year-olds can marry with their parents' permission. In many ways, we recognize in these provisions that young people are maturing earlier now than a generation or two ago—and **this maturity may not be only social and personal, but political, too.**

Many young people today, with their extended education, are as politically well informed at 16 and 17 as many adults. This age group is directly affected by policies concerning university entrance, tuition fees, and employment. **It may be that they would benefit from instruction in the main differences between the political parties and their policies.** If this was in place, and given the rights that they have already, *it would seem sensible to extend the right to 16-year-olds to choose the politicians who make the decisions that affect them.*

The final sentence of the first paragraph—the first of two intermediate conclusions—is the *pivot* of the argument: it is where the social and personal reasons for giving 16-year-olds the vote give way to the political reasons. (The first political reason—that many young people are as politically well informed as many adults—is one that you could support with *evidence* of a sort yielded by a simple questionnaire administered to a representative sample of 16-year-olds, and a sample of 'adults'.)

This argument further illustrates the job that an intermediate conclusion might do:

232. Hans and Sophie Scholl were leaders of a group of undergraduate students called the White Rose, at the University of Munich. This was a humanist, non-violent resistance movement against the National Socialist regime. The Scholl siblings were caught distributing anti-Nazi leaflets, in February 1943, and handed over to the Gestapo. Within a matter of days they had been tried and executed by guillotine. **The Scholls were representative of what is finest in German intellectual culture.**

    It might be said that the German bourgeoisie of today is more in tune with currents of intellectual, cultural, and political life—they are, in a word, better educated—than the middle class in Britain. It is likely that the same thing can be said of their forebears in 1943. This is what is so taxing about the question that has been posed again and again: *how is it that a German middle class, as educated as it was, could have signed up to the hate-fuelled, totalitarian savagery of the National Socialists?*

    Adapted from an extract of an article by<br>DAVID POUNTNEY, The Guardian, 5 March 2011

The emboldened intermediate conclusion shifts the focus of the argument from the Scholls to the social class that they represented: it is the point at which the *specific* becomes the *general*.

Here are two further instances of where an intermediate conclusion has this pivotal function (you will need to allow for the fact that Argument 233 was published in 1847; by 'vital', in his second sentence, the writer means 'animate', or 'living'):

233. When we consider our own animal frames, 'fearfully and wonderfully made', we observe in the motion of our limbs a continual conversion of heat into living force, which may be either converted back again into heat or employed in producing an attraction through space, as when a man ascends a mountain. Indeed, the phenomena of nature, whether mechanical, chemical, or vital, consist almost entirely in a continual conversion of attraction through space, living force, and heat into one another. Thus it is that order is maintained in the universe—nothing is deranged, nothing ever lost, but the entire machinery, complicated as it is, works smoothly and harmoniously. And though, as in the awful vision of Ezekiel, 'there are wheels within wheels', and everything may appear complicated and involved in the apparent confusion and intricacy of an almost endless variety of causes, effects, conversions, and arrangements, yet is the most perfect regularity preserved—the whole being governed by the sovereign will of God.

JAMES PRESCOTT JOULE, English physicist, 1847

> **10c.** What might you identify as the intermediate conclusion in Argument 233, and how would you justify your choice?

God does not figure in this 21st-century argument about energy:

234. There is a gap in our future electricity supply, so the Royal Society is to consider the existing and potential sources of energy at our disposal. Some people are taking the view that only nuclear energy can fill the gap; but we know the drawbacks of this source of energy, and cost is one of the more significant. The government is already subsidizing the industry, and is finding out that the setting up and decommissioning costs are greater than we had been led to think.

There are alternative routes that we could take, but they will involve radical thinking. First of all, we might ask ourselves whether the National Grid is the best way of transmitting power throughout the country. Wind turbines might not be beautiful, but they compare favourably with the pylons that carry power-lines across some of our finest landscapes. Secondly, we should take energy conservation seriously: we could all use electricity more efficiently; insulation of buildings could be undertaken more comprehensively; and waste heat from industrial processes could be harnessed for domestic use.

The Royal Society has a host of possibilities to look into, not the least of them the generation of energy at the local level by photo-electrical cell technology. Almost any solution to the problem of the energy gap is going to be better than the nuclear option.

Adapted from a letter to *The Scotsman*, May 2005

> **10d.** Is there an intermediate conclusion in Argument 234? If so, what job does it do?

# Alternative inferences

You will be fairly sure what your main conclusion will be before you begin writing—indeed, you will probably give a foretaste of it in your opening **Statement**. You may even decide upon one or more interme-diate conclusions in the planning process.

It is not always clear what the main conclusion of an argument is: I was not sure about what James Gordon Bennett's main conclusion was, in Argument 6, way back in Chapter 1—and I am still not sure. Bennett might not have been sure himself.

The claims of others that you give an account of in **Argument A** might change your mind about what your conclusion will be; or your own reasons, in **Argument B**, might not look quite so powerful on the page as they had seemed at the outset. For these and other reasons (see Chapters 6 and 7) it is as well to bear in mind that *more than one possible conclusion might well be drawn at the end of an argument, however well conducted that argument might be.*

Evidence might seem conclusive:

235. Francis Bacon didn't always tell the truth about his painting life. He said he worked entirely by 'chance' and 'accident', yet the secrets of his studio revealed since his death include plans for

paintings, rough sketches, and precise sources for images—such as the photograph of a plucked and trussed chicken from the Conran cookbook that he directly copied on to a canvas. Evidently his work was more thought-out and intellectual than he liked to make it look.

JONATHAN JONES, art critic, *The Guardian Weekend*,
6 September 2008. © Guardian News & Media

It may be 'evident' to another critic, on the basis of the same studio secrets, that had Bacon's paintings been produced by 'accident' or by 'chance', rather than by copying images from a cookbook, we might think even more highly of them than we do. Evidence can point in more than one direction.

The budget airline Ryanair thought that the evidence of passenger figures was pretty conclusive when it paid for a full-page advertisement in national newspapers to lambast the British government (the BAA was the British Airports Authority, now Heathrow Airport Holdings Ltd):

236.

---

### OVER 4 MILLION FEWER PASSENGERS AT BAA'S UK AIRPORTS IN 5 MONTHS AS £10 TRAVEL TAX DEVASTATES GB TOURISM

| | BAA UK AIRPORT TRAFFIC |
|---|---|
| JAN–MAY 2008 | 56.8m PASSENGERS |
| JAN–MAY 2009 | 52.4m PASSENGERS |
| **TOURISM LOSSES** | **4.4m PASSENGERS** |

THE BELGIAN & DUTCH GOVERNMENTS HAVE SCRAPPED THEIR TRAVEL TAXES

THE GREEK & SPANISH GOVERNMENTS ARE REDUCING AIRPORT FEES TO ZERO

BUT STILL THE UK GOVERNMENT IS TAXING TOURISTS AND DESTROYING TOURISM

### SCRAP THE UK'S £10 TOURIST TAX BEFORE BRITISH TOURISM LOSES EVEN MORE PASSENGERS!!

---

A 7.75 per cent drop in tourist numbers as a result of the £10 tourist tax certainly looks like a government own-goal. It might be remembered, though, that one British bank (Northern Rock) was taken into public ownership in February 2008, and the government persuaded another (Lloyds) to take over a third (HBOS) in January 2009—and between these dates (September 2008) Lehman Brothers filed for bankruptcy. The financial world was in turmoil, so it is perhaps not surprising that tourist numbers fell. Ryanair's inference from the data was not 'wrong', but it was not the only 'right' one.

You might have come to another conclusion than the one that this writer came to ('Kenmure' was William Gordon, 6th Viscount Kenmure, commander of the Jacobite forces opposed to the union of Scotland with England):

237. Kenmure came upon the scaffold and looked with all the courage and resolution of an old Roman. He walked about the stage with a great deal of concernedness. Two clergymen attended him upon the stage and prayed, he being a Protestant. When he was beheaded his body was put into a coffin. What he said I have not heard. There was no disturbance made at all, while the mob were as quiet as lambs, nor did there seem to any face of sorrow among the multitude.

It is very moving and affecting to see a man that was but this moment in perfect health and strength sent the next into another world. Few that die in their bed have so easy an end of life.

DUDLEY RYDER, British politician and judge, 1716

Kenmure himself, for all his Roman stoicism, might have preferred, on balance, to die in his bed.

Scotland was prized, but it was India that came to be the jewel in the crown:

238. It is only when you get to see and realise what India is—that she is the strength and the greatness of England—that you feel that every nerve a man may strain, every energy he may put forward, cannot be devoted to a nobler purpose than keeping tight the cords that hold India to ourselves.

LORD GEORGE CURZON, English statesman,
later Viceroy of India, 1893

His reference to 'England' would suggest that Curzon had forgotten that India was held in the name of Victoria, Queen of Great Britain and Ireland. He seems also to have overlooked whatever Indians themselves might have thought when they saw and realized what India was.

Relations between causes and effects (as we saw in Chapter 4) may sanction a variety of inferences. There is huge interest in drilling for oil and gas in the Arctic as climate change reduces the amount of sea ice in the region. Early in 2013, a Shell vessel, the *Kulluk*, ran aground in Alaska, and, though there was no oil spillage, it was judged that safety procedures were inadequate. The UK government gave the drilling its full support.

UK Member of Parliament Joan Walley called for the government to oppose drilling for oil and gas in the Arctic:

239. This government is complacently standing by and watching new oil and gas drilling in the region, even though companies like Shell cannot prove they could clean up an oil spill in such harsh conditions. The government has failed to provide a coherent argument to support its view that exploring for oil and gas in the Arctic is compatible with avoiding dangerous climate destabilisation.... The rapidly disappearing Arctic sea ice should be a wake-up call for this government to tackle climate change, not pave the way for a corporate carve-up of the region's resources.

JOAN WALLEY MP, Chair of the Environmental Audit Select Committee, 2013

> **10e.** This is the inference that Joan Walley draws from the drilling for oil and gas in the Arctic. What might an oil company, and what might the UK government, infer from the discovery of substantial deposits of oil and gas in the region?

Even statistical 'evidence', though, as we saw in the Ryanair case, is notoriously open to interpretation. In 2008, tests of 560,000 5-year-olds in the UK seemed to 'show' that:

- one in seven children could not write their own names after one year of school;
- nearly 80,000 5-year-olds found it difficult to hold a pen properly, and write simple words like 'mum', 'dad', and 'cat';
- 'thousands more' could not recite the alphabet or count to ten;
- fewer than 50 per cent of the children reached targets in basic numeracy, communication and language, personal skills, physical development, and creativity;
- 49 per cent of the children met the targets in all these areas.

Adapted from an article in *The Independent*, 19 September 2008

What might we infer from these figures? We might infer—if we are pessimists—that too many 5-year-olds are failing to meet the targets set; or that there is something badly wrong with teaching in reception classes. On the other hand—if we are optimists (or faithful to the principle of charity)—we might infer that the targets are unrealistically high; that it is too early to test children at the age of 5; or that education at this age ought not to be about literacy and numeracy at all.

Much will depend, where the inference you make is concerned, on whether you are a glass half-full, or a glass half-empty person.

Here is some more statistical 'evidence', this time concerning how much Britons drink, and what their alcohol consumption is doing to them, and to the National Health Service. The information derives from an analysis of government figures by the Centre for Public Health at John Moores University, Liverpool.

- 10 million Britons admit to drinking more than the weekly limits recommended by the government (21 units for men, 14 units for women; the glass of wine in the picture might be one and a half units);
- in 2008/9, no fewer than 606,799 people were admitted to hospital for alcohol-related reasons—that is more than 1,500 men and women every day;
- between 2006 and 2009 11,000 men died of liver disease; cirrhosis of the liver has increased by a factor of ten over recent decades;
- alcohol abuse claims, on average, seven months of the lives of every man and woman in Britain, and up to two years in some areas;

- one in three men and one in six women are described as 'hazardous drinkers'; 9 per cent of men and 4 per cent of women are 'alcohol-dependent';
- 415,059 crimes attributed to alcohol abuse were committed in 2009/10, a rise of 65 per cent in five years.

Adapted from an article in the *Daily Mail*, 1 September 2010

> **10f.** What might you infer from this information? Is there one main conclusion that you would come to?

# Quotation and referencing

I have done a lot of quoting in this book, and you will probably quote material from a number of authors in the course of laying out **Argument A**—your evaluation (or 'review of the literature') of how other writers have answered your question.

It is one thing to refer to the ideas of another author, and another to quote his or her actual words. Why might you include quotations in what you are writing? Are quotations good in themselves? Churchill thought so:

240.  It is a good thing for an uneducated man to read books of quotations. *Bartlett's Familiar Quotations* is an admirable work, and I studied it intently. The quotations when engraved upon the memory give you good thoughts. They also make you anxious to read the authors and look for more.

WINSTON CHURCHILL, *My Early Life*, 1930

For all his love of quotations, Churchill is quoted far more than he ever quoted others. He did not need to borrow anyone else's words when he had ringing words of his own. Most of us, though, are less authoritative (and have less authority) than Churchill—and we have other work to do. You may well quote for the same reason that Montaigne did. First, though, he gives examples of how not to do it in what amounts to an early crack at **plagiarism**—the attempt to pass off others' work as one's own:

Chrysippus, the philosopher was in the habit of dropping into his writing not just passages but entire works by others, including for example the whole of *Medea*, by Euripedes; Apollodorus, too, said that if everything that was not his was edited out of his work, there would be nothing left. Epicurus, by contrast, never included a single quotation in any one of the three hundred volumes that he bequeathed to us.

I have seen some writers clothe themselves in other men's armour to the extent that only their fingertips are showing. They create work that is made of bits and pieces of the work of classical authors—an easy job for an educated man who is writing about something simple—and pretend that what they have stolen is their own. This is foolish, and worse, since in winning the admiration of those who are ignorant, they lose that of the learned—and only the respect of an intelligent audience is worth anything. As for me, I would rather do anything than that. I quote only to make myself clear.

MICHEL DE MONTAIGNE, 'On the Education of Children', 1580

Those who plagiarize the work of others generally give themselves away. Robin Cook praises the work of Geoffrey Bowman among those who draft UK parliamentary bills:

> With few resources, they do a remarkable job and their work has been much plagiarised by the new democracies of the East. Geoffrey tells us that Azerbaijan copied one of their bills word for word. They were able to identify it as a copy because it even included the clause on its application to Northern Ireland.
>
> ROBIN COOK, *The Point of Departure*, London: Simon & Schuster, 2003

Two European presidents (one Hungarian, the other German) have lost their jobs in recent years because they were found to have plagiarized their PhD theses.

A Word of Advice

You won't do a Chrysippus, then; but you needn't do an Epicurus, either. What is vital is that whoever reads your argument is able to tell the difference between what is yours and what is not yours. If you quote (or *paraphrase*, or *translate*) the words of others you must make it obvious that this is what you are doing.

You might quote a saying, or proverb, or adage without naming its author, as Joule did in the first line of Argument 233 (he was quoting from Psalm 139, thus giving support to Cameron's first reason in Argument 228), and as Teddy Roosevelt did:

241. There is a homely old adage which runs: 'Speak softly and carry a big stick; you will go far.' If the American nation will speak softly, and yet build and keep at a pitch of the highest training a thoroughly efficient navy, the Monroe Doctrine* will go far.

THEODORE ROOSEVELT, US President, in a speech, April 1903

\* Of 1823, that the Americas should be free from European intervention.

He said it was a West African adage (or saying); but it seems Roosevelt, himself, was its author. Perhaps by calling it an 'old' adage, he thought to make it the more undeniably 'true'. If so, it was an innocent deception.

Authors who wrap the printed or spoken words of others in quotation marks do not 'pretend that what they have stolen is their own' (Montaigne, 1580); but if they do not name those others they are deceivers of a kind. The following passage is taken from a book about schizophrenia (whose author I shall not name):

> In addition to the exaggerated emotions that are experienced by individuals with schizophrenia, there is also evidence that some people affected with this disease have difficulties in assessing emotions in other people. A recent review of studies in this area asserted that 'there has been a growing literature suggesting that schizophrenics differ substantially from controls in processing emotional communication.' One research technique used to demonstrate this is to ask individuals with schizophrenia to describe the emotions of people in photographs, which is frequently a difficult task for them.

Did the author quote from the 'recent review' because he had no 'evidence' of his own? Does the fact that the reference to 'a growing literature' appears to be a quotation impress us more than if the author had used his own words? Are we expected to take the review and its 'evidence' on trust?

Mrs Beeton does name the authorities to whom she appeals, though they are strangers to us, 150 years and more later. Here are two passages from her *Book of Household Management* (see Argument 199 in Chapter 8), in which she appeals, in turn, to a bishop and to a judge:

242. The necessity of practising economy should be evident to everyone, whether in the possession of an income no more than
sufficient for a family's requirements, or of a large fortune which
puts financial adversity out of the question. We must always
remember that to manage a little well is a great merit in housekeeping. 'He is a good waggoner,' says Bishop Hall, 'that can turn
in a little room. To live well in abundance is the praise of the
estate, not of the person. I will study more how to give account of
my little than how to make it more.' In this there is true wisdom,
and it may be added that those who can manage a little well are
most likely to succeed in their management of larger matters.

243. The housekeeping accounts should be balanced not less than once
a month—once a week is better; and it should be seen that the
money in hand tallies with the account. Judge Halliburton never
wrote truer words than when he said—'No man is rich whose
expenditure exceeds his means, and no one is poor whose incom-
ings exceed his outgoings.'

ISABELLA BEETON, *Book of Household Management*, 1861

> **10g.** How effective do you
> judge Mrs Beeton's appeals
> to authority to be in these two
> instances?

Neither Bishop Hall nor Judge Halliburton would have had much to
say about household management, as such. A quotation has more
impact when the author quoted is an authority in your chosen field.
The soldier Arthur Wellesley, later the Duke of Wellington, quoted the
words of the soldier-cavalier Philip Stanhope, 1st Earl of Chesterfield,
in 1810:

As Lord Chesterfield said of the generals of his day, 'I only hope that
when the enemy reads the list of their names, he trembles as I do'.

Somehow, this quotation from Chesterfield has come down to us as:
'I don't know what effect these men will have upon the enemy, but, by
God, they frighten me!' This version carries more punch; but it is wise
to be faithful to an author's actual words if you want to inspire trust.
Here—honestly, and unusually—a writer confesses to misquoting:

I used to quote Churchill as declaring that a first-rate mind was
one that could maintain two opposing ideas at the same time. It

certainly sounded Churchillian to me until someone better read pointed out that this quotable quote is by F. Scott Fitzgerald. At first this disappoints, because the quote, to me, seems to argue for political nuance, for subtlety and precision in state affairs.

DAVID SIMON, The Guardian Weekend,<br>6 September 2008. © Guardian News & Media

What F. Scott Fitzgerald actually wrote was:

> The test of a first-rate intelligence is the ability to hold two opposed ideas in the mind at the same time, and still retain the ability to function.
>
> F. SCOTT FITZGERALD, 'The Crack-Up', in Esquire, 1936

There is not much here about political nuance, or subtlety and precision in state affairs. It is possible that David Simon had been thinking of this famous line by Orwell:

> *Doublethink* means the power of holding two contradictory beliefs in one's mind simultaneously, and accepting both of them.
>
> GEORGE ORWELL, Nineteen Eighty-Four, London:<br>Secker & Warburg, 1949

Here, state affairs are, indeed, paramount—there is nothing about a first-rate mind or intelligence. But self-deception can be innocent, too.

You will not be attempting to quote from memory; but why (if there are so many pitfalls) quote at all? It is often enough to name authors and to characterize their views in your own words. But there are also good reasons for quoting the words they use, in moderation:

- to show that you have taken comprehensive account of how others have responded to the question that you are seeking an answer to;
- to demonstrate that you are not alone in your views, and that you have considered authors who agree with you, and who disagree;
- to appeal for support from an author whose authority in the field would be agreed by everyone;
- to do justice to an original thought that you might fear to misinterpret by rewording it;
- to represent an idea that is expressed succinctly and tellingly, so that you feel that you could not improve upon it.

There are conventions in place to guide writers in how to set out quotations, and how to reference these quotations, and you may have adopted one of these (or be required so to do). A quotation will ordinarily figure in text something like this:

> The English philosopher John Locke has had a far-reaching influence, yet, as Magee points out, 'much of what Locke said had already been said by others, for example Descartes—the view of the whole universe as a colossal machine, the division of the world into matter and minds, and so on' (Magee, 1988: 121).

The words quoted are enclosed in single inverted commas, and the *author's surname* is given in brackets, together with the *date of publication*, and the *number of the page* from which the quotation is taken. If it is a quite short quotation, as the one here is, it can be comfortably incorporated into the text. If on the other hand, it is a longer quotation—of, say, 50 words or more—then it may be better to indent it, and give it, as it were, a separate paragraph, as I have done throughout this book. An alternative in-text reference is, of course, the **footnote**: in this case, a superscript number[1] would direct the reader to the full book reference at the foot of the page.

Such references might, alternatively, be collected at the end of a section, as **endnotes**. What is crucially important is that every quotation in the text should be referenced there, and the full publishing details of that reference should be given either in footnotes, or endnotes, or in a **bibliography** at the very end of the work.

A Word of Advice

There should be no reference in the text that is not in such a bibliography, and there should be no item in the bibliography that is not referred to in the text. *There should be a perfect match between in-text and end-of-text references.*

Generally, the items in the bibliography are listed in alphabetical order, by the author's or editor's name (or if there is no named author or editor, by the name of the institution publishing the work). Books, journals, and websites might be collected together, or be kept separate. Again, there are conventions that apply to the setting out of a

---

[1] Magee, Bryan (1988) *The Great Philosophers*, Oxford: Oxford University Press, p121.

bibliography to which you might be locally required to adhere; but generally, the format is not very unlike what follows:

## Bibliography

Austin, J.L. (1962) *How to Do Things with Words*, Oxford: Oxford University Press.

Ayer, A.J. (1936) *Language, Truth and Logic*, London: Penguin Books.

Baggini, Julian and Lawrence Krauss (2012) 'Philosophy v Science: which can answer the big questions of life?' in *The Observer*, London, 9 September 2012.

Carel, Havel and David Gamez (eds) (2004), *What Philosophy Is*, London: Continuum.

Devlin, Keith (1997) *Goodbye Descartes*, New York: John Wiley.

Dreyfus, Hubert (2007) '*From Gods and Back*', available at: <https://archive.org/details/Philosophy_6_Spring_2007_UC_Berkeley>.

Evans, Jules (2012) *Philosophy for Life: And Other Dangerous Situations*, London: Rider Books.

Sometimes the date of publication is at the end of the reference (though it helps to have the date after the author's name if you are making reference to more than one of the author's works). What matters is *consistency*, and that you enable your reader to go to the sources that you have used should he or she wish to do so.

What guidelines might you take away from this chapter?

---

> ➤ Some reasons that you put forward will be **independent** of each other;
>
> ➤ others will be **interdependent**, or **joint** reasons—these will naturally go together;
>
> ➤ place reasons in a simple-to-complex, or other logical order;
>
> ➤ bear in mind that an **intermediate conclusion** can act as a herald to the main argument, or as a useful pivot in an argument;
>
> ➤ take care to allow for **alternative inferences** from the evidence that you present;
>
> ➤ there are good reasons for including **quotations** in your argument, in moderation;
>
> ➤ there should be full references to all sources used so that all are attributed, and traceable, by being listed in a **bibliography**.

It only remains now to unite all these end-of-chapter summaries in one composite diagram and to lay out a couple of complete responses to questions that aspire to be 'effective', if not to be knock-down arguments.

# A summary of recommendations for effective argument made in this book

Frame your title as a **Question**

---

**In an opening Statement**

➤ Define key terms that you will use.

➤ Be precise about the scope of your argument.

➤ Make your assumptions and your point of view—your position—explicit.

| **Argument A** | → | **Argument B** |

**Argument A**

Here you are laying out the argument(s) that you will counter. Identify the conclusion(s) and the reasons that support it (or fail to do so):

$R_1 \rightarrow R_2 \rightarrow R_3$ (etc.) $\rightarrow$ C.

➤ Select reliable, credible, expert sources.

➤ Look for straw men, overstatement, confusion between causation and correlation, mistaken conditions.

➤ Be alert to questionable appeals to the past or to feelings.

Judge whether the evidence is strong enough to justify the conclusion. Apply the principle of charity.

**Argument B**

Re-examine your position in light of what you have read. Reflect on what evidence you have at your disposal:

➤ Your examples, experience (anecdote?), facts, factual claims, statistical evidence.

➤ Judge how far this is corroborated by reliable sources.

➤ Distinguish what is certain, probable, plausible, possible, from what is believed—what is opinion and what prejudice.

➤ Be aware of bias in your position, of where you might be over-simplifying and arguing from principle.

➤ Order your reasons so that they flow, one from another.

Consider whether an **Intermediate Conclusion** might mark a turning point in your argument.

Come to your **Main Conclusion**—one supported by each item of your evidence—making allowance for alternative inferences.

Ensure that all quotations from and paraphrases of other authors' work is attributed, and that in-text references match those in your **Bibliography**.

# Exemplar arguments

'Exemplar' does not mean 'exemplary'. The two arguments that follow are not presented as models of their kind; they are intended simply to exemplify the pattern of an argument in the Summary of Recommendations diagram. The first is labelled (and runs to just over 1,000 words); the second (of over 2,000 words) is not.

# 1 Should all young people have the opportunity of going to university?

[Statement] We might take it that 'all young people' means everyone between the ages of about 18 and 25. There used to be a clear, near-universal understanding of the 'idea of the university'; but there might not be unanimity about this now. The idea has certainly been subject to change in the UK, and the UK will provide the background for this paper. I shall argue that all young people should have the opportunity of going to university, as long as we accept that the experience will not be the same for everyone.

[Argument A] The ancient universities were very much the model for the idea of a university; so when J.H. Newman came to write about *The Idea of a University* in 1858, he had (Catholic) Christian gentlemen in mind; knowledge for its own sake; and an education that was rather generalist than specialist. The university was for the few; for the intellectual elite. Many secular, 'civic' universities were established in the UK in the century after Newman wrote, but it was not until the late 1950s, with the founding of Keele University, and then of Sussex, in 1961, that thinking began to change in any radical way. There was still a feeling that 'universities should be concerned with the pursuit of knowledge for its own sake' (Brook, 1965: 10); but it was acknowledged that, thanks to the expansion of the university sector, large numbers of students were beginning to enter university 'who would never have been to university but for the expansion' (ibid:* 47). The North American view, that university was about bringing students to 'a higher level of personal development', was contrasted with the view that 'in the last resort, the scholar is a man apart, and that he ought to be so' (Fulton, 1964: 14). This was the 'ivory tower' view of the university. Its defenders would argue that **[R1]** the nation only needed a limited pool of graduates, and that **[R2]** only a minority of school-leavers were capable of benefiting from university education.

**[Argument B]** In 1999, Prime Minister Tony Blair set a target of '50 per cent of young adults going into higher education in the next [i.e. the present] century'. He gave as his reason that 'in today's world there is no such thing as too clever' (Gill, 2008), or in other words that **[R1]** one cannot have too much education. He might also have claimed with some justice that **[R2]** a mature economy needed more young people to have graduate-level skills; and he might have pointed to **[R3]** our competitors, the United States, Germany, Japan, where a larger percentage of young people went to university than in the UK. It should be noted that Blair did not speak of school-leavers only; nor did he refer to universities only, but to 'higher education'. Even if all higher education is delivered in universities, **[Intermediate Conclusion 1]** there is no reason why a 'university' today should mean what Newman meant by it.

Compulsory education was introduced in the UK in 1880 in part because children below the age of 10 were no longer employable. It might be said that, **[R4]** in the 21st century, school-leavers without some further qualification will not be employable. It has been a prime defect of the English education system as a whole that it has privileged 'academic' over 'vocational' education, and that it has separated 'education' from 'training'. It is doubtful whether any learning can be said to be undertaken 'for its own sake'; and if there is research that has no use whatsoever, the researcher is perhaps rather to be pitied than respected. Learning does not have to take place in a residential ivory tower, for three or four full-time years, nor does it require that teaching be face to face. **[Evidence]** The Open University is the UK's biggest, with 250,000 students, 70 per cent of whom are in paid employment (Open University, 2013). What makes the Open University unique is that 'for most courses you don't need any previous qualifications' (ibid*). The university seeks to be open as to the age, the previous experience and the location of the student—nearly 21,000 of the university's current students are overseas, receiving tuition electronically, and peer-support in online forums. **[R5]** There is, then, plenty of 'room' for more students; and, though demand for places in the UK dropped by 6.64 per cent in 2012 when fees were raised, the number of applicants (653,637) was higher than the number in 2009 (639,860)—and it was reported by the Universities and Colleges Admissions Service that **[R6]** student demand was up again, by 3.5 per cent, in 2013 (UCAS, 2013).

Of course, **[IC2]** it only makes sense to offer the opportunity to enter some form of higher education to those young people who wish to take it up; it is most unlikely that the 1944 rallying cry for 'secondary education for all' will be replaced by a call for 'university education for all', just because the institutional capacity and growing student demand are in place. Nevertheless, **[Main Conclusion]** there are many sound reasons for making the opportunity to go to university available to all young people, on the understanding that there will be those who will prefer an alternative path, and there will be others who delay entry until they are not so young.

* ibid—short for *ibidem* (Lat.), the same (in this case, the same source as the previous one).

## Bibliography

Brook, G.L. (1965) *The Modern University*, London: André Deutsch.

Fulton, Sir John (1964) 'New Universities in Perspective' in David Daiches (ed.), *The Idea of a New University*, London: André Deutsch.

Gill, John (2008) 'Labour concedes that it won't deliver its 50% target on time' in *Times Higher Education*, 17 April 2008.

Open University (2013) <http://www.open.ac.uk>, accessed 31 January 2013.

UCAS (2013) <http://www.ucas.ac.uk>, accessed 31 January 2013.

# 2 Is it ever justifiable for a 'western' democracy to invade another sovereign territory?

Powerful nations have invaded less powerful ones throughout history, and they have justified their invasions by reference to the standards of their own time. Most often, power (and the wealth that flowed from it) was justification enough. Since the second of two wars to end all wars, the west, at least—though it has not stopped invading—has needed 'better' reasons for doing so. I shall confine myself to the post-1945 world, therefore, and consider mainly the military actions of the United States, the UK, and France, whether or not they acted under the aegis of NATO or the United Nations.

As a Briton I cannot but understand events through British eyes, and as a result of reading mostly British sources of information. From this point of view, I believe there have been invasions of sovereign territory that can be justified as a last resort.

Those who argue against intervention might well base their opposition on a principled understanding of 'sovereignty': of the right of a nation to determine its own path. 'Armed force shall not be used, save in the common interest': these words feature in the preamble to the UN Charter. British attempts to battle against insurgents in Malaya, and French attempts to do the same in Indo-China, looked to the Americans like a simple reversion to old-style imperialism:

> It is nothing less than tragic [that] we should be forced to choose between following in the footsteps of Anglo-French colonialism in Asia and Africa or split our course away from theirs (Cohen and Major, 2004: 869).

So said Secretary of State John Foster Dulles on 1 November 1956. The United States had not been a colonial power before 1945, so it could justify its actions in Korea (1950–3) and later in Vietnam by reference to the felt need to support one domino after another falling to communism. Dulles was speaking in the context of Anglo-French action in Egypt following Nasser's nationalization of the Suez Canal in July 1956. UK Prime Minister Anthony Eden was all for a swift response, and his cabinet backed him. Nasser was a dictator like Hitler and Mussolini and he must not be 'appeased' as they had been. 'With dictators you always have to pay a higher price later on, for their appetite grows with feeding' (Robinson, 2012: 116): this was Eden's view. A canal-users' association was formed, but Eden was obliged to refer the declaration of this group to the United Nations. According to Edward Heath, Selwyn Lloyd (Eden's foreign minister) 'believed he could have got a settlement at the United Nations. Eden held a different view' (Heath, 1999: 167). Eden was determined that Nasser should not be allowed to 'get away with it' because, in the words of another of his ministers, if he did: 'The whole Arab world will despise us … It may well be the end of British influence and strength for ever. So, in the last resort, we must use force and defy opinion, here and overseas' (Macmillan, 2003: 587). And then there was oil: 80–90 per cent of oil supplies to Western Europe came from the Middle East. 'If Nasser gets away with it, we have had it' (ibid: 590). These were not reasons for military invasion of Egypt that satisfied the Americans; and they have failed to find favour with commentators ever since.

Motives for invasion of this sort make justification difficult. Then there is the issue of legality—and this cannot be separated from the question whether or not invasion is sanctioned by the United Nations. Even Dulles had been of the opinion that the canal-users' declaration could be 'railroaded' through the Security Council (ibid: 590). The United States made no attempt to consult with the United Nations in 1964, however, when it committed itself to defending South Vietnam against the North. It might have seemed like a heroic enterprise until it became plain not only that might was not 'right', but that it was not succeeding in its aims. Vietnam was a very costly and very public failure. 'Television brought the brutality of war into the comfort of the living room,' wrote Marshall McLuhan. 'Vietnam was lost in the living rooms of America—not on the battlefields of Vietnam' (Cohen and Major, 2004: 887). If Kennedy had been able to justify sending military advisors in 1962, there could be no justification for the years of destruction that followed; yet, in spite of the determination of the United States to avoid 'another Vietnam', the Americans invaded Somalia in 1992, Afghanistan in 2001, and Iraq in 2003. The justification for the Somali invasion was that the rule of law there had broken down, and people were starving. The justification for the Afghan invasion was '9/11'. UK intelligence chief Stephen Lander 'felt the pressure on the Americans to respond quickly, even immediately, would be enormous. Afghanistan was the obvious place' (Campbell, 2007: 561). It was obvious because it was here that the perpetrator of 9/11, Osama bin Laden, and his al Qaida henchmen were hiding and training the jihadists who—now that the cold war was over—were the new threat to the west. Iraq was less 'obvious' (though it should not be forgotten that Clinton had sanctioned four days of Baghdad bombing, in the 1998 'Desert Fox' action, as a warning to Saddam Hussein to cooperate with UN weapons inspectors). 'Tony Blair was pretty clear that we had to be with the Americans' (ibid: 630) in 1998, and subsequently. One question was what purpose was to be served by invading Iraq: was it regime change, or was it Saddam's supposed 'weapons of mass destruction'? Another was whether or not invasion required UN sanction. According to Campbell, the United States and the UK had a different understanding of UN Security Council resolutions, 'the US thinking they have existing cover, us [the UK] believing we need a new one for foolproof legal cover' (ibid: 612). That the UK Attorney General decided under pressure in March 2003 that the invasion would be 'legal' is unlikely to persuade historians that it was 'justified'.

The case against invasion by western countries of sovereign territories would seem to be a strong one—and there must always be a presumption that force will not be used. Nevertheless, there have been instances where inaction might have seemed less justified than forceful intervention. Though the Argentine invasion of the Falkland Islands in April 1982 did not threaten Britain's national survival, and though Mrs Thatcher sent the naval Task Force because she was 'certain that Britain's standing in the world depended on retaking the Falkland Islands', knowing that 'if she did nothing her government was doomed' (Robinson, 2012: 173), the islands were 'sovereign' British territory, and the islanders had no desire to be anything other than British. Even the party leader whom Margaret Thatcher had displaced, Edward Heath, agreed that 'since British territory had been violated, international law recognized our right to use force' (Heath, 1999: 580). The Americans were not altogether sure about that right (how did these islands, so near to Argentina, come to be British in the first place?); but Reagan was won over; the Security Council passed Resolution 502 calling for the Argentinians to withdraw; and the European Community imposed trade sanctions against the Galtieri government. The Falklands campaign was, in an important sense, justified by its confronting an unlikeable dictator, and by its (albeit costly) success.

When yet another dictator, Saddam Hussein, invaded the sovereign territory of his neighbour Kuwait, in August 1990, and its ruler called for help, the case for military action was surely unanswerable. Within weeks, the United Nations imposed sanctions against Iraq and empowered armed forces to ensure that they were applied. At the end of November, Security Council Resolution 678 set 15 January 1991 as the date by which the Iraqi army must withdraw. Throughout December, as the new UK premier John Major writes: 'diplomatic efforts to prevent war continued without much hope that they would be successful' (Major, 1999: 223). Though the Democratic majority in the US Congress still argued in favour of long-term sanctions; though Russia and China 'muttered frustrated dissent from the sidelines' (ibid: 227); and though Mitterrand of France launched a surprise diplomatic initiative in New York without informing the Americans or the British (ibid: 232), we can surely acknowledge that the mission of American, British, Saudi, and Egyptian forces was justified—even though two of these countries were not western democracies.

The situation throughout the 1990s in the Balkans was less clear-cut, but the imperative to 'do something' was even more strongly felt—this was Europe, after all. European Community monitors had tried to keep the peace between Serbs and Muslims in Bosnia, following the EC's recognition of Croatia's independence (1991); and in 1992, a UN protection force (UNPROFOR) was given the limited mandate to protect refugee and humanitarian convoys. By this time, according to a BBC journalist, 'the war was already beyond the reach of diplomacy', and the UN peacekeepers found that they were little more than 'bystanders' (Bell, 1996: 136). Bell comments acidly: 'The UN Security Council is better at passing resolutions than at providing the means to implement them' (ibid: 179). Thus, when a mortar bomb killed 70 civilians in Sarajevo in February 1994, the United Nations called upon NATO to be its 'Bosnian enforcement agency' (ibid). By 1999, when it came to expelling the Serbs from Kosovo, 19 nations came together to fight a war from the air that was justified by all but the Serbs and Russians. Robinson observes, interestingly, that 'victory in Kosovo did more than convince Tony Blair of the moral value of military action against dictators' (Robinson, 2012: 268). Hence his decision to act against rebels in Sierra Leone, in 2000, and his (less happy) contribution to the Iraq invasion of 2003.

Britain acted alone (though under UN auspices) in Sierra Leone; the British and French acted in concert in Libya (in 2011); and the French acted alone (with logistical support) against Islamists in Mali in 2012, at the request of the government in Bamako. François Hollande claimed that 'recent UN Security Council resolutions provided the legal framework for him to respond to the request' (Chrisafis et al, 2013). He also claimed the backing of 15 West African states which, it was anticipated, would assume responsibility for security in Mali in the longer term. As Sarah Diffalah wrote in Le Nouvel Observateur: 'France is doing all it can to accelerate the deployment of African forces on the ground. The resolution of the Malian conflict should be an African matter' (Diffalah, 2013). In Le Monde, ex-President Giscard d'Estaing was quoted as expressing a familiar anxiety: 'I want to guard against an evolution of the French action into something neo-colonialist' (Châtelot, 2013).

Plainly, it is easier to justify invasion of a sovereign state when its ruler is an oppressive dictator; and it is easier to justify 'invading' the sovereignty of a state whose ruler seeks help from aggression whether from within or beyond the state boundaries. What is most unsatisfactory is that there is no framework for deciding internationally when an action might be justified, and by whom that action should be taken.

The question focused on 'western' democracies: all too often Russia and China are left out of account (to say nothing of other nations—some of them nuclear-capable). Do the governments of western democracies ask themselves how they would feel if Russia or China took it upon themselves to right what they might consider wrongs, using military force? If we are to justify such force, we must devise a mechanism for reconciling swiftness of action that is genuinely 'in the common interest' with approval that is as near universal as possible.

## Bibliography

Bell, Martin (1996) *In Harm's Way*, London: Penguin Books.

Campbell, Alastair (2007) *The Blair Years*, London: Hutchinson.

Châtelot, Christophe (2013) in *Le Monde*, online, available at <http://www.lemonde.fr>, accessed 16 January 2013.

Chrisafis, Angélique, Afua Hirsch, and Nick Hopkins in *The Guardian*, 12 January 2013.

Cohen, M.J. and John Major (eds) (2004) *History in Quotations*, London: Cassell.

Diffalah, Sarah (2013) in *Le Nouvel Observateur*, online, available at <http://tempsreel.nouvelobs.com>, accessed 16 January 2013.

Heath, Edward (1999) *The Course of My Life*, London: Coronet Books.

Macmillan, Harold (2003) *The Macmillan Diaries: The Cabinet Years* (ed. Peter Catterall), London: Macmillan.

Major, John (1999) *The Autobiography*, London: HarperCollins.

Robinson, Nick (2012) *Live From Downing Street*, London: Bantam Books.

What in the second of these two arguments would you judge to be:

a. the most important claim-as-reason (or item of evidence) in Argument A;

b. the most important claim-as-reason (or item of evidence) in Argument B;

c. an intermediate conclusion (there may be more than one);

d. the main conclusion?

# Responses to Questions

The following are not presented as 'answers' to questions raised in the book; rather they are my own considered judgements, as open to further question as yours may be.

# 1 What do you do when you argue a case?

**1a**. I rather expect a nil response to this question.

**1b**. Lippmann appears to make six distinct claims. The fifth would seem to be the main claim: that Roosevelt is without any important qualifications for the office of president.

**1c**. Marr does argue: his **P** appears to be that not having an understanding of today's world is ridiculous; his **Q** that, therefore, there is a case for writing, and reading, a history of the world. His claim is that to attempt to write such a book is an enormous undertaking, but that from an understanding of how we got here, we can better understand the 'here'. So, he concludes, the undertaking is worthwhile. Much of the explanation is in the final sentence.

**1d**. His reasons might have been: (a) look what chaos lighting the torch of war in 1914 brought upon Europe; and (b) Europe in 1935 is a tinderbox of unstable governments, deep-seated resentments and unresolved border disputes; it is a multiple car crash waiting to happen.

**1e**. Obama asks himself: What's holding America back from investing in its infrastructure, and coming first in the competition?

Marr asks himself: Why under heaven would one want to do anything so ridiculous as to write a history of the world?

**1f**. Perhaps the one reason why you might not need to word or reword your title as a question is that you are merely asked to *explain* something—to *account for* something; in this case, whilst you are not being asked to argue, exactly, you will be giving reasons, and so you will be reasoning.

**1g**. Perhaps that: civil war, with its attendant bloodshed, is the least desirable way to settle a dispute.

**1h**. His question would seem to be: What can we best do to bring about the Ireland that the freedom-fighters of 1916 died for?

And his conclusion: 'We of this generation must see to it that our language lives. [That would be the resolve of the men and women of 1916]'.

(The sentence in brackets may or may not be thought to be a constituent part of the conclusion.)

# 2 How will you make yourself clear?

**2a**. 'Think Bike' comes to mind. British motorists are encouraged to do this, and in particular on motorways; but it is not clear who should 'think bike' (lorry drivers, motorists, or bikers), and what 'thinking bike' might involve (avoiding bikes, making way for them, or simply being aware of them).

**2b**. 'Well-regulated militia' might have been defined: did it mean a professional army; or conscripts recruited in time of war; or ordinary citizens, at any time? Only in the last case would security seem to call for 'the people' to be permanently armed—and it might be questioned whether 'the people' would include children, adolescents, the mentally unstable, and those who never would qualify as conscripts in time of war. What should be the extent of the regulation? And, finally, would 'arms' exclude weapons that had far more than a defensive or sporting purpose?

**2c**. 'Gay', 'cool', 'green', 'intelligence', 'partner', 'consume'—these are all words that have changed in meaning, or whose meaning has been extended, within the last generation or so.

**2d**. He appears to have assumed that only males can be politicians; that it is given to only a certain sort of male to understand government—even, perhaps, that only one, 'orthodox' understanding would be acceptable; and that a politician is thought better of some years after his death. You might have discerned others.

**2e**. By his use of the word 'primordial', Wright is assuming that the argument against female suffrage is a priori, or self-evident; it is part of the fabric of the world as we know it. Men and women are constitutionally different; they always have been, and they always will be—this seems to be the assumption.

**2f**. Mussolini assumes that nobility consists in physical courage—in aggressive manliness; that might is right.

The BNP assumes that globalization is to blame for Britain's employment problems, and that it is in the power of government to act against it.

Kafka assumes that all readers seek what he seeks in a book, and that, like him, we need to be shocked out of our icy torpor.

**2g**. He suggests that men and women are motivated to live together in marriage (i.e. that it is natural), yet that civilized society has difficulty obliging men and women to remain married—because it is *un*natural. Can it be natural to marry, yet unnatural to remain married?

**2h**. The use of the same word in the two contexts appears to weaken his argument: in comparing the tyranny of Nero and Tiberius with that of 'your next-door neighbour', Bagehot overstates the case against the neighbour (who may tyrannize only two households) and so renders humorous what might have been a serious point.

**2i**. The five imperatives appear to be placed in a random order. Having issued the first, none of the other four is really necessary: non-membership cancels the obligations of membership. Reasons are given for three of the five demands—but they all say much the same thing.

**2j**. The four aims are placed in ascending order of manageability, or long-term significance; and in chronological order of the likelihood of their being achieved.

# 3 What case have others made?

**3a**. Ruskin might have mentioned that no one has a right to anyone else's property; that the rich are the last people to have a right to more; that the right of the rich to their property was probably asserted by might in the first place, and therefore it may not be justly maintained in its entirety; and finally he might have pointed out that the most grossly unequal societies are the ones with most social problems.

**3b**. Claim A is that American football is a 'mindless bout of mayhem between brutes got up in spacemen outfits'. His counter-claim is that it is an 'open-air chess game dismissed as warfare'. His conclusion is that American football is 'the most scientific of all outdoor games'. He supports his conclusion by suggesting that the game is misunderstood; that criticism of it is 'facetious'; and that it takes time to appreciate its finer points. The comparison with chess is a further 'reason'.

**3c**. The conclusion seems to be that Irish parents should involve themselves more in their children's study of mathematics. He gives as the reason for this conclusion the research done by a private firm in the United States and England that shows that giving assistance with homework, keeping up with the curriculum, and laying on extra tuition, as in Singapore, is what helps most.

**3d**. It seems reasonable to infer that democracy will not come 'any time soon' to the Middle East. Whether this is because of the intolerance of the dominant religion is another matter. Was religion in England any more than the outward trappings of power that would have been oppressive whether or not the Church was harnessed to the state? In order to judge whether we can hope that democracy will take root in the Middle East, we would need to know what the strength is of secular (non-religious) forces in each country: can we be sure that the conditions for democracy are as bad or as good in Tunisia as they are in Kuwait? And are there other factors than religion at work in the Middle East that frustrate the development of democracy?

**3e. Argument A** is that psychology has given us greater understanding of our motives, and made us more honest with ourselves. His reasons for scepticism about psychology are what he sees as the privileging of instinct over reason, and the illegitimacy of distinguishing between aspects of mind that are better understood holistically.

**3f.** A 'western' historian would be suspicious of such a text because it is written from a single, ideological point of view, with a propagandist purpose. It claims that there is just one 'history of Russia', and that there is no room for interpretation. The very business of the historian—as Wilde pointed out—is to rewrite it, that is, to reinterpret the data in light of new research findings.

**3g**. They might have pointed out that no one is an expert in political ethics; that thinking citizens in a democracy all have a contribution to make to state policy—that, in fact, politicians may be the last people to pronounce on what is ethical and what is not, since power may corrupt their judgement. The professors were as well qualified as any Israelis of the time to advise the prime minister.

**3h**. One might go to a publicly funded, university-based research institute working in this field; and/or to specialist groups working under the aegis of the United Nations, or other non-commercial international organization.

# 4 What do you make of these arguments?

**4a**. In my own view, Sauven's (Argument 62) is the stronger argument. Sir David King may be right about some 'greens': that they would like us to live as we lived in pre-industrial times. But is a standard of living for everyone 'based on a large energy consumption' sustainable? Surely not. Sauven may be too ready to dismiss nuclear energy, but we certainly need to plan for a standard of living that everyone in the world can aspire to without destroying the planet in the interests of the lucky few.

**4b**. Spencer overstates his case by lumping together all the men (and some women) who are out of work as good-for-nothings. He does not pause in his invective to consider that there might have been some men—even many men—who had no work because there was no work to be had; or because they were sick or disabled; or because their own or their employer's business had failed. There is a sort of straw man in Spencer's description of the workless: no one would rise to the defence of such men (or women).

**4c**. Footballers' behaviour is unlikely to be either a cause of, or to be correlated with, classroom misbehaviour. The second factor (lack of parental responsibility) is far more likely to be a cause, and possibly a major one. If there was a reluctance in the 1960s and 1970s to enforce the sort of classroom discipline that had been common in the years before, things had changed by 2005. If there was then (and now?) a systemic problem of misbehaviour (even 'loutishness') in schools it is more likely to be correlated with a general decline in deference to authority in the wider society, and with the emergence of influential adolescent subcultures.

**4d**. It does seem that creativity thrives—even, perhaps, excels itself—in adverse conditions. One thinks of the inspired music and literature of dissidents in Soviet Russia; the work of Romantic poets and musicians who died young after troubled lives; the poems and paintings of war poets and artists. Conservative, static times may not be cradles of invention.

**4e**. R1 and R2 in **Argument A** are reasons why many had an 'ivory tower' view of universities—and it was such a view that could be seen as *conditions* that obtained, or as *causes* that restricted entry into higher education. They were the **P**; the restriction was the **Q**.

R1, R2, and R3 in **Argument B** were all *conditions* for the expansion of higher education that had obtained since the 1960s (long before Blair's 50 per cent target); R2 and R3 can also be regarded as *causes* of the further expansion after 1999.

**4f**. Customs, habits, attitudes handed down to us may not suit present circumstances. Our success as a species has been the result of our ability to adapt to new challenges. An appeal to tradition is likely to be one that recommends retaining, or returning to, a practice that had its origins in the past, and that was fitting in the past: that it was relevant then is no guarantee of its relevance now.

**4g**. Perhaps you do not have a subject that you would call your own; still, you can probably think of people whose names inspire confidence in one or more fields of study.

**4h**. Marx in Argument 93 is appealing to his readers' appetite for choice, variety, and freedom of action in a fair and open society. Argument 94 is appealing to consumers' love of leisure, comfort—the 'good life'. It also appeals to their wish to economize (and to a dislike of airports). Both arguments appeal to the pleasure principle—to hedonism.

**4i**. De Barros appeals to Portuguese nationalism and a particular understanding of 'rights'—reciprocal rights among Europeans, unilateral rights as between Portuguese and everyone else. Gladstone appeals to a vision of the future, to destiny, to greatness, and to the conviction of divine sanction.

# 5 How will you support your case?

**5a**. If by 'secondary drinking' we mean the effects of a drinker's habit on others, we might list those injured or killed by a drunk driver; those assaulted by one whose drinking made him aggressive; the family of an alcoholic who suffer loss of money and affective engagement at the hands of the drinker; police and public-health resources drawn on disproportionately by drinkers—and, doubtless, many others. The effects of secondary drinking on others may be greater than the effects of others' smoking; yet the effects of smoking in pubs would be greater on others in the pub at the time. They would be inconvenienced by the smoke, and might die of its effects, yet not have been the victim of particular smokers.

**5b**. Sleeping behind windows without curtains or blinds is a merely personal preference of no significance. The wisdom of sleeping with one's windows open in the winter may depend upon the severity of the winter; and this applies to sleeping outside. Doing this in the depths of winter is an idiosyncrasy bordering on the perverse. The final point about boyish 'bad dreams' invites laughter. Baden-Powell's example is one that few would choose to follow.

**5c**. It was discovered that it took a certain time for a certain quantity of water, heated at a constant rate and intensity, at sea level, to come to the boil. The time, the quantity, the rate and intensity, and the point at which the water boiled all had to be measured, though—all had to be defined on scales that had themselves to be defined. (You may need to make allowances for the fact that I am not a physical scientist.)

**5d**. The author of Argument 111 intended to refer to the novels of Henry James, William's younger brother. I know this because it was I who made this silly mistake. I knew full well that William James was a philosopher and psychologist, to whom no novel has ever been ascribed. The mistake does not affect my conclusion. The mistake that the author of Argument 112 makes actually strengthens his conclusion (that 'Historical context can be very important in interpreting and evaluating an argument'): Malthus wrote his *Essay on the Principle of Population* 11 years before Charles Darwin was born (1809). The author has got his historical contexts (not merely names) the wrong way round.

**5e**. You would need to select a sample of about 1,000 people. About half would need to be male and half female, since left-handedness may be correlated with gender—though it is unlikely. Age is also unlikely to be a factor, but, to be on the safe side, it might be as well to include in your sample roughly equal numbers of young people, middle-aged, and elderly subjects. Beyond this simple stratification, it should be enough to place yourself in a busy urban location and ask passers-by, randomly, whether they are left or right-handed. (You would need to tally responses in $2 \times 2 \times 3 = 12$ separate cells.)

**5f**. The 'eight out of ten Britons' turn out to be people who already have health-insurance cover. The 'two out of three' people appear to be from the same sample. This is not a sample of the British population at large; it is a sample of the minority of people (we are not told how big or small it is) who have opted out of the National Health Service. It is not, therefore, representative of all Britons. We are not told how big the (possibly self-selected) sample was.

**5g**. We can cite as historical facts the dates of the beginnings and endings of reigns and regimes; of the signing of treaties; and of meetings and celebrations. We can name figures who proved to be agents and victims of change; and we can identify events that played a critical role in larger movements. There are 'historical facts', but (like most facts) these are only the raw materials of our knowledge. Disagreement enters by the same door as interpretation of the significance of these facts.

**5h**. The first might best be corroborated by instancing what learning monks and nuns advanced; the works of art they patronized; and the developments in agriculture they promoted. The second claim we have to take largely on trust—if we are not to believe the disparaging and self-interested claims made by Henry VIII's commissioners. Possibly the best evidence for the third claim would be an assessment of what was lost at the dissolution: fine buildings, libraries, charitable work, accommodation for travellers, local crafts, employment, and food production.

# 6 How much can you be sure about?

**6a**. Ten years is not long, so 'massive' change in that time is improbable. Technology will change, but the changes will be based, recognizably, on present-day research and development. There are about half a million places in UK universities each year; so there are probably going to be five million more students in the coming decade. On current trends, the number of low-skilled jobs will fall; but it is unlikely that as more students graduate, their degrees will earn them salaries commensurate with those of the past.

**6b**. Claim a is plausible; claim b is highly unlikely; claim c is possible; claim d is so probable as to be certain (perhaps, indeed, it is necessarily the case); claim e is somewhere between possible and plausible; and claim f is very probable.

**6c**. 'Poland is a member of the European Union, therefore Poland subscribes to the rule of law.'

**6d**. His first sentence ('Criticisms which stem from some psychological need of those making them don't deserve a rational answer') seems to be his major premise. It cannot be called a fact: who is to say that such criticisms stem from some psychological need of the critic? Who is to say that such criticisms are irrational? Who is to say that they do not deserve a rational answer? Who is to say what is a rational answer? Freud the psychoanalyst is writing in defence of psychoanalysis. His argument is deductive, and *tu quoque* (see Chapter 8).

**6e**. 'Then we should not need to rely on offensive nuclear deterrence. *So, we should develop missiles that could intercept and destroy enemy missiles, defensively.*'

**6f**. Not being a logician, for me the answer has to be no. When sentences are factual claims, as opposed to facts, only evidence of a scientific kind, and/or very wide agreement indeed, will make facts of them—or truths. Even Hodges the logician has his doubts about whether it makes sense to divide 'life' into what is True and what is False. One may wonder whether logic can be 'honest' when it proceeds as if it does.

# 7 How much is a matter of belief?

**7a**. He is justified in his first sentence where his own case is concerned—and perhaps in respect of others of his class trapped in loveless, arranged marriages. It may also be fair to say, in general, that marriage is more 'complicated' than friendship because it involves the conjoining of whole families, not just two individuals. His reflections on the fitness of women for marriage are not justified, however: this is very much a male point of view, and one reinforced by the contemporary teachings of the Church concerning the moral weakness of Eve, the first woman, and the secondary status of women.

**7b**. My own point of view would have to be that of a national of a country that has long been allied with the United States—with which it has a 'special relationship', nurtured by history, language, and shared interests. It would also have to be that of a critical friend who has witnessed the failure of US foreign policy in numerous theatres.

**7c**. I would agree with him that when we say we 'believe' something, we are making a factual claim for which there may be little or no evidence. We may, indeed, only be expressing an inexpert opinion. I would hesitate, however, before calling anything 'necessarily true', or any truth 'fundamental'.

**7d**. The three letter-writers are expressing opinions, but those opinions may well spring from a belief shared with Caro that much modern art is 'damned stupid'. Though Caro (in conversation) is dismissive, his is an 'expert opinion'—the judgement of a practitioner. Pater's argument, likewise, is a judgement born of a settled, informed belief.

**7e**. Along with his point of view, Lamb's prejudices would have been caught from the dominant culture: from an insular, English respect for Jews and Judaism, but a suspiciousness of them deriving from old charges of deicide, and from unfamiliarity. His prejudice against the Scots was the product of a history of conflict, exploitation, even collective contempt.

**7f**. There is no real contradiction: Horgan admires scientific findings because we can and do make practical use of them. Tariq Ali seeks to correct the popular impression that scientists pursue their researches high-mindedly; he is honest about the motives of scientists, but he does not cast doubt on the wonderful usefulness of their findings.

**7g**. If, as Planck says in Argument 165, we are 'part of nature', it is difficult to study our own biological workings—but to study those of plants and the 'lower' animals, as Wells does, is less problematic; but we are so much more a part of history, because history is about the behaviour of people like ourselves—our ancestors—so our feelings, and our biases, are in play. Perhaps 'objectivity' (and therefore 'truthfulness') is easier the further down the food chain one goes, and the further back in time.

**7h**. We live in a more interdependent world than Wilson did. Apart from the obvious cases in which compassion demands that we help to feed the hungry in economically and climatically disadvantaged countries, or in which we try to protect a helpless people from a despotic ruler, shared interests demand that we prevent particular countries from overfishing the seas, or from exterminating an animal species, or from polluting the air that we all breathe.

**7i**. We must be careful not to conflate two meanings of the word 'principle': Darwin is using the word to mean theory. He does not want a pre-existing theory to cloud the lens through which he observes the world. On the other hand, a principle (in the sense in which it is used in this chapter) too firmly held may well have the same obscuring effects on efforts to be objective.

# 8 Are you over-simplifying the issue?

**8a**. McCarthy exhibits in this name-calling a spitefulness that demeans his argument. It makes it look as if he does not like what Dean Acheson is saying merely because he does not like Dean Acheson—and he does his best to give 'ordinary' (unsophisticated, mid-western) Americans cause to dislike him, too.

**8b**. It may be that, where an *ad hominem* observation is relevant to the matter of the argument, it may be acceptable. It may be relevant to a critique of his argument, for instance, that Adolf Hitler shouted hysterically when he spoke to the German people, revealing mental instability, or aggressiveness.

Most of Webb's charges (shallowness, vulgarity, dreariness, and so on) fail to register because they are not supported by examples or explanation. The one that does stick is that Shaw fell for 'second-rate' women. We would need to know who these women were, though, before we could judge whether this was fair comment.

**8c**. The conclusion seems to be: Abdelbaset al-Megrahi should have served his full life sentence. The letter-writers might, alternatively, have concluded that the prisoner had already cost the British (and especially the Scottish) taxpayer quite enough already, and that it might have looked bad if he had died in a Scottish prison. These particular letter-writers are unlikely to have concluded—as certain investigators have—that Abdelbaset al-Megrahi was not the real culprit, but a Gaddafi stooge.

**8d**. Machiavelli says a prince must be feared or loved; might he not simply be respected? And might there not be sinners who know themselves to be sinners (Pascal)?. Morris does not help his case when he talks vaguely about 'Nature' (see Chapter 2); and there are many degrees of beauty and ugliness—and there is simple utility. Lenin, too, talks in terms of absolutes: it is perfectly possible to live freely in a 'state'. There is no either/or trade-off between butter and guns (Goering)—and few would hold that the opposite of socialism is imperialism (Norway is a capitalist country, but not noticeably imperialistic).

**8e**. Stebbing herself presents us with a third possibility: opposition. Indifference is another (if we accept that acquiescence is a conscious act). It may be, in spite of what Hardy says, that we live on knowledge that we have acquired for ourselves—or from other non-professionals.

**8f**. No, in both cases. De Tocqueville cannot have met all the English (not even all Englishmen), and Macmillan cannot have met all Americans—or even heard about them all. Not all the English are obsessed by social status (and they were not in 1840); and (surely) not all Americans are 'impatient, mercurial, panicky'; Americans, after all, gave us the modern sense of the word 'cool'.

**8g**. Many 'impressionist' paintings (such as Monet's *Impression, Soleil Levant*, of 1872) were considered to be ugly at first, so Cocteau was, perhaps, right in this respect. Do we, though, consider 'flapper' fashion of the 1920s to be ugly? Or Christian Dior's 'New Look' of the late 1940s and 1950s? Both have, in some measure, become 'classics', or (dare I say it?) 'iconic'.

**8h**. It is probably not the case that *any* good housekeeper could understand the problems of running a country. Mrs Thatcher was not any good housekeeper. Besides, a housekeeper faces problems on a very much smaller scale, and possibly alone: she (and it is a 'she' who is being talked about here) does not have to be a 'leader' of millions of other housekeepers, with other ideas than hers about how to run a home.

**8i**. Houses and stones are certainly familiar (though bricks are more familiar still nowadays), and stones and facts are both 'hard' and there are many of them in a house and in science, respectively. We can envisage a house: it can stand concretely for the abstract building that is science; and the 'pile' and the 'collection' are alike in their haphazardness. All in all, there seem to be more strengths in the analogy than weaknesses.

**8j**. The argument is not very persuasive. There is a very particular (health) reason why tobacco advertising might be restricted, or banned outright. There is no (health or other) reason why such a ban would lead to a ban on advertising of other (non-life-threatening) products. The very premise of the argument is suspect: gradual erosions of liberty can scarcely lead to its *total* loss—even in a totalitarian state (*pace* Orwell's fictional *Nineteen Eighty-Four*), freedom of thought cannot ultimately be controlled.

# 9 Does your argument hang together?

**9a**. The first line implies that we have all thought critically to some extent before we study 'critical thinking', as such. The second line implies that 'critical thinking' is difficult for many people at first. The first line is intended to be reassuring; the second may be off-putting—so they are not easily reconciled. There is some contradiction.

**9b**. In the first extract it is clear that Gladstone knew enough about the 'Irish problem' to want to avoid antagonizing the Irish Church. In the second, we are told that he knew nothing about the problem. These claims do not seem to be compatible. In the first, he seemed to be conscious that he might damage his party; in the second, the thought of doing so does not seem to occur to him. The repetition of the phrase ('lead the Liberal Party to martyrdom') seems to emphasize the contradiction.

**9c**. Can an appeal often give 'weak' support to a conclusion, yet be 'strong'? Or should we infer that an appeal gives 'weak' support in most cases, but a strong one in a few? Perhaps; but the two judgements may well leave us confused about whether 'appeals' are acceptable or not.

**9d**. The two claims, that we construct our own truth and that we construct our own reality, are declared to be 'false', on page 4. On page 39, the authors are at pains to report that perception acts as a filter between truth/reality and our conscious minds—that we do construct truth/reality, and that it is vital that we do. There does appear to be a discrepancy between the claims on page 4 and the findings on page 39.

**9e**. The red herring is the (perhaps beguiling) idea that physical-science laboratories might be shut down for a decade without loss. It is even implied that the work of physicists and chemists is an obstacle to humanitarianism. Might it not have been more relevant to suggest that armaments factories, or the offices of popular newspapers, or parliament itself be closed down? On the other hand, is it necessary to close *any* institution down in order to foster human decency?

**9f**. Mitchell's conclusion seems to be: we should hold fast to our objective to increase development aid so as to meet the UN target. His final point does appear to elevate self-interest to the same level as the moral imperative to save children's lives, and therefore to rob some of that imperative of its all-sufficient force.

**9g**. The word 'so' is not enough to make an argument of this set of claims: Mussolini gives no reason for his assertion that opposition to fascism is out of place. He simply says it is unnecessary, senseless, superfluous, and that it will not be tolerated. If the non-argument is not circular, it is certainly repetitious.

**9h**. Williamson appears to question why philosophers have not used the 'notion of knowledge', instead of using surrogate, 'more basic notions' (alone or in combination) like 'belief', 'truth', and 'justification'; yet at the beginning of the extract, he acknowledges that philosophers have not really succeeded in saying what knowledge 'really' means. This is the reason for their using the surrogate terms. The problem seems to lie in the assumption that there is a 'correct' reading of what we mean by knowledge, and that other readings will be 'wrong'.

# 10 How will you lay out your case?

**10a**. There is a certain link between reasons one and four (the imperative to explore), and between two and three (the need to assert power). The Committee sandwiches two rather mean reasons between two grander ones. Then, in the first sentence of the final paragraph (an intermediate conclusion), it claims that it is the 'mean', military reasons that have made the grander, all-of-humanity reasons, possible.

**10b.** The 'personal' reasons: a, c, e, and f might come first—and the order of reasons a, c, and e matters little; f is a useful, general, summarizing reason, so is appropriately the last of the four. Then the more 'political' reasons b and d, in this order, might take us into the next stage of the argument.

**10c.** The intermediate conclusion in Joule's argument (introduced, notice, by the conclusion indicator 'thus') seems to be: 'order is maintained in the universe'. Until this point, Joule has claimed that energy is converted from and into heat continually. Following this intermediate conclusion, he claims that, in spite of the appearance of confusion, all is divinely regulated.

**10d.** The intermediate conclusion seems to be: 'There are alternative routes that we could take, but they will involve radical thinking'. This claim turns the argument from one that is critical of nuclear energy to one that explores two alternative 'better' ways of filling the energy gap.

**10e.** The oil company would welcome the opportunity to open up new oilfields in a region that is increasingly hospitable to drilling; obviously, to add to oil and gas reserves is good business. At the same time, it will not want to antagonize governments and environmentalists, in the way that BP did in the Gulf of Mexico in April 2010. The UK government, like other governments, is well aware of the consequences of burning fossil fuels in the not-so-long term, yet it is concerned to ensure that energy supplies are maintained. It is politically imperative that the lights be kept on.

**10f.** One might infer that government advice is being ignored by a large section of the population; that alcohol abuse has damaging consequences for the individuals concerned and for the National Health Service; and that unhealthy drinking habits may lie behind much of the crime and violence in society. One's main conclusion would have to be that (in common with many other 'developed' countries) *Britain has a drink problem.*

**10g.** In both cases, the quotations take us away from the matter in hand: in the first, Mrs Beeton was writing specifically about economizing in a domestic setting; Bishop Hall both specifies—the 'good waggoner'—and generalizes; but he does not add anything to Mrs Beeton's point about 'practising economy'. In the second example, Mrs Beeton makes a specific point about balancing household accounts once per month. Judge Halliburton merely states the obvious in a 'truth' that has general application. The quotation is something of a distraction.

# Exemplar argument 2

## Is it ever justifiable for a 'western' democracy to invade another sovereign territory?

**a.** I think I would judge the fact that there was doubt at the highest level about the objectives of the invasion of Iraq, and about whether it was covered by international law as the most important claim-as-reason in **Argument A** ('One question was what purpose was to be served by invading Iraq...Another was whether or not invasion required UN sanction'). The invasion seems to have been less easily justifiable by its objectives and by its outcome than any other post-war invasion by western democracies—though Vietnam runs it a close second.

**b.** The strongest support for the claim that invasion may be justified is probably the intervention in Kuwait, in 1990 ('Saddam Hussein invaded the sovereign territory of his neighbour Kuwait...the case for military action was surely unanswerable'). Help was called for by the ruler of the invaded territory; a plain wrong had been done; and the action was (arguably) proportionate—and successful. No bystander state could raise serious objections to the intervention since it delivered on an unambiguous UN warning.

**c.** 'The case against invasion by western countries of sovereign territories would seem to be a strong one'. This intermediate conclusion is a summary comment on **Argument A**. There are other similar interim judgements that might be called intermediate conclusions: e.g. 'The Falklands campaign was, in an important sense, justified by its confronting an unlikeable dictator, and by its (albeit costly) success'. In the penultimate paragraph, the second of the two sentences ('What is most unsatisfactory is that there is no framework for deciding internationally when an action might be justified, and by whom that action should be taken') is more obviously an intermediate conclusion; but both halves of the first sentence might qualify, too.

**d.** The main conclusion could be said to be embedded in the second sentence of the second paragraph ('...there have been invasions of sovereign territory that can be justified'). The final two sentences in the last paragraph are a kind of gloss on this claim.

# Index

Included in this index are: subjects of arguments; authors of arguments and claims (in capitals); and semi-technical terms (in bold).